HOUSING

4th edition

Mike Egan

Institute of Financial Services
IFS House
4-9 Burgate Lane
Canterbury
Kent
CT1 2XJ

T   01227 818649
F   01227 479641
E   editorial@ifslearning.com

Published by the Institute of Financial Services. The Institute of Financial Services is the official brand of the Chartered Institute of Bankers, a non-profit making registered educational charity.

The Chartered Institute of Bankers believes that the sources of information upon which the book is based are reliable and has made every effort to ensure the complete accuracy of the text. However, neither CIB, the authors nor any contributor can accept any legal responsibility whatsoever for consequences that may arise from errors or omissions or any opinion or advice given.

Typeset by Kevin O'Connor

Printed by Antony Rowe Ltd, Wiltshire

© The Chartered Institute of Bankers 2003    institute of financial services

ISBN 0-85297-737-9

Contents

Contents

Housing

Introduction

Housing

The Concept of the Course

This is a practical course written for students studying for banking and finance qualifications and also for practitioners in the financial services who are looking for a practical refresher. The framework of this study text is structured so that many will find it to be the most coherent way of learning the subject.

Each chapter or unit of the Study Text is divided into sections and contains:

- learning objectives
- an introduction, indicating how this subject area relates to others to which the reader may have cause to refer
- clear, concise topic-by-topic coverage
- examples and exercises to reinforce learning, confirm understanding and stimulate thought
- often a recommendation of illustrative questions to try for practice.

Study Units

Each of the main units consists of study notes designed to focus attention upon the key aspects of the subject matter. These notes are divided into convenient sections for study purposes. The key sections of which for this subject are:

Social Structure and the National Housing Stock

- Social Structure and Social Change
- The Nature of the Nation's Housing Stock

Development of Housing Policy

- Background and Present Framework
- Housing Policy Issues and Trends
- Partnership of Public and Private Sectors

Housing Administration and Finance

- Housing Agencies
- Terms of Tenure, Tenants' Rights and Rent Control and House Sales

Accessing Information

Although the workbook is designed to stand alone, as with most topics, certain aspects of this subject are constantly changing, ie policy, statistics and legislation, and the author has brought this edition up to date during 2003. Therefore it is of great importance that students should keep up to date with these key areas and access the Web (www.odpm.gov.uk).

It is anticipated that the student will study this course over a six-month period, reading through and studying approximately two units every three weeks. However, it should be noted that as topics vary in size and as knowledge tends not to fall into uniform chunks, some units in this workbook are unavoidably longer than others.

The masculine pronoun 'he' has been used in this Workbook to encompass both genders and to avoid the awkwardness of the constant repetition of 'he and/or she'.

Study Guide

In the next few pages, we offer some advice and ideas on studying, revising and approaching examinations.

Studying

As with any examination, there is no substitute for preparation based on an organized and disciplined study plan. You should devise an approach that will enable you to get right through this Study Text and still leave time for revision of this and any other subject you are taking at the same time. Many candidates find that about six weeks is the right period of time to leave for revision – enough time to get through the revision material, but not so long that it is no longer fresh in your mind by the time you reach the examination.

This means that you should plan how to get to the last chapter by, say, the end of February for the April sitting. This includes not only reading the text, but making notes and attempting the bulk of the illustrative questions at the end of the units.

We offer the following as a starting point for approaching your study.

- Plan time each week to study a part of this Study Text. Make sure that it is 'quality' study time: let everyone know that you are studying and the you should not be disturbed. If you are at home, unplug your telephone or switch the answerphone on; if you are in the office, put you telephone on 'divert'.

- Set a clearly defined objective for each study period. You may simply wish to read through a unit for the first time or perhaps you want to make some notes on a unit you have already read a couple of times. Do not forget the illustrative questions.

- Review your study plan. Use the study checklist a couple of pages on to see how well you are keeping up. Do not panic if you fall behind, but do think how you will make up for lost time.

- Look for examples of what you have covered in the 'real' world. If you work for a financial organization, this should be a good starting point. If you do not, then think about your experiences as an individual bank or building society customer or perhaps about your employer's position as a corporate customer of a bank. Keep an eye on the quality press for reports about banks and building societies and their activities.

Revising

- The period which you have earmarked for revision is a very important time. Now it is even more important that you plan time each week for study and that you set clear objectives for each revision session.

- Use time sensibly. How much revision time do you have? Remember that you still need to eat, sleep and fit in some leisure time.

- How will you split the available time between subjects? What are your weaker subjects? You will need to focus on some topics in more detail than others. You will also need to plan your revision around your learning style. By now, you should know whether, for example, early morning, early evening or late evening is best.

- Take regular breaks. Most people find they can absorb more if they attempt to revise for long uninterrupted periods of time. Award yourself a five minute break every hour. Go for a stroll or make a cup of coffee, but do not turn on the television.

- Believe in yourself. Are you cultivating the right attitude of mind? There is absolutely no reason why you should not pass this exam if you adopt the correct approach. Be confident: you have passed exams before so you can pass this one.

The Day of the Exam

- Passing professional examinations is half about having the knowledge, and half about doing yourself full justice in the examination. You must have the right technique.

- Set at least one alarm (or get an alarm call) for a morning exam.

- Having something to eat but beware of eating too much; you may feel sleepy if your system is digesting a large meal.

- Do not forget pens, pencils, rulers, erasers and anything else you will need.

- Avoid discussion about the exam with other candidates outside the exam hall.

Tackling the Examination Paper

First, make sure that you satisfy the examiner's requirements

Read the instructions on the front of the exam paper carefully. Check that the exam format has not changed. It is surprising how often examiners' reports remark on the number of students who attempt too few – or too many – questions, or who attempt the wrong number of questions from different parts of the paper. Make sure that you are planning to answer the right number of questions.

Read all the questions on the exam paper before you start writing. Look at the weighting of marks to each part of the question. If part (a) offers only 8 marks and you cannot answer the 12 marks part (b), then do not choose the question.

Do not produce irrelevant answers. Make sure you answer the question set, and not the question you would have preferred to have been set.

Produce an answer in the correct format. The examiner will state in the requirements the format in which the question should be answered, for example in a report or memorandum.

Second, observe these simple rules to ensure that your script is pleasing to the examiner.

Present a tidy paper. You are a professional and it should always show in the presentation of your work. Candidates are penalized for poor presentation and so you should make sure that you write legibly and lay out your work professionally. Markers of scripts each have dozens of papers to mark; a badly written scrawl is unlikely to receive the same attention as a neat and well laid out paper.

State the obvious. Many candidates look for complexity which is not required and consequently overlook the obvious. Make basic statements first. Plan your answer and ask yourself whether you have answered the main parts of the question.

Use examples. This will help to demonstrate to the examiner that you keep up-to-date with the subject. There are lots of useful examples scattered throughout this study text and you can read about others if you dip into the quality press or take notice of what is happening in your working environment.

Finally, make sure that you give yourself the opportunity to do yourself justice.

Select questions carefully. Read through the paper once, then quickly jot down any key points against each question in a second read through. Reject those questions against which you have jotted down very little. Select those where you could latch on to 'what the question is about' – but remember to check carefully that you have got the right end of the stick before putting pen to paper.

Plan your attack carefully. Consider the order in which you are going to tackle questions. It is a good idea to start with your best question to boost your morale and get some easy marks 'in the bag'.

Introduction

Read the question carefully and plan your answer. Read through the question again very carefully when you come to answer it.

Gain the easy marks. Include the obvious if it answers the question and do not spend unnecessary time producing the perfect answer. As suggested above, there is nothing wrong with stating the obvious.

Avoid getting bogged down in small parts of questions. If you find a part of a question difficult, get on with the rest of the question. If you are having problems with something the chances are that everyone else is too.

Do not leave the exam early. Use your spare time checking and rechecking your script.

Do not worry if you feel you have performed badly in the exam. It is more likely that the other candidates will have found the exam difficult too. Do not forget that there is a competitive element in exams. As soon as you get up and leave the exam hall, forget the exam and think about the next – or, if it is the last one, celebrate!

Do not discuss an exam with other candidates. This is particularly the case if you still have other exams to sit. Put it out of your mind until the day of the results. Forget about exams and relax.

Housing

1

HOUSING STOCK AND LAND

Objectives

After studying this unit, you should be able to:

● explain how the stock of housing is affected by both quantity and quality;

● distinguish between the demand and the need for housing stock;

● write about local housing strategy and housing investment plans;

● describe the tenure of the housing stock;

● explain the need for green belt land and be aware of the arguments both for and against building on such land;

● write notes on 'sustainable communities'.

1.1   Introduction

Apart from food, water and warmth, one of the main human requisites is adequate shelter. In this text we shall look at both the quality and quantity of the housing stock and at the same time consider population trends. However, there is an important difference between these two factors.

● Population trends take place more or less independently of the government (both central and local) or any other organization. The best that can be done is to try to predict future trends and react to them.

● Housing stock is, on the other hand, a controllable commodity – at least in theory. If it has shortcomings in a particular area, then something can be done about it.

● To summarize, the population cannot be adjusted to fit the housing stock whereas the housing stock can be manipulated to fit the population.

Before we proceed, what are your initial thoughts on the quality and quantity of the country's housing stock? How do you think population trends will develop in the next couple of decades? Do you think that there is adequate housing for everyone?

In this unit we shall look at the features of the national housing stock. How many dwellings exist throughout the country? What sort of dwellings are they? What do we mean by the term 'dwelling'? Could they house all the national population? This last question involves an important distinction between the two terms 'housing need' and 'housing demand'. We shall consider this distinction next. Let us first consider what a dwelling is.

Dwelling units are defined as a structurally separated room or rooms occupied by private households of one or more people and having separate access or a common passageway to the street.

1.2 The Demand for Housing

The demand for housing is represented by the number of dwellings that can be purchased, rented or otherwise occupied by the present population, within its current economic situation. In effect, it is the housing demanded by the population which that population can afford.

To measure housing demand, it is only necessary to watch the market forces at work and to gather statistics from building societies, banks, housing associations, local authorities and from the National Census. Other data is also available in publications such as *Social Trends*. In both this and the next unit we shall consider some of this statistical information.

1.3 The Need for Housing

The need for housing is far more difficult to quantify and has a deeper social significance. For example a low-income family might need a three-bedroomed house, but may not be able to afford it. Their requirement for a house would be counted as housing need, but not as housing demand. On the other hand, a wealthy single person may be able to afford a three-bedroomed house, but does not really need it: his requirement would be included in housing demand, but not housing need.

Local housing authorities have to take account of housing need rather than housing demand. They have to try to quantify what the population actually needs in the way of housing, rather than what it appears to want as reflected in the usual round of housebuying and renting. We need to note here that the Local Government and Housing Act 1989 provides that local authorities are no longer required to keep a housing stock. As you work through this study text, this will become apparent with the transfer of many of the local authorities' housing stock to housing associations and other forms of ownership.

Clearly organizations have a much harder task in trying to measure housing need than if they were trying to measure housing demand. To measure housing need, we must look at the social structure of the population, such as at the age of the residents, their family structure, economic circumstances and so on. This is a very difficult task. It is not made any easier by the fact that the make-up of the population is constantly changing as we shall see as we work through this text.

Think of your own family network. How has it changed in the last few years? Has it affected the housing need? Have members of the family moved in search of better employment prospects?

Local housing authorities are obliged to review the housing needs of their districts on a yearly basis. What they have to do is try to reach a rough estimate of how many additional dwellings are required, according to a supply and demand formula. (It is perhaps unfortunate that the word 'demand' is used, when we know that what local housing authorities really want to know about is housing 'need'.)

Let us look for a moment at the supply and demand factors. The first point to bear in mind is that the number of houses needed is not directly related to the size of the population, but to the number of households in the population. The Chartered Institute of Public Finance and Accounting explains the effect of this complication very well:

> A prediction of the number of households over a period of time is a complex calculation depending on a number of variables. As a start a prediction must be made about the size of the population in the time period involved, using all information about birth and death rates and migration from one area to another... Having established the likely size of the population, this has to be analysed into a number of expected households, for this is the figure which, when adjusted for joint use of a dwelling by more than one household and for single-person households, will form the basis of the calculation of housing need in terms of the number of units required.

So the 'demand' can be roughly calculated as:

present number of separate households

plus natural increase or decrease in household population

plus immigration into the district

less emigration from the district

plus an estimated number arising from the fact that populations tend now to break down into smaller households often as a result of a breakdown in a family relationship.

The government uses a General Needs Index and a Housing Needs Index to assess housing needs on a national and on a localized level. Numerical representations are produced and indices are used as statistical methods to provide a rendering of housing needs across the country, regions of the country and particular local authority areas. The statistics take in deprivation, housing conditions, excess demand above supply, over- and under-occupation etc. Currently the indices indicate that resources should be concentrated in the South East and London. The indices also compare one council's performance against another.

Both the Office of the Deputy Prime Minister and the Housing Corporation use the indices in allocating resources to those areas and local authorities which need them most and in allocating funds to housing associations.

1.4   The Supply of Housing

The 'supply' is the size of the existing stock, bearing in mind that the stock may well be:

- increased over the relevant period by new building or by improvement and conversion programmes;

- decreased over the relevant period by wastage or obsolescence and demolition. A reduction should also be calculated to take account of 'voids' and 'second homes', in order to arrive at a sensible figure for total stock available. (A 'void' is a property not physically occupied. It might, for example, be a vacant council dwelling awaiting new tenants, or it could be a vacant private sector dwelling waiting to be sold. A second home is one used as a 'holiday' home, eg many such dwellings are found in areas of natural beauty (ie Lake District) or by the sea and are used as 'retreats' by city dwellers.)

Once the local housing authority has estimated the supply and demand, the remainder of the calculation is simple enough:

Demand less supply   =   total housing requirement needed to provide every potential household with appropriate accommodation.

It is very important to realize that applying the supply and demand method gives only an estimate of housing need. You must remember that it is virtually impossible to arrive at a precise, or even reasonably accurate figure for true housing need because it involves so many different social factors. However, the supply and demand method at least gives local housing authorities a practical way of planning their housing strategies. If additional housing is required, local housing authorities have to consider where such developments should be.

The Surplus of Dwellings

We shall return to local housing strategies shortly. First, it is useful to illustrate the point that housing need and demand are not the same with the startling news that, statistically, there is actually a surplus of dwellings in England. In December 2002, there were 623,000 vacant dwellings in the private sector. At the same time there were 86,000 vacant local authority dwellings; 38,000 empty housing association dwellings and 16,000 other public sector vacant dwellings.

Initially your thoughts may be that these figures are extremely high, especially when so many people are homeless and live on the streets. We shall look closer at reasons as to why so many dwellings are empty later but we can say briefly here that some are unfit and cannot be used and this applies to both public and private-sector properties.

If we look for a moment at the private-sector dwellings, 45% of these were vacant because they were in the process of being sold – these are known as 'frictional' or 'transitional' vacancies. Similarly in the public sector, 60% are between lettings and essential to allow mobility.

We shall look later in this unit at a variety of housing statistics.

Information on housing can be gathered from a wide area of statistics as we shall see as we work through this study text. One useful source of information is the English House Condition Survey.

The latest survey was carried out in 2001. This survey was the eighth of a five-yearly series undertaken by the government. The survey assesses the condition of the housing stock together with improvements made. It also assesses how poor conditions are distributed across different types of dwellings, households and areas. These surveys provide the government with the major source of information on the country's housing stock and assist in the development and monitoring of policies directed towards the repair, improvement and energy efficiency of that stock.

Table 1.1: English housing stock: December 2002		
Owner-occupied	14,901,000	70%
Local authorities	2,708,000	13%
Registered social landlords (mainly housing associations)	1,467,000	7%
Private rented sector	2,190,000	10%
	21,266,000	100%

Note: Some 220,000 households in England have a second home, most of them (87%) owned.

Source: Office of the Deputy Prime Minister

The housing stock in the UK increases by less than 1% per annum in spite of an increasing number of households. Most of the money spent on housing each year is in respect of existing dwellings, many of which were built before the Second World War. This is irrespective of whether the property is owner-occupied, social housing or privately rented. Housing costs are in the form of rent or mortgage repayments and as such constitute the largest single item of regular expenditure.

For those who have studied economics, housing is a durable commodity (ie long-lasting and resists wear compared with other commodities such as cars, washing machines etc.). As such houses last for many, many years and consequently not only retain their value but with inflation, actually increase in value.

Houses are the most popular dwelling type and account for 80% of all dwellings. These range from small terraced properties to large detached properties. Flats account for 20% of dwellings although the proportion of flats in the rented sectors (private and social) is much higher than in the owner occupied stock (9%). The ratio of houses to flats varies from area to area and also across the different tenures; flats tend to be concentrated to the greatest extent in the rented sectors. In England there are nearly four million rural dwellings (20% of the housing stock) and these dwellings are in better condition than those in urban areas. (Similarly there are fewer vacant dwellings in rural areas).

However, rural areas lack affordable housing. This is partly caused by lower average incomes for those working in rural areas compared with those working in urban areas. Many new households cannot afford to enter the rural housing market and consequently rural homelessness and out migration has increased.

As such rural areas are becoming increasingly polarised between richer newcomers who can afford the high housing costs and the indigenous population who are being priced out.

There is an imbalance between the north and the south of England. Some inner cities areas in the north have a surplus of dwellings. Northern towns including Manchester, Newcastle and Middlesbrough have been demolishing new social housing built for either local housing authority or housing association tenants because people do not want to live in the blighted parts of the town.

The opposite in happening in the south, in particular in the south-east, where there is a severe housing shortage many would be home owners cannot afford to start on the property ladder because of the high prices demanded.

The 2001 English House Condition Survey shows that between 1996 (when the last survey was carried out) and 2001 nearly two million dwellings changed tenure, the biggest movements being between owner-occupation and private renting (600,000 dwellings in both directions); the transfer of some local housing authority stock to registered social landlords (350,000) and the sale of local authority dwellings to their occupants through the Right to Buy (see Unit 9) (200,000).

Table 1.2: English housing stock: Rural areas December 2002

	England as a whole	Rural areas
Owner-occupation	70%	74%
Local authorities	13%	12%
Registerd social landlords (mainly housing associations)	7%	3%
Private rented sector	10%	11%

Source: *Office of the Deputy Prime Minister*

There has been a theoretical surplus since the early 1970s. If we were to delve further we would see a similar trend also for the United Kingdom.

We have this surplus of dwellings and yet people are sleeping rough in towns and cities and more recently in the countryside. Can you think why this happens?

We all know that there is a housing problem in the country – the homeless frequently feature in the news and documentaries on television and radio. Let us look at how we have a surplus number of dwellings in this country:

- very often the vacant dwellings are in the wrong part of the country;

- they are often the wrong type, for example where a three-bedroomed dwelling is required and only a bedsit is available (this is known as 'mismatch');

- people have second homes, for example by the sea or in the countryside (an estimated 40% of the dwellings in Keswick, in the heart of England's Lake District, and 16% of those by Lake Windermere, England's largest lake, are second homes and many are owned by people living in the Manchester area). As at December 2002, there were 220,000 households with second homes. It means that 1.0% of households in England owned more than one dwelling for their own use in 2002;

- many houses are 'voids', that is empty pending a considerable amount of work being carried out to restore them to good condition;

- dwellings may be vacant pending sale, often being caught up in the 'chain' when the various purchasers buying houses from others are held up for legal documents and so on. (Note here that the government is considering ways of expediting house sales – this is covered later in the text.);

- dwellings left empty pending road-widening schemes etc;

- local authority and housing association dwellings left empty pending new tenants;

- local authority and housing association dwellings left empty pending monies being made available for improvement works;

- local authority dwellings kept vacant as part of the National Mobility Scheme (which is dealt with in the next unit) under Housing and Organizations Mobility and Exchange Services (HOMES);

- Ministry of Defence and other central government tenancies (although a number of Ministry of Defence dwellings have been sold recently);

- undesirable dwellings, for example tower blocks;

- undesirable areas as a result of crime, vandalism, drugs etc;

- property empty pending inheritance;

- property not within financial reach of people needing accommodation;

- property deliberately kept empty for personal or speculative reasons;

- shortage of particular tenures and especially affordable social housing.

As you can see dwellings are vacant for a variety of reasons, the most common being that they are awaiting sale. This is understandable when most dwellings in the country are in private ownership (either owner-occupied or privately rented). The English House Conditions

Survey shows that 80% of vacant dwellings are in private ownership. Public sector dwellings which are vacant are more likely to be of recent construction than those in the private sector. The public sector 'high-rise' or tower block flats built mainly in the 1960s and early 1970s tend to be difficult to let.

Surprisingly perhaps, 40% of vacant dwellings are in the south east where demand for accommodation is higher. In Greater London alone 105,000 homes stand empty (2002), a figure equivalent to the entire housing stock of Lewisham in London.

In 2002 the number of dwellings exceeded the number of households by about 750,000. Yet this picture is not as rosy as this implies as we have seen above there are many reasons for this 'surplus'. The regional distribution of supply and demand was not equally spread. The measured number of households understates the number of units needing accommodation, ie a couple living with one set of parents whilst awaiting to get accommodation of their own. Such households are known as 'hidden' or 'concealed' households.

Table 1.3: The number of vacant dwellings by tenure in England: December 2002

Type	Number	% of total housing stock
Private*	623,000	3.6
Local authority	86,000	3.1
Housing association	38,000	2.6
Government owned	16,000	18.0
TOTAL	**763,000**	**3.6**

*owner-occupied and privately rented dwellings

Source: *Office of the Deputy Prime Minister*

It is worthwhile noting here that the Empty Homes Agency, a charitable organization, is funded by and works with local authorities in devising strategies to get vacant housing back into use.

In December 1999, the government established the Empty Property Advisory Group in order to identify practical ways to influence behaviour, raise the profile of empty property and possible changes to the existing tax framework.

Unused social housing puts a strain on the public purse because of the need to maintain and secure empty homes. When council blocks are entirely empty, money is paid for security to keep out squatters. Steel shutters, the usual approach, can cost more than £4,000 a year. Empty homes could be brought back into use if the current law on VAT was changed. At present VAT is waived for people building new homes but charged on those repairing old housing stock. This from an economic point of view encourages building on green field land rather than repairing existing homes.

In March 2001, the government announced that VAT would be cut from 17.5% to 5% on all repair and refurbishment works to properties which had been empty for three years or more. This initiative will make many potential schemes to reuse empty homes financially viable.

Council Tax regulations have been amended from 1 April 2000, to provide that empty dwellings requiring major renovation, that have been exempt from Council Tax for one year, are now subject to the standard 50% Council Tax levied on other unoccupied dwellings. This is an endeavour by the government to bring vacant housing back into use.

Housing Stock

Nearly half of our housing stock was built before the Second World War; 20% being built before the First World War and 20% before the Second World War. The early years of the last century saw mainly terraced housing. This changed at the end of the Second World War to semi-detached dwellings. Since 1965, the trend has been for detached dwellings or purpose built flats. Currently of the 135,000 dwellings built in 2000/01 most had three or more bedrooms (80%), 19% had two bedrooms and 1% had just one bedroom.

This trend clearly reflects the aspirations and desires of owners to have a spare bedroom, a storage room or a home office to allow people to work from home thus deriving the benefits of information technology and e-mails!

Table 1.4: Date of dwelling stock by Region – England – December 2002					
Year built	Before 1919	1919 to 1944	1945 to 1964	1965 to 1984	1985 or later	All dwellings thousands
	%	%	%	%	%	%
North East	12	22	29	25	12	1,135
North West	23	22	24	20	11	2,980
Yorkshire and the Humber	19	19	26	25	11	2,166
East Midlands	20	17	21	27	15	1,807
West Midlands	13	22	27	26	12	2,230
East	15	13	26	32	14	2,318
London	28	33	16	16	7	3,087
South East	18	16	22	29	15	3,379
South West	24	13	21	26	16	2,164
England	20	20	23	25	12	21,266

Source: Office of Deputy Prime Minister

Considerable amounts of money were given by local authorities to owners for repairs to the older private sector housing stock in the late 1970s and early 1980s. In spite of these sums spent there remain around 1.5 million dwellings unfit. This represents 7% of the housing stock. These dwellings are more likely to be the older dwellings and concentrated in older urban centres and privately owned. You must, however, consider that significant problems are found on some local authority housing estates, usually as a result of poor design and difficulties in maintenance.

The Local Government and Housing Act 1989 defined through a new fitness standard whether a property is fit for human habitation. This standard replaced, redefined and extended the previous fitness standard contained in the Housing Act 1985.

We need to look at the standard of fitness laid down in the Local Government and Housing Act 1989. This states that a dwelling is unfit unless it has:

· a piped water supply;

· a wash basin with hot and cold water;

· a fixed bath or shower and an internal wc;

· drainage and sanitation facilities;

· facilities for cooking and food preparation, including a sink with hot and cold water and waste disposal facilities;

· adequate natural and satisfactory artificial lighting, heating and ventilation;

· substantially free from rising damp, penetrating damp and condensation.

In addition the dwelling must be structurally stable and in adequate repair.

Another expression used when looking at fitness standards is the term 'amenities' or rather the term 'lacking amenities'. By this we mean lacking those amenities which are classed as standard in legislation. The Housing Act 1985, section 508 defines standard amenities as:

- a fixed bath or shower (see notes 1 and 2);

- a hot and cold water supply at a fixed bath or shower (see notes 1 and 2);

- a wash-hand basin;

- a hot and cold water supply at a wash-hand basin;

- a sink;

- a hot and cold water supply at a sink;

- a water closet (see note 3).

   Notes:

1. A fixed bath or shower shall be in a bathroom, unless note 2 applies.

2. If it is not reasonably practicable for the fixed bath or shower to be in a bathroom but it is reasonably practicable for it to be provided with a hot and cold water supply, it need not be in a bathroom but may be in any part of the dwelling which is not a bedroom.

3. A water closet shall, if reasonably practicable, be in, and accessible from within, the dwelling or, where the dwelling is part of a larger building, in such a position in that building as to be readily accessible from the dwelling.

With the additional money provided for repairing the private housing stock, the condition of the country's dwelling stock has continued to improve. However 207,000 dwellings lack a basic amenity; this represents approximately 1% of the housing stock. Of this figure 100,000 dwellings still lack an internal wc.

Table 1.5: Condition of the dwelling stock – England 1971 – 2001

	1971	1976	1981	1986	1991	1996	2001
Lacking basic amenities*	17.4%	8.9%	5.0%	2.5%	1.0%	1.0%	0.9%

* Dwellings lacking a bath/shower and/or inside w.c.

Source: English House Conditions Survey 2001

In spite of slum clearance programmes during the last century, there are still over 1.5m homes classed as unfit. The late 1960s and early 1970s saw a decisive policy shift away from demolishing towards renovation. (See Unit 10.) However, the level of renovation and improvement fell in the 1980s and 1990s and the condition of the housing stock is rapidly deteriorating. This needs addressing with both regard to local authority dwellings and owner occupied properties. The Labour government is endeavouring to address the public sector issue but cut backs on grant aid places the onus on improving owner occupied properties clearly on the owners.

One of the latest buzz-words to note is the term 'decent home'. This arises out of the English House Conditions Survey. It is best if we consider what is not a decent home, ie:

- unfit;
- in disrepair;
- in need of maintenance;
- insufficient thermal comfort.

The number of these types of dwellings has fallen from 9.4m (46% of all) in 1996 to 7.0m (33%) in the 2001 English House Conditions Survey. The most common reason why dwellings do not reach the standard is because they do not provide a reasonable degree of thermal comfort – 5.6m homes (80% of all non-decent dwellings) fail on this; 4.3m (62%) fail for this reason alone.

Of the 7m, 1.6m are social dwellings, the remainder (5.4m) are in the private sector and are either owner occupied (4.3m) or privately rented (1.1m).

The average cost to make a home decent is £7,200 meaning a total cost of £50bn. Many of the local authority dwellings will be transferred to housing associations; 125,000 are expected to be transferred in 2003 and a further 180,000 subject to arm's length management bids.

Housing

Clearly the tenure with the worst housing conditions is the private rented sector where more than 20% of the occupied dwellings are estimated to be unfit (compared to 7% of total dwellings). Those dwellings most likely to be in poor condition are pre-1919 terraced houses. One in twelve residential properties are in need of major repair or lack standard amenities.

The quality of the stock should, of course, be improved but would cost money. The stock could be improved by

- providing grant aid to owners;

- tax incentives for improvements, major repairs and added amenities;

- target grant funding to those in most need;

- greater extent of estate action programmes in the public sector (see Unit 11) through the increased use of private funding, perhaps by the involvement of housing associations and other agencies;

- clearance and redevelopment of housing which is too expensive to renovate, possibly with the help of housing associations and the attraction of private funding.

There is now broad agreement between professionals on some of the links between poor housing conditions and ill-health and these links are summarized as follows:

Housing defect	Health risk
Inadequate heating facilities	Bronchitis, pneumonia, stroke, heart disease, hypothermia, accidents
Damp and mould growth	Respiratory and other diseases
Inadequate ventilation	Respiratory complaints, carbon monoxide poisoning
Lack of hygiene amenities	Infections
Inadequate kitchen facilities	Accidents, food poisoning
Disrepair	Accidents, fire, infections
Structural instability	Accidents
Inadequate lighting	Accidents
Overcrowding	Infections, stress
Inadequate means of escape	Injury or death from fire
Hazardous materials (eg asbestos)	Cancer

As you can see poor housing conditions such as damp, mould, condensation and cold persist and can cause poor health. This then becomes a knock-on effect for health and social services with hospitals treating a rising level in asthma and respiratory problems and tuberculosis.

Those living in poor housing conditions often suffer mental stress. All these issues need addressing and it is the economy as a whole that bears the cost of productivity lost through illness.

It is estimated that because of the low rate of clearance of obsolete dwellings, coupled with the low number of dwellings being built today, just 130,000 in 2001, the lowest since 1924 (excluding the Second World War period) that dwellings will now have to last more than 7,500 years before they are replaced!

The government is currently looking at the way dwellings are judged fit for human habitation. It wishes to replace the current 'blunt instrument' of a straight pass or fail with a sliding scale. Under the present standard, as referred to above, a dwelling is unfit if it fails in one requirement. The new scale would award points against each requirement, depending on the danger posed, and local authorities would take action on homes below a certain point on the scale.

The government are looking towards a Housing Health and Safety Rating System. This is based on a health and safety risk assessment of hazards identified within a dwelling. The assessment is based upon the likelihood of an injury from a hazard occurring and the outcome of that injury. These two elements combine to provide a hazard score that allows the risk of different hazards to be compared.

This has been brought about by the high number of accidents in the home. In 2000, there were 4,000 domestic deaths arising from falls, fire suffocation, poisoning etc. In that year, there were 1.08m falls reported within dwellings. These accidents cost the National Health Service £300m per annum. The government is also well aware that there are each year up to 30,000 excess winter deaths due to cold homes.

Primary legislation would be required to replace the fitness standard by the Housing Health and Safety Rating System and this could form part of the Housing Bill 2003 (see Unit 5).

1.5   The Role of Local Authorities

Under the Local Government and Housing Act 1989, there is an annual duty placed upon local housing authorities to consider the housing conditions in their area and the need for any action to be taken. This not only includes its own stock but private sector housing as well. The local authorities must make sure that the best use is made of all housing in their areas. Local housing authorities must assess local needs and produce comprehensive housing strategies in partnership with tenants, residents and other members of the local community.

Since the Housing Act 1988 (which we shall look at later in Unit 4), housing associations have become the main providers of new social housing.

Somehow local housing authorities have to find a way through the conflicting mass of housing figures, population statistics and unquantifiable social factors in order to come up with a sensible strategy for tackling the problems of housing. In addition there are limited financial resources available. We have already seen how analysis of supply and demand can help to give some idea of the scale of the problem. On top of that, housing authorities also have to consider:

- policies in other fields which could conceivably affect the housing situation, such as those concerning schools, transport, social services or sewage;

- whether there is sufficient land available for their own needs and those of other public agencies, as well as for builders and developers generally.

Social housing has become stigmatized both in the public perception and reality. Often social housing is poorly located, away from transport routes and other amenities. Social housing estates are seen as the core of social exclusion and many combine high levels of unemployment with poor educational attainment by children and high crime levels.

The incoming Labour government introduced a Comprehensive Review of Spending across the whole spectrum of public expenditure. This was published in July 1998 and the key features were as follows:

- significant additional resources through the Capital Receipts initiative;

- accent on regeneration through the New Deal for Communities;

- investment in renovations and improvement of existing local authority housing stock;

- promotion of public/private partnerships in housing;

- increased tenant involvement through Tenant Participation Compacts (see Unit 8).

Local Housing Strategy and Housing Investment Plan

One of the most important ways in which local authorities attempt to summarize the various factors affecting housing is to produce a Housing Investment Programme (HIP). As its name implies, a HIP also puts local authority housing strategies into financial terms.

In order to put HIPs into context we need to look back to the period just after the Second World War when under the Labour government of 1945-51, a cheap money policy was pursued. Local authorities were able to borrow monies for various aspects of their work (including housing) at very low interest rates from the Public Works Loans Board. Under the Conservative regime which followed interest rates were increased and local authorities actively encouraged to borrow on the open money markets using the Public Works Loans Board as a last resort.

A Labour government was returned to power in the mid-1960s and in 1967 there was the devaluing of the pound. Consequently the government announced a package of public expenditure cuts in January 1968. Further public expenditure cuts were delivered by the Conservative government between 1969 to 1974.

During the mid-1970s inflation was running high; interest rates were likewise high and volatile so the Labour government introduced under the Housing Act 1974 a system of annual local authority bids and allocations from central government with regard to improvement expenditure. In 1976, the government announced that the system would be extended to all capital spending on housing with effect from the financial year 1977-78. The system to be used would be known as Housing Investment Programmes.

The idea that local authorities should set out a detailed plan for their forthcoming housing activities was first put forward in the 1977 Green Paper *Housing Policy*. This indicated that there were advantages to both central and local government by adopting the concept of HIPs. The Green Paper claimed:

> *It will provide a means of controlling public expenditure while allowing resources to be allocated selectively with regard to variations in local housing requirements. Within the context of national policies and standards it will increase local discretion by putting greater responsibility for deciding the right mix of investment on the local authorities. For instance, they will be able to decide for themselves the right balance to be struck between acquiring and if necessary renovating existing houses and building new ones.*

> *It will give authorities an incentive to seek the most cost effective mix of spending programmes to meet their requirements. It will encourage local authorities to adopt a comprehensive approach to housing provision including provision for those in special needs. It will provide some flexibility to alter spending within a financial year and from one year to another as circumstances change, thus improving the use of time resources and cash when unforeseen opportunities or problems arise.*

The Green Paper also stated:

> *Local authorities will be asked to prepare comprehensive local housing strategies. The strategies will be based on assessments of the full range of housing needs in each area, taking account of policies in other fields – such as transport and employment, health and social services – within the broad framework of development plans. Local housing strategies will involve a wide variety of action in both public and private sectors, and will call for further development of existing working relationships between local authorities and all other bodies concerned with housing in their areas, such as the Housing Corporation, registered housing associations, local house builders, building societies, new town corporations, county councils and tenants' and community organizations ...*

In the same year, Housing Investment Programmes (HIPs) were initiated by a government circular. The circular (DOE 63/77) described HIPs as:

> *... designed to enable local authorities to present coordinated analyses of housing conditions in their areas and to formulate coherent policies and programmes of capital spending on public housing. Within the framework of national policies and resources available, this system will enable local authorities to produce solutions that accord most closely to their assessment of local need.*

A local authority has to prepare its HIP annually. Back in 1977 local authorities were required to set out their proposals for housing investment for the following four years; however, this period has since been reduced to two years.

Because they were intended to cover every aspect of housing activity within the district, HIPs were seen as a new form of housing plan, which would help both local and central government.

● Local authorities can obtain a much clearer and more comprehensive picture of the housing situation in their districts. This in turn helps them to draw up a housing strategy and, of course, to cost their proposed housing activities.

● Central government can use the information contained in HIPs to allocate resources efficiently.

These plans have been restructured into what are called Local Housing Strategy and Housing Investment Plans which basically is a three year rolling programme presented to the Government Office for the region.

The Plan still identifies local housing need, considers policies for all housing tenures in the area including enforcing standards in the private rented sector and makes a bid for capital approval.

Local housing authorities are required to complete these plans each year within the context of national, regional and local policy priorities and developments and establish the framework for delivering housing related services over the next three years. The government's Housing Policy Statement shows its commitment to housing, social inclusion and community development.

To achieve sustainable solutions, the Housing Strategy needs to bring together measures that tackle not just housing but also health, the environment, local economic conditions, social inclusion, crime and safety, local employment, training initiatives and various other initiatives. To achieve this, links are necessary with other programmes – community care, forging links with local agencies such as health authorities and the police and involvement with regeneration projects. These objectives are achieved by joint ventures and partnerships.

Mixed Communities

The government is committed to creating mixed communities wherever appropriate rather than areas of exclusively high cost or low cost, to increasing the supply of affordable housing and to creating a greater choice of housing types.

Affordable housing is where the rent or price is permanently reduced, directly or indirectly, by means of subsidy from the public, private or voluntary sector and which is provided or managed by a registered social landlord.

Builders now have to include affordable housing in any development of 16 or more houses in London and 25 or more elsewhere.

The idea behind mixed tenures is to combat social exclusion and avoid concentrations of deprivation. It would help to change the image of social housing, particularly if all homes are built to the same specification, with the same external elevations. Ultimately mixed tenures would protect the value of the investment in social housing.

There will be certain obstacles to be overcome:

● homeowners are generally less keen on mixed tenure than social housing tenants;

● developers are unwilling to take the marketing risk of 'pepper-potting';

● like all housing developments, mixed tenure schemes require an active property market to ensure the successful sale of homes;

● previous mixed tenure schemes have separated out the social housing from the owner-occupied to meet the marketing needs of the developer – this does not encourage integration between residents of different tenures.

Sustainable development: Local Agenda 21

Homes produce 25% of the CO_2 emissions in the United Kingdom, consume significant amounts of energy and water resources and produce large amounts of waste. Many of the materials used in construction are natural non-renewable resources or toxic.

At the Rio de Janeiro Earth Summit in 1992, world leaders agreed on an action to tackle the major threats to the environment and improve people's quality of life. It is known as Local Agenda 21 and is a plan for achieving 'sustainable development', ie development that meets the needs of the present without compromising the ability of future generations to meet their own needs. There is a need to deal with the growing problems of pollution, waste and loss of natural resources. Environmental problems and their solutions are interdependent on social and economic issues such as poverty and health. It promotes an integrated response to social, economic and environmental issues, particularly through the development of locally based initiatives.

1.6   Housing Statistics

Wide-ranging statistics on housing stock are available but it would be inappropriate for us to delve too deeply into the mass of available housing stock statistics here. Probably the most important point to remember is that there are three main ways in which they may be presented. These are:

● by tenure;

● by total completions over a period;

● by total stock figures.

Tenure

Tenure describes the terms on which households occupy their homes. People usually own or rent dwellings. Many own dwellings but have an outstanding balance which they owe to a building society, insurance company, bank or other lending institution. This is repaid with interest at regular intervals. Others rent properties from local housing authorities, housing associations or private landlords. Thus the way in which people 'hold' property is known as **tenure**.

Some people occupy a dwelling without either owning it or paying rent. Examples are live-in servants, farm workers, clergymen and some policemen who are required to live in certain properties by the nature of their employment. They are said to do so under what is known as a 'service tenancy'.

As we go further into this book, we shall see how housing tenure has changed. Housing tenure is linked closely to social class and economic status, eg professionals are far more likely to reside in detached dwellings (37%) than unskilled workers (7%). Those households consisting of lone parents with dependent children are more likely to rent their property than to own it and in most cases the renting would be from either a local authority or housing association.

It is interesting to note here that housing tenure depends very much on the age of the head of household. In 2002, 40% of households where the head of household was under 25 were living in the private rented sector. In particular, private rented furnished properties were in demand by those under 25. People over 65 tend to own their own property outright, many having repaid their mortgage on retirement. Those living in furnished accommodation are the most mobile (ie moving between properties) with 50% of 16–24 year olds living at their address for less than a year, compared to 57% to outright owner occupiers who remain in their homes for at least 20 years. Similarly, 25% of local authority tenants have been in their homes for at least 20 years. Basically, as we have seen there are three principal types of housing available in the UK; these are:

- owner occupation – people living in their own homes
- social housing – housing provided for rent at below market level
- private renting – housing rented from a private landlord

It is useful to look briefly at each of these areas now.

- **owner occupation**

Owner occupation has increased rapidly since the beginning of the last century and particularly so since the Second World War. Currently 70% of households in England own their own homes either with a mortgage or outright. The figure for Scotland is 62%, in Wales 72% and in Northern Ireland 68%. Since 1981 to date the number of owner occupied properties in the UK has doubled.

Owner occupation has increased because of the popular image of ownership providing both control and autonomy. It offers more freedom and choice than other tenures. It is clearly regarded as the most profitable investment that ordinary people can ever make and the profit element of house purchase is often the discussion at dinner parties or even on the beaches when holidaying abroad! It is also far easier to obtain credit if an owner occupier.

As a direct result of the dramatic increase in owner occupation since the Second World War, inheritance is becoming increasingly important as a form of wealth accumulation. Properties owned by parents are left to children who are usually owner occupiers themselves. Such properties are sold immediately in most cases with half the money being invested; a third of the money is used for buying or improving a property and the rest for general spending. With such wealth accumulation the 'rich get richer and the poor get poorer' as the wealth is distributed amongst the higher social classes. What is also becoming very apparent is that children of home owners tend to marry other children of home owners and these children will, in due course, stand to gain from two inheritances.

- ● **social housing**

Renting from local authorities increased from 19% in 1951 to 30% in the early 1970's; this was a direct result of major local authority house building programmes during that period.

Council tenants can now purchase their dwellings as indeed can some housing association tenants.

Council housing is now just 13% of the country's housing stock. This decrease is as a direct result of the Right to Buy whereby over 1.4m dwellings in England (1.8m in Great Britain) have been sold coupled with transfers of local authority dwellings to Registered Social Landlords. Since 1988, nearly 500,000 such dwellings have been transferred; the main reason for the transfers being financial. Because of the backlog of repair work in the local authority housing stock, transferring is often seen as the best way to bring about improvements by bringing in private investment.

- ● **private rented sector**

The private rented sector has declined rapidly since the Second World War. Back in 1951, 52% of dwellings were privately rented, this figure dropped to just 6% in the late 1970's. This collapse of the private rented sector was caused by landlords selling, when gaining possession, into the owner occupied market. Landlords had been unable to increase controlled rents for many years. At the time of introduction of the Right to Buy in 1980, there were 400,000 houses in the private rented sector with controlled rents; under the Housing Act of that year, these were converted to regulated tenancies whereby fair rents would be set irrespective of the condition of the properties.

In a further endeavour to revitalise the private rented sector, the government introduced new types of tenancies which we shall look at later in Unit 8.

As a result of these initiatives the private rented sector was revitalised to some extent. Private rented sector accommodation increased further with the massive slump in the owner occupied market in the late 1980s. Whereas previously landlords had taken the opportunity of selling properties into the owner occupied market when they gained vacant possession, this proved difficult at that time with falling house prices. Many landlords held onto properties waiting for house prices to rise again.

Since that period a further initiative has been introduced; the Buy to Let which was launched in 1996. This initiative set up by the Association of Residential Lettings Agents (ARLA) has been actively supported by leading mortgage lenders. It is estimated that 15% of dwellings purchased in the South East are under the Buy to Let initiative.

Table 1.6 indicates the tenure of dwellings in the European Union.

Table 1.6: Dwelling stock in the European Union

	Owner Occupied %	Rented %	Other %
Austria	56	41	3
Belgium	74	23	3
Denmark	51	45	4
Finland	60	30	10
France	55	39	6
Germany	31	69	–
Greece	76	20	4
Ireland	81	14	5
Italy	76	22	2
Luxembourg	70	26	4
Netherlands	53	47	–
Portugal	64	28	8
Spain	82	11	7
Sweden	39	44	17
United Kingdom	68	32	–

Source: *Office of Deputy Prime Minister*

Housing Costs

House prices have continued to rise in the new century. The average dwelling price in the UK in 2003 was £127,412 (an increase of 28% on 1999 prices). House prices vary throughout the different regions of the country.

Prices are highest in the London area where the average price of £210,958 is nearly three times the average house price in the North East (£72,701). In the North West, the average price is £81,816; in the West Midlands £101,307 and the East Midlands £90,990. You need to note that these prices are average across the board prices including all types of dwellings. A detached house in London in 2003, would fetch almost £500,000, four times the cost of a detached house in the North East.

The average sale price of £127,412 is 5.2 times the average salary. This is the highest ratio since the comparison was first made 50 years ago. It suggests that families and first time buyers have been prised out of the market. The 5.2 figure is worse than the previous highest index figure of 5.0 seen during the last property boom of 1989 which was followed by a devastating bust which fuelled a recession and plunged thousands of homeowners into the misery of negative equity – owing more on their homes than the properties were worth on the market. The long term average for this ratio is 3.6 but with the exceptionally low interest rates at present, a figure of 4% is sustainable.

City analysts now predict a fall of prices by as much as 15%–20% from the middle of 2004; this would be necessary to get the rate back to an average ratio of 3.6.

Any drop in house prices is not expected to see the misery of the last bust in the early 1990's which was coupled with rising unemployment and a wide recession. During this period many people handed back their keys to the lenders after they lost their jobs and could not afford to meet rising mortgage repayments.

With high house prices, savings can be made in terms of hard cash if people are willing to travel some distance to work. Savings on house prices more than make up for the cost of commuting. To give some comparisons let us consider a property in West London selling at £337,910 to similar properties in various commuter belts (see Table 1.7).

Table 1.7: Correlation of house prices and distances from London

Area	Price of Property	Distance in miles from London	Savings per mile
Reading	£188,547	41	£3,643
Milton Keynes	£167,707	55	£3,095
Southampton	£161,637	77	£2,289
Swindon	£157,842	82	£2,196

Table 1.7 shows a clear correlation between house prices and the distance from London. Similarly prices of properties further from the City or the bright lights of the West End are cheaper.

A survey undertaken in 2003, showed that the location and quality of life services or blights affect the value of a property.

These are summarized below:

Positives (within 3 miles)	**Negative – things to avoid**
● main line railway	● run-down/derelict houses
● motorway/dual carriageway links	● airport flight path
● top state school	● derelict land
● open countryside/park	● pungent takeaway
● restaurants/pub/nightlife	● late licence drinking/music venue

Positives (within 3 miles) (cont.)	Negative – things to avoid
• quality food stores	• busy road
• good NHS hospital	• waste/refuse station
• sports club/exercise facilities	• poorly-rated comprehensive school
• post office/bank	• local authority housing
• cinema/entertainment	• electricity pylons
	• prison
	• railway line
	• mobile phone/telecom masts

London has the lowest percentage of dwellings in the lowest valuation bands. These valuation bands were set out following the introduction of council tax which replaced the community charge in England and Wales in April 1993. The amount of council tax payable is dependent on the valuation band allocated to the dwelling; the lowest band is A and the highest is H. Sixty-eight per cent of dwellings were in the lowest three council tax bands in 2003. The North had the greatest percentage in bands A to C with 86 per cent compared to the South East which had the lowest at 49%.

Council taxes are raised by local authorities to part fund the services they provide. The amount payable depends on the value of the property they occupy. Those on low income can receive assistance in the form of Council tax benefits.

New house building in England

Another way of describing stock figures statistically is to show how many dwellings have been completed (built), year by year. Examples of this kind of statistic are given in Table 1.8.

The number of dwellings build each year has dropped significantly in recent years as indicated in Table 1.8.

Table 1.8: New house building in England: December 2002

	1979	1997	2002
Private	118,000	128,000	126,000
Local authority	75,000	300	400
Housing association	16,000	21,000	13,500
Total	209,000	149,300	139,900

Source: Department of the Deputy Prime Minister.

The number of owner-occupied dwellings continues to rise, but more slowly in recent years. The 1980s saw increases in owner-occupation due to the Right to Buy initiative of the incoming Conservative government in 1979.

We referred to mortgages briefly earlier. Let us look further into this now.

Approximately 75% of all houses purchased are with the aid of a mortgage loan facility. There are various types of mortgages, the main methods being:

- repayment;
- endowment; and
- interest only.

Repayment mortgages are usually for 25 years and are those that provide for regular monthly payments whereby over the life of the mortgage, the debt and interest are entirely repaid.

Endowment mortgages are those where interest is paid on the loan and at the same time contributions are made to an insurance policy which in due course should repay the outstanding amount at the end of the mortgage term. The popularity of endowment mortgages peaked in 1988 when they accounted for 83% of all new mortgages. However now endowment mortgages account for just 17% of all loans. This is as a direct result of investments not growing fast enough to repay the capital borrowed.

In 2003, 25% of the 250,000 mortgage endowments maturing that year were insufficient to pay off the home loans they were supposed to. The shortfall spells catastrophe for home owners who faced being plunged into debt, plundering other savings or switching to a repayment mortgage to make good the shortfall. Consequently some owners could be forced to work into their retirement.

Nowadays mortgage interest rates are often fixed for the first few years of a loan before they become variable; currently most mortgages are of this type. It is quite common now with the changing mortgage market for borrowers to shop around for the best deals. In 2002 nearly 50% of new loans were for people re-mortgaging existing homes.

When there is a boom in the housing market, there tends to be an increase in the ratio between house prices and average wages/salary. The norm is 3.5; this went as high as 4.98 in the late 1980s.

As far as privately-rented dwellings are concerned, this reached its lowest level in 1988 at just 8% of the total number of dwellings. In an endeavour to revitalize the private rented sector, the government enacted the 1988 Housing Act. This abolished rent regulations in relation to new lettings and weakened the security of private tenants. The number of dwellings privately let has subsequently revived and now stands at 10% of all dwellings (Table 1.1).

Local authority lets have dropped from 29% in England to just 13% between 1981 and today. There has been an increase in the number of housing association lets because of the transfer of some local authority housing stock.

Stock Transfers

In 2003, the Commons' Public Accounts Committee revealed that homes transferred to housing associations were being handed over for too little money, short changing the public purse by millions of pounds. The Committee also found that for each house transferred, the tax payer spent at least £1,300.

The Committee noted that council housing managers often moved with their housing stock becoming housing association managers and increasing their salaries by 20% to 30%. This gave them an incentive to recommend transfers. The Committee further noted that many tenants felt pressured to vote for a switchover because their homes had fallen into disrepair and that they had no other hope of getting them renovated. Although the policy had been introduced to give tenants more choice, in fact they had no choice of landlord, with the housing association merely replacing the local authority.

Under the stock transfer programme, housing associations pay for the homes with private loans secured against money they expect to get from rents over the next 30 years

Total

Perhaps the most important statistic relating to the housing stock is simply the number of dwellings in existence. These will be the basic figures that demonstrate (in conjunction with population statistics) whether there is a surplus or deficit of total dwellings.

There are two important points to remember about housing stock statistics.

- The statistics themselves do not pretend to be spot-on. There are always inaccuracies caused by errors in information collected and by the rounding of figures. Nevertheless they are a good indication of the broad situation of the housing stock.

- No single statistical table tells the full story of the housing stock. For example, a table showing the total stock might reveal a surplus of dwellings – but only in conjunction with another table on the size of the population. In any case, the surplus might be more apparent than real, as another table on housing stock by tenure might show.

Completions of new dwellings continue to drop; the reasons for this are as follows:

- the government wish local authorities now to be enablers and provide housing as a last resort; hence local authority starts have dwindled as this has become a reality;

- subdued levels of housing association activity throughout the period;

- the depressed housing market conditions generally resulting in private speculative starts plummeting.

Table 1.8: Tenure by length of time at current address 2000/01

Great Britain	Percentages					
	Under 1	1–4	5–9	10–19	20 years	All
Owner-occupied	year	years	years	years	or more	
Owned outright	3	10	9	21	57	100
Owned with mortgage	8	30	22	18	12	100
Rented from social sector						
Local authority	10	28	17	20	25	100
Housing association	11	33	24	20	13	100
Rented privately						
Furnished	48	35	9	5	3	100
Unfurnished	28	43	12	7	11	100
All tenures	9	25	17	22	27	100

Source: Social Trends

Owner-occupation

Let us look further at owner-occupation: currently 70% of dwellings are classed as owner-occupied and many of these will be subject to a mortgage. As we might expect, the highest rate of owner-occupation is in the south-east of England where 73% of dwellings are owner-occupied (excluding the London area).

In spite of falling house prices in late 1989 and the early 1990s, people still purchase property as an investment. Status is also involved: it is always interesting to see how quickly the purchasers of council dwellings improve their properties by the addition of a new front door or double glazing, for example. There have been, in the past, limited tax advantages under the MIRAS system. This was phased out in April 2000 following the 1999 Budget.

We shall see in the next unit that it is easier to move around the country in search of employment if you are an owner-occupier rather than a council tenant.

1.7   Future Demand for Housing

We must now consider what the future demand for housing might be. In 1996 the Environment Secretary announced that 176,000 additional homes were required annually. This follows the publication of figures estimating that there will be up to 4.4 million extra households between 1991 and 2016. Such increase represents a 20% increase in the numbers of dwellings in the country. This is equivalent to building 27 more Milton Keynes. Various organizations consider that this is underestimating the need for new homes. However in 1999 the government revised the number of extra households from 4.4 million to 3.8 million.

This revised figure of 3.8 million households equates to a need for building 150,000 new dwellings each year. At first this figure may seem very high but it is not when compared with the number of dwellings built over the last 30 years:

Housing

1960s   3.5 million

1970s   3.0 million

1980s   2.0 million

In fact the scale of development that is likely to be required is less than at any time since the Second World War.

The projected 3.8 million new households would consume 1.6 billion litres of drinking water a day, generate 4 million tonnes of solid waste each year and require 80 new quarries.

The extra 3.8 million households are estimated to be as a result of the following:

- 46% population growth;
- 21% changes in age structure;
- 33% changing social behaviour.

Of the growth 80% are expected to be single-person households:

- arising from divorces/separation;
- people choosing to live alone;
- people living longer and outliving their partners.

The Green Paper *Household Growth – where shall we live?* raised the question of where and whether to meet the housing needs generated by the growth in households.

The government hopes that many of these new dwellings will be built on derelict urban 'brownfield' sites and not virgin land. It is the government's intention that 60% of the dwellings will be built on urban land by:

- using old buildings;
- conversion of offices into flats;
- using derelict buildings;
- using old hospitals;
- using disused airfields.

The House Builders Federation in a publication in August 1997 entitled *New Homes because Britain deserves better – An agenda for the New Government* estimated that meeting the needs and other uses of the increase in households would increase the urban area of England from 10.6% in 1991 to 11.9% in 2016.

As stated above, the Labour government hopes to reclaim enough land to build 60% of the total on derelict urban 'brownfield' sites. Assuming that finance is available, where will they be built? Currently in England and Wales all the dwellings are built on just 12% of the land, which leaves almost 9/10ths of the land available for building on.

Positive planning depends on the availability of land for development or redevelopment; but Great Britain is a small island and the land is therefore limited in extent. The density of population is high for a small island. The aim of town and country planning legislation is to ensure that land is used in the best possible way for the benefit of the community, including reconciling the often conflicting needs of agriculture, development, housing, communication and recreation.

The direction of a national housing policy, however, has a profound influence on planning courses and on the use of land. Following the Conservative regime in 1979, this direction had been towards increasing home ownership and an important part of this process had to be making more land available for developers.

The cost of land is a vital factor in all housing development and this, in the free market which increasingly prevails, inevitably reflects scarcity value. Such value can be derived from permission to develop having been given under planning legislation to certain sites and not to others and often from the location of a site and its desirability or otherwise for development which would give a good economic return.

Green Belt Land

Those who have studied economics at some time will realize that there is a relationship between housing stock and land. In a large country like the United States, where there are wide expanses of land available, the cost of accommodation is not that high because there is little competition for the value of the land. On the other hand, in England a high price is placed on good building land, especially in the south-east of the country. This is because England is a small country with limited land available for building houses upon, unless we venture into the green belt. This is something we shall consider now.

The idea of a 'green belt' – a belt of land around a town or city which should remain undeveloped and unspoilt – is not new. It first gained prominence in 1898 in a vision set out by Ebenezer Howard in his book *Tomorrow: a Peaceful Path to Real Reform* (this book was subsequently republished in 1902 and retitled *Garden Cities of Tomorrow*). The intention was to build low-density units of limited size protected by permanent green areas but linked in groups to form larger towns and cities of 250,000. Suitable factories would be built in a confined area.

This, of course, was completely at variance with the congestion, squalor and lack of planning that existed whereby workers' housing was packed in among factories, mines and mills.

The idea of green belt land remained, however, a remote one until 1935, when the pressures of housing development turned it from an ideal into a necessity.

The first official proposal 'to provide a reserve supply of public open spaces and recreational areas and to establish a green belt or girdle of open spaces' was made by the Greater London Regional Planning Committee in 1935. A few years later in 1938 the Green Belt (London and Home Counties) Act promoted the idea of a green belt around London. The preamble of the Act stated that its intention was *to make provision for the preservation from industrial and building development of areas of land in and around the administrative county of London to confer powers for that purpose upon the London County Council and certain other authorities and persons and for other purposes.*

The Act dealt mainly with technical arrangements for acquiring land, together with powers that local authorities and/or individuals could have over land acquired and so on. New provisions for compensation in the 1947 Town and Country Planning Act allowed local authorities to incorporate green belt land proposals in their first development plans. Then in 1955 a government circular invited local planning authorities to consider the establishment of green belts around their areas. Precisely why this was necessary and how it was supposed to work was succinctly explained at the start of the circular itself:

1. I am directed by the Minister of Housing and Local Government to draw your attention to the importance of checking the unrestricted sprawl of the built-up areas and safeguarding the surrounding countryside against further encroachment.

2. He is satisfied that the only really effective way to achieve this object is by formal designation of clearly defined green belts around the areas concerned.

3. The Minister accordingly recommends planning authorities to consider establishing a green belt wherever this is desirable, in order;

(a) to check further growth of a large built-up area;

(b) to prevent neighbouring towns from merging into one another;

(c) to preserve the special character of a town.

4. Wherever practicable a green belt should be several miles wide, so as to ensure an appreciable rural zone all round the built up area concerned.

5. Inside a green belt, approval should not be given, except in very special circumstances, for the construction of new buildings or for the change of use of existing buildings for purposes other than agriculture, sports, cemeteries, institutions standing in extensive grounds or other uses appropriate to a rural area.

Although the preservation of green belts was generally upheld, development pressures gradually led to some relaxation of the early restrictive policies. A government booklet issued in 1962 contained the statement: 'The Green Belt conception implies no further building except where there is a positive argument for allowing it'. Where, on appeal, 'positive arguments' were put and accepted, developments permission were allowed.

Since the early 1980s there has been increasing controversy over green belts. A draft circular *Green Belts* issued in August 1983 as part of a 'Memorandum on Structure and Local Plans and Green Belt' gave rise to considerable concern because its proposals were seen by many as an outright attack on green belt and urban containment. While the House of Commons Environment Committee investigated green belt and housing land policy early in 1984, an amended green belt circular emphasized government support of green belt and a modified form of the circular was issued in June 1984 stressing urban renewal aspects and recognizing the use of green belt designations within the boundaries of conurbations.

Today the green belts now cover approximately 1,556,000 hectares, about 12% of England. There are 14 separate green belts varying in size from 486,000 hectares around London to just 700 hectares at Burton on Trent.

In January 1995 the government produced a 'Planning Policy Guidance Note' setting out policies on different aspects of planning and as far as green belt is concerned this guidance note:

- states the general intentions of Green Belt policy, including its contribution to sustainable development objectives;

- reaffirms the specific purposes of including land in Green Belts with slight modifications;

- gives policy a more positive thrust by specifying for the first time objectives for the use of land in Green Belts;

- confirms that Green Belts must be protected as far as can be seen ahead, advises on defining boundaries and on safeguarding land for longer-term development needs; and

- maintains the presumption against inappropriate development within Green Belts and refines the categories of appropriate development, including making provision for the future of major existing developed sites and revising policy on the re-use of buildings.

We have already seen that the fundamental aim of Green Belt policy is to prevent urban sprawl by keeping land permanently open; the most important attribute of green belts is their openness – they help to protect the countryside, be it agriculture, forestry or other use. government guidance states the following purposes of including land in Green Belts;

- to check the unrestricted sprawl of large built-up areas;

- to prevent neighbouring towns from merging into one another;

- to assist in safeguarding the countryside from encroachment;

- to preserve the setting and special character of historical towns; and

- to assist in urban regeneration, by encouraging the recycling of derelict and other urban land.

Once Green Belts have been defined, the use of land in them has a positive role to play in fulfilling the following objectives;

- to provide opportunities for access to the open countryside for the urban population;

- to provide opportunities for outdoor sport and outdoor recreation near urban areas;

- to retain attractive landscapes, and enhance landscapes, near to where people live;

- to improve damaged and derelict land around towns;

- to secure nature conservation interests;

- to retain land in agricultural, forestry and related uses.

Once the extent of a green belt has been approved it should be altered only in exceptional circumstances. If such an alteration is proposed, the Office of the Deputy Prime Minister needs to be satisfied that the local authority has considered opportunities for development within urban areas contained by and beyond the Green Belt land. There has been some housing development on such land and the pressure of an expanding population, which in turn creates pressure on housing, has made such development inevitable.

More than 100 square kilometres of green countryside (an area the size of Bristol) is built over every year. Since the Second World War, an area larger than Greater London, Berkshire, Hertfordshire and Oxfordshire combined has been built on. At this rate 20% of England will be urban by 2050.

Indeed the government have approved developments of vast new estates at Stevenage in Hertfordshire and at Newcastle. However, the government has stated that the proportion of new homes built on 'brownfield' sites will be 60% over the next decade and appointed Lord Rogers of Riverside to lead a task force to identify recyclable land (see Unit 10). (Lord Rogers, the London peer, was the architect of the Millennium Dome.)

This 60% figure was stated in the government's planning policy guidance note PPG3 published in March 2000; the purpose being to put an end to suburban sprawl by encouraging higher densities and ensuring that local authorities allocated 60% of new homes to brown field sites. Currently, this figure of 60% is not being met by local authorities; the government wants this target achieved by 2008.

As stated earlier in this unit, VAT charged on urban development invites the building industry to concentrate on the countryside.

Although in theory green belt land should not be developed except in very special circumstances, in practice some of the land has been used for housing development.

The green belt is a sensitive issue, but the argument at its core is straightforward enough: should the green belts be maintained, or should they give way to the need for more housing?

- The argument for maintaining green belts is that they represent a relatively unspoilt part of the environment and make towns and cities a better place in which to live. Pressure groups such as Friends of the Earth and and the Council for the Protection of Rural England subscribe to this view. Perhaps a majority of the voting public does too, because, back in 1987, Nicholas Ridley (the Environment Secretary) said that 'the general presumption against development in the green belt remains firm'. Such arguments were used in a vain attempt by protestors to stop the destruction of trees and wildlife in the Newbury By-Pass demonstration in 1996.

- The argument against green belt land is that there is a greater need for housing development than there is for unspoilt countryside. Certainly this is the view of house developers, who might also argue that houses could be constructed more quickly and more cheaply in green belt areas, using economies of scale. Presumably it is also the view of those who would like to move to a new house, rather than stay cooped up in old cities. Another argument against the green belt is that, if it were opened up for development it would provide not only housing but also an outlet for industry, and therefore result in the creation of new jobs.

In practice, the green belts have been welcomed by most government ministers as a way of stopping the continued outward growth of cities and of preserving city character, promoting agriculture, stimulating recreation and protecting amenities.

What remains uncertain is what alternative action should be taken if the green belt land really is to be preserved. Certainly its maintenance does little, of itself, to preserve the inner cities or to prevent further urban decay. Perhaps schemes such as the London Docklands Development Corporation in the East End of London might be one way of addressing those particular problems. In the meantime, people's desire to have building and other environmentally hostile projects situated as far away as possible from where they happen to be living has given rise to a new term of abuse: the 'NIMBY' syndrome ('not in my back yard').

It is interesting to note here a loophole in the planning laws to build homes on green belt land. Surprisingly, the regulations allow executive homes to be built in green belt areas if they are designated as farm houses. A case has been made by the Council for the Protection of Rural England (CPRE) for these rules to be amended, so that developers must prove that the houses are for farmworkers, since purchasers of land are classed as 'hobby farmers'.

If the subject of green belt land turns up in an examination, you must be sure to give both sides of the issue. Do not let your personal view colour your answer. There is no right or wrong solution to the problem: one policy leads to more housing and less countryside, the other maintains the countryside and curtails development.

Perhaps the only certainty about the green belt issue is that the pressure to develop is going to grow. That is inevitable given the rising population and increasing housing need. Some say that the development of land is inevitable: only time will tell if they are right.

Arguments for retaining green belt land:

- protects against towns and cities encroaching upon each other and against urban sprawl;
- assists with urban regeneration by forcing the government and local authorities to concentrate on redeveloping towns and cities as opposed to building on 'Green Field' sites, eg London Docklands Development Corporation;

- provides opportunity for outdoor sports and outdoor recreation;

- protects countryside from development and allows agriculture, forestry and nature reserves to be maintained;

- preserves historic towns;

- assists in the maintenance of nature conservation by allowing a home for wildlife and a natural environment generally;

- traffic, air, noise and light pollution would be greater if green belt land was released to build on because many occupants would have to travel into the inner towns and cities to work unless they were lucky enough to find local employment;

- environmental arguments such as the destruction of trees and wildlife as in the Newbury By-Pass;

- retains attractive landscapes and enhances landscapes near to where people live;

- creates a greater imperative to regenerate inner cities and towns.

Arguments for releasing green belt land:

- continuing growing demand for more housing as a result of people living longer, more divorces, children leaving home younger than previously cannot be met by redevelopment, etc. of urban areas;

- green belts inhibit development by not allowing the spread of housing industry;

- economies of scale would permit housing to be built at a reasonable price;

- the development of green belt land would create jobs from the outset in rural areas;

- there is insufficient land in urban areas on which to build sufficient dwellings;

- lower building costs because of clean sites;

- greater freedom of design due to more options in the land development.

The government is committed to improving our inner cities and protecting our countryside. John Prescott, Deputy Prime Minister, has gone on record by saying in February 1998.

> We must reclaim our city centres for people. Most people want to live in towns and cities because of their work, their families and the amenities they provide. But many people have been put off by a mixture of rundown public services, poor transport, dilapidated streets, a fear of crime and poor standards in schools. Better planning can put the heart back into urban living; but of course we must also tackle the range of problems in housing, crime, education and transport, to improve the framework for our communities...together we can bring a better way of living to our towns and cities and protect our countryside.

Contaminated land

Laws about contaminated land were introduced in the Environment Act 1995. The Environment Agency estimates that there could be 200,000 problem sites in the United

Kingdom on a total of 300,000 hectares. The pollution covered is both industrial – old asphalt sites and docks, etc. – and natural – such as radon and methane gas. Local authorities are now required to identify such land.

New rules on contaminated land require that the original polluter, eg gas works, steelworks, and chemical factory etc. must pay for the cost of cleaning up the pollution. This could mean the treatment of the contaminated land with chemicals or merely the provision of new topsoil and replacing the old soil. If the original polluter no longer exists or cannot pay then the developer is liable. If the local authority cannot get the developer to pay, then the homeowner has to pick up the tab.

Sustainable Communities: Building for the future (The Sustainable Communities Plan)

The government's 'Sustainable Communities (The Sustainable Communities Plan)' was launched in February 2003, and sets out a long term programme of action to tackle the pressing and worsening problems face by some of the communities in the U.K. As such £22bn has been earmarked to:

- solve the housing crisis;
- end homelessness;
- bring down house prices;
- preserve the Green Belt that has so far stopped London from sprawling out of control;
- increase Green Belt land;
- revive the cities;
- create a spirit of neighbourliness.

This will include:

- £5bn for more affordable housing including £1bn for homes for key workers;
- £300m to encourage modern build housing;
- £500m for deserted and rundown housing areas in the North and Midlands;
- £2.8bn to improve social housing;
- £201m for improving the local environment.

It sets out action to provide good quality homes in places where people want to live, at a price people can afford and in a way that protects the countryside. This means an end to poor housing and bad landlords. Included in this is affordable housing for key workers (nurses, teachers, policeman etc) in high demand areas.

In meeting the additional housing need in the South East, the government have allowed the following growth areas:

- Ashford (Kent) – 31,000 dwellings;
- area around Milton Keynes to Luton, Bedford, Kettering and Northampton – 370,000 dwellings;
- a corridor stretching from London via Stansted to Cambridge – 500,000 dwellings;
- Thames Gateway stretching from the east of the capital along both shores of the estuary (North Kent and South Essex) – 100,000 dwellings.

The government also proposes to address the abandonment of some homes in the North of England and the Midlands by demolishing thousands of empty homes on decaying estates and turning land into parks and open spaces. More powers are to be given local authorities to seize empty homes.

Sustainable communities is all part of the government's drive to raise the quality of life for the communities through increasing prosperity, more employment, better public services, tackling crime and anti-social behaviour etc.

The Sustainable Communities Plan makes clear that there are three routes open to local authorities who need to seek additional investment for part or all of their stock to deliver decent homes: Stock Transfer, Arm's Length Management Organizations (ALMOs) and the Private Finance Initiative (PFI).

Euro

It is very difficult to predict what will happen to the British housing market in the future because of the uncertainty within the current Labour government as to whether Britain should join the Euro. Lower mortgage interest rates are paid in the European Union but many countries have high property taxes.

Britains are generally more likely to own their own homes than those in Europe. However, they are likely to borrow more to buy them. As we have seen most have short-term flexible mortgages because they are cheap. If Britain joined the Euro, home owners with mortgages would be more vulnerable to fluctuations in the interest rate decided by the European Central Bank. Any sharp increase in rates in Europe would not affect the borrowers because they have long-term fixed rate mortgages, whereas British homeowners would see the mortgage payments soar if interest rates increased.

Before joining the euro, there is a need to address the mortgage interest issue and endeavour to get long-term fixed-rate loans; this could cost the average family thousands of pounds extra over a 25-year term.

Currently the Chancellor of the Exchequer is considering higher property taxes to take the heat out of the housing market and put brakes on spiralling prices.

'The Way Forward for Housing'

The government set out its proposals for modernising housing so that everyone has the opportunity of a decent home in its Housing Policy Statement published in December 2000.

This Statement followed a consultation document *Quality and Choice – a decent home for all* published earlier that year.

The government's policy for housing includes:

- for social housing, a wider range of landlords providing high quality services, charging fairer rents and increasing the choice for tenants;

- extra investment for local authorities to improve their housing stock with additional funding available to authorities which achieve excellent standards and establish arm's-length arrangements for the management of their housing;

- support for continued transfer of council housing to non-profit-making registered landlords, where the tenants agree;

- an increase in Private Finance Initiative schemes for housing;

- reforming lettings policies to give tenants more choice over where they live;

- reforming social sector rents to make them fairer, more coherent and affordable;

- promoting best practice for landlord in the private sector and considering options to tackle the minority of bad landlords;

- promoting more affordable housing, in particular through the Starter Home Initiative;

- improving housing benefit to give better customer service and tackle fraud and error;

- tackling housing-related social exclusion for example rough sleeping.

Starter Homes Initiative

In 2001, a report was published by the London Assembly entitled *Key Issues for Key Workers*. It is in the long-term interest of employers to work, not only with each other, but with lenders and developers, both private and public, to meet the housing needs of key workers, ie nurses, police, teachers etc. The report recognizes that many key workers are priced out of the market yet do not qualify for social housing. The report noted that the average price of a property in London was equivalent to 8.6 times a nurse's annual salary. For fire fighters and teachers the ratios were almost as daunting, standing at 7.7 and 6.7 respectively. The knock-on effect is that these key workers move to other areas leaving a chronic shortage of workers in highly priced areas.

The government Starter Home Initiative, launched in September 2001, is helping up to 10,000 key workers in urban and rural areas where house prices are high. The initiative offers key workers an average subsidy of £25,000 to buy homes costing up to £100,000. It is available up to March 2004. Assistance is in the form of equity loans, interest free loans and shared ownership. Equity loans are lump sums given to the key worker at the outset which are repaid not on the usual monthly basis but when the property is sold, ie if a loan of £10,000 is made, representing 10% of the value of a £100,000 home, then the key worker has to pay back a tenth of the property's value when it is sold. The type and amount of assistance available varies from area to area dependent on the scheme being offered by local scheme managers. Applicants have to demonstrate that they would not be able to afford to purchase a home without assistance. There is no age limit on applicants but they must be first time buyers in a household earning less than £35,000.

One of the disadvantages of the scheme is that there are both income tax and national insurance implications. Generally speaking, cash grants paid to an employee by reason of his/her employment by either an employer or a third party are treated as taxable income (under PAYE) and Class 1 National Insurance Contributions would also be paid up to the upper earnings limit for the pay period. The taxable amount is calculated by reference to the difference between the interest payable on the loan and the 'official rate'. As a rough guide an interest free taxable loan of £25,000 would give rise to an employee tax benefit of £1,062 (£25,000 x 4.25%) in which tax at the basic rate would be £233.75 including additional national insurance of about £137.

Reforming Home Buying and Selling

In December 1999, the government launched a pilot scheme in Bristol for improving home buying and selling. The government are keen to take steps to rid us all of the more infuriating aspects of house purchase. As a result a number of local estate agents in Bristol participated in the scheme that hinges on the preparation of a special vendor's pack to speed up the whole process for anyone who is doing the buying.

Traditionally, the buyer is responsible for undertaking searches, obtaining Land Registry entries and commissioning a survey of the property. These tasks are undertaken once an offer has been agreed and then time drags on as property professionals pass bits of paper to each other. This is a crazy back-to-front way of doing things; it inevitably slows down the process when the information does become available and causes people to seek to renegotiate or change their minds. The vendor's pack cuts through all this by getting the vendor to prepare much of the legal work, searches, draft contract, title deeds, replies to standard search enquiries, relevant planning and building control consents and surveyor's report on the condition of the property.

For Conveyancers involved in the pilot scheme, it meant that their working practices had to change because the pack assembly required the immediate carrying out of tasks rather than the traditional method of waiting for somebody else to do something.

Although the aim of the pilot was not to test the speed of the transaction, information was being collected on how quickly exchanges of contracts were being reached. The average length of time taken to get from offer acceptance to exchange was 48 days. This was slightly faster than the national average (62 days). Conveyancers reported that sellers were in a position to exchange much quicker than this but time was lost waiting for others in the chain to proceed. Only two of the 65 sales where offers had been received had failed. This represents about 3% of sellers pack transactions. Nationally, an estimated 28% of transactions fail after an offer has been accepted.

The government tried to introduce this in the Homes Bill 2002, but this failed because of lack of Parliamentary time. The draft Housing Bill 2003 now contains among other things, ways to speed up the house buying and selling process.

Summary

In this unit we have considered the supply of and the demand for housing stock, including some of the available housing stock statistics. We have looked at the difference between housing demand and housing need, plus how this need can be estimated and planned for by local authorities. Finally, looking to the future demand for housing, we have outlined the arguments both for and against the development of green belt land.

2

DEMOGRAPHIC FACTORS

Objectives

After studying this unit, you should be able to:

- name the sources of the various statistics available, concerning both housing and population;

- describe the needs of the vulnerable groups;

- outline the difficulties encountered by first-time buyers;

- explain why some people need to move home in pursuit of employment.

2.1   Introduction

There are two major factors which have a bearing on housing policy. These are:

- the quality and quantity of housing stock, which is theoretically controllable; and

- the size and changing composition of the population, which is not controllable.

In order to work out what needs to be done in the field of housing, the size and composition of the population has to be ascertained and then some predictions must be made as to how it is likely to change in the future. In this unit we shall look at how this is done and at what the current predictions are.

Demography

Students need to be aware of demographic changes and forecasts, but what do we actually mean by **demography**? *The Concise Oxford Dictionary* defines demography as the 'study of statistics of births, deaths, disease, etc., as illustrating conditions of life in communities'.

The reason why demography is included in the syllabus should now be obvious: by studying figures on the size and structure of the population, it should be possible to develop a housing strategy to cope with predicted changes in those population figures.

In housing, we need to look at more than just births, deaths and disease. We must examine the composition of the population in some detail, in order to find out whether any special housing is required.

2.2   Sources of Statistics

Population and housing statistics are available from a number of sources. The main ones are as follows.

National Census

The National Census takes place every ten years in this country. It began in 1801 and, with the exception of 1941 because of the war, has taken place every ten years since then. The latest available figures for the Census relate to 2001. Until recently, collating information from the National Census was time-consuming, taking a number of years to produce information which was often out of date by the time it was produced. With the advancement of information technology, statistics can be analysed far more quickly.

The National Census in 2001 comprised the following topics, some of which had not previously been included:

Personal Topics

1. Name

2. Address of enumeration

3. Usual address

4. Sex

5. Date of birth

6. Marital status/relationship

7. Relationship in household

8. Country

9. Scottish Gaelic language (Scotland only)

10. Welsh language (Wales only)

11. Ethnic group

12. Address one year ago

13. Term-time address of students

14. Economic position/employment status

15. Occupation

16. Industry of occupation

17. Hours worked weekly

18. Address of workplace

19. Means of travel to work

20. Higher education qualifications

21. Long-term illness/carers

Household Topics

22. Dwellings classification

23. Type of accommodation

24. Tenure

25. Number of rooms

26. Bathroom and wc

27. Central heating

28. Number of cars or vans

29. Lowest floor level of accommodation (Scotland only)

The next Census will be held in 2011.

Government Statistics

Useful government sources of information for students of housing include:

- publications such as *Regional Trends* and *Social Trends*, published by the Stationery Office;
- surveys, which are occasionally carried out by the government, of the numbers of males and females employed in different industrial groups;
- statistics on gross annual earnings, compiled by the Department of Work and Pensions;
- housing and construction statistics, produced by the Office of the Deputy Prime Minister.

Some of these statistics were used in Unit 1.

Local Authority Statistics

Examples of records kept by local authorities, which are relevant to housing are:

- planning applications and approvals;
- applications for mortgages;
- applications for tenancy of local authority dwellings;
- house condition surveys;
- homelessness statistics;
- housing and council tax benefit claimants.

Pressure Groups

Various pressure groups keep statistical information on the numbers of people in the particular category in which they are interested. For example:

- Mencap (Royal Society for Mentally Handicapped Children & Adults) keep details on the numbers of mentally handicapped people and the Mental Health Foundation keeps similar statistics together with those of people with learning difficulties;

- organizations such as RADAR (Royal Association for Disability and Rehabilitation) keep records of people with disabilities;

- Age Concern and Help the Aged keep data on the numbers of elderly people;

- Women's Aid and Gingerbread keep records of one-parent families;

- Shelter maintains statistics on the number of homeless people.

Records Kept by Other Organizations

Several other organizations keep records which contain housing information: for example, building societies, banks, universities, trade associations and institutions such as the Chartered Institute of Housing and the Institution of Civil Engineers.

2.3   Definition of Terms

Before going on to look at actual demographic statistics, there are some more terms we need to look at. These are:

- households and families;
- lone-parent families;
- homeless persons;
- socioeconomic status;
- dependent population;
- immigration;
- divorce.

Households and Families

The word 'household' is a common one, but what exactly is a household in the present context? Is it the same as a family? Technically the answer is no. Government documents define a household as:

> *... a person living alone or a group of people who have the address as their only or main residence and who either share one meal a day or share the living accommodation.*

A family, on the other hand, is defined as:

> ... a married couple, or cohabiting couple, either with or without their never-married child or children (of any age), or a lone parent together with his or her never-married child or children. A lone parent ... is a married parent whose spouse does not reside in the same household or any single, widowed or divorced parent.

In other words, a household is a group of people who live and eat together, whereas families consist of a married or cohabiting couple (with or without children) or a lone parent (with children). In practice, most households consist of a single person or a family.

Children are defined as:

> never-married people of any age who live with one or both parent(s). They also include stepchildren and adopted children (but not foster children) and also grandchildren (where the parents are absent).

Dependent children are defined as:

> those children who are never married in families who are aged 16 or aged 16-18 and in full-time education.

There are an estimated 20,715,000 households in England, this figure is projected to rise to 24,000,000 by 2021. The breakdown of the 20,715,000 households is as follows:

North East	1,079,000
North West	2,823,000
Yorks and The Humber	2,092,000
East Midlands	1,740,000
West Midlands	2,155,000
East	2,264,000
London	3,121,000
South East	3,346,000
South West	2,097,000

The number of households in Great Britain has tripled since the Second World War whereas the population has only increased by 50%. This is because more people live alone and households are getting smaller.

You can see by Table 2.1 how the number of one person households has increased dramatically over the last 40 years in Great Britain, with 7m people living alone. This figure is partly reflected by the decline in marriage, the rise in separation and divorce, as well as people marrying for the first time at an older age as well as the desire of many to have independence.

Table 2.1: Household formation

Great Britain	1961	1971	Percentages 1981	1991	2001
One family households					
Living alone	4	6	8	11	12
Couple –					24
No children	18	19	20	23	39
Dependent children	52	52	47	41	9
Non-dependent children only	12	10	10	11	10
Lone parent	3	4	6	10	5
Other households	12	9	9	4	5
Total population (millions)	51.4	54.4	54.8	56.2	57.2

Source: Social Trends

The average size of a household in Great Britain is 2.4 compared to 2.9 in 1971.

This reduction is due to:

● increasing elderly population living alone;

● increasing number of young people living alone, especially men;

● increasing divorce rates (creating smaller households);

● falling family sizes.

Table 2.2: Households: by size

Great Britain	1961	1971	Percentages 1981	1991	2001
One person	14	18	22	27	29
Two people	30	32	32	34	35
Three people	23	19	17	16	16
Four people	18	17	18	16	14
Five people	9	8	7	5	5
Six or more people	7	6	4	2	2
All households (=100%)(millions)	16.3	18.6	20.2	22.4	24.1
Average household size	3.1	2.9	2.7	2.5	2.4

Source: Social Trends

The proportion of teenage girls becoming pregnant continues to increase. Almost 90% of the births to teenage mothers were outside marriage.

However, with increased participation by women in higher education and the labour market, coupled with greater choice and effectiveness in contraception, have encouraged the trend to late child bearing and lower fertility.

Women aged 25–29 are the most likely to give birth but since 1992 those in the age group 30–34 have been more likely to give birth than those aged 20–24.

Lone-parent Families

A lone-parent family is defined as:

> *... one parent, irrespective of sex, living with his or her never-married dependent children, provided these children have no children of their own. Married lone mothers whose husbands are not defined resident in the household are not classified as lone parents because evidence suggests that the majority are separated from their husband either because he usually works away from home or some other reason that does not imply the breakdown of marriage ... Couples describing themselves as married or common-law married but who are in fact cohabiting are coded and counted as married.*

Homeless Persons

Homelessness was originally defined in the Housing (Homeless Persons) Act 1977, which was consolidated into the Housing Act 1985. Changes were made to the legislation under the Housing Act 1996 and further changes implemented under the Homelessness Act 2002. A person is homeless if:

- they have no accommodation available for their occupation anywhere in the world;

- they cannot secure entry to it;

- their occupation of it is likely to result in violence or threats of violence from someone else who has resided there;

- their accommodation consists of a vehicle or movable structure and they cannot park it, or moor it if it is a boat;

- they are likely or will become homeless within 28 days.

The accommodation must be reasonable for the person who is to occupy it.

Accommodation should be regarded as available for a person's occupation only if it is available for occupation by him together with

a) any other person who normally resides with him as a member of his family; or

b) any person who might reasonably be expected to reside with him. However it is not reasonable for a person to continue to occupy accommodation if it is probable that this will lead to domestic violence against him, or against (i) a person who normally resides with him as a member of his family, or (ii) any other person who might reasonably be expected to reside with him.

Legislation goes on to specify certain groups who have a priority need:

- a pregnant woman or a person with whom a pregnant woman resides or might reasonably be expected to reside;

- a person with whom dependent children reside or might reasonably be expected to reside;

- a person who is vulnerable as a result of old age, mental illness or handicap, or physical disability or other special reason or with whom such a person resides or might reasonably be expected to reside. This includes those in danger of physical or sexual abuse or who have fled violence;

- a person who is homeless or threatened with homelessness as a result of an emergency such as flood, fire or other disaster;

- 16 and 17 year olds;

- care leavers aged 18–24;

- people assessed as vulnerable because of an institutionalised background such as former prisoner.

If a local housing authority has reason to believe that a person is homeless or threatened with homelessness, it must make enquiries to satisfy itself:

a)   whether he is eligible for assistance; and

b)   if so whether any duty, and if so what duty, is owed to him.

The local housing authority needs to make enquiries as to whether the applicant has a local connection with another local housing authority in England, Wales or Scotland; if so, the applicant will be informed in writing and the local housing authority in question will also be notified.

As well as having a 'priority need' (referred to above), a person must have a local connection with the Council where they are seeking housing, ie they must show why they have approached that particular local authority.

This 'local connection' could be that:

i)   a person is or was a resident of that area;

ii)   a person is employed there;

iii) a person has family connections with the area;

iv)   there are special circumstances such as a family returning from abroad or people wishing to return to an area in which they were brought up or had lived for a considerable length of time in the past.

A person becomes intentionally homeless if he deliberately gives up accommodation he already had which he could reasonably continue to occupy. Therefore a person becomes threatened with homelessness if he deliberately does or fails to do anything the likely result of which is that he will be forced to leave the accommodation which is available. An example of making oneself intentionally homeless is the failure to heed warnings to control children, leading to eviction because the family caused a nuisance and an annoyance to neighbours; *R v Salford City Council ex p Devenport* (1983).

Similarly intentionally homeless could include an applicant disposing of her home as a result of having obtained a mortgage by deliberately supplying false information to the building society.

In *R v Barnet London Borough Council ex p Rughooputh*, the applicant, in an attempt to raise money for a business venture, obtained a £46,000 mortgage on her flat from Skipton Building Society by falsely stating she was at work and earning £18,000 per annum. The business failed leading to the building society taking proceedings against the applicant and obtaining possession. As a homeless person the applicant applied to the council for accommodation. Under the Housing Act 1985, the council was required to ascertain the cause of the homelessness and whether it was a result of a deliberate act by the applicant. There was a fraudulent application made for a mortgage. It was not possible to hold that a fraudulent act such as that done by the applicant was done in good faith and consequently she was not regarded as homeless.

Legislation provides that every local housing authority shall secure that advice and information about homelessness, and the prevention of homelessness, is available free of charge to any person in their district. The Authority may give to any person by whom such advice and information is provided on behalf of the Authority assistance by way of a grant or loan.

Where a local authority considers that an applicant may be homeless, eligible for assistance and in priority need, it is under a duty to secure accommodation pending a decision as to what further duty may be owed. Figure 2.1 summarizes those duties.

Figure 2.1: Homelessness: Summary of duties owed by local authority

Not eligible for assistance	→	No duty owed
Eligible for assistance, but not homeless or threatened with homelessness	→	No duty owed

Figure 2.1: Homelessness: Summary of duties owed by local authority (*continued*)

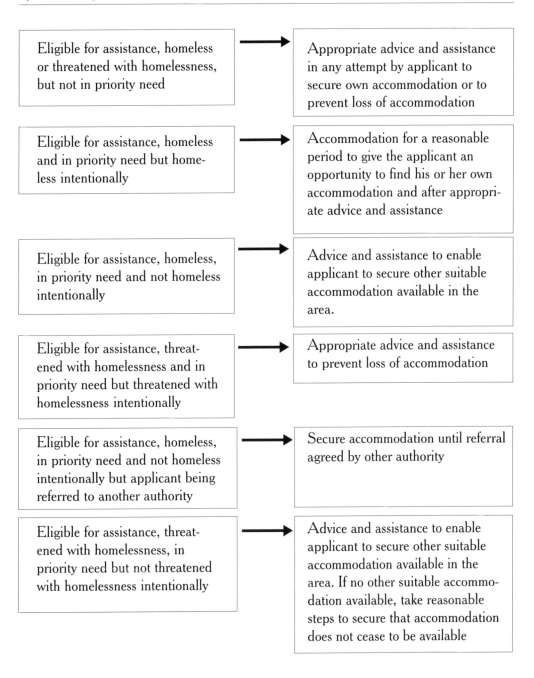

Eligible for assistance, homeless or threatened with homelessness, but not in priority need	Appropriate advice and assistance in any attempt by applicant to secure own accommodation or to prevent loss of accommodation
Eligible for assistance, homeless and in priority need but homeless intentionally	Accommodation for a reasonable period to give the applicant an opportunity to find his or her own accommodation and after appropriate advice and assistance
Eligible for assistance, homeless, in priority need and not homeless intentionally	Advice and assistance to enable applicant to secure other suitable accommodation available in the area.
Eligible for assistance, threatened with homelessness and in priority need but threatened with homelessness intentionally	Appropriate advice and assistance to prevent loss of accommodation
Eligible for assistance, homeless, in priority need and not homeless intentionally but applicant being referred to another authority	Secure accommodation until referral agreed by other authority
Eligible for assistance, threatened with homelessness, in priority need but not threatened with homelessness intentionally	Advice and assistance to enable applicant to secure other suitable accommodation available in the area. If no other suitable accommodation available, take reasonable steps to secure that accommodation does not cease to be available

A person who ceases to be owed the duty under the legislation may make a fresh application to the authority for accommodation or assistance in obtaining accommodation.

An applicant has the right to request a review of:

a)   any decision of a local housing authority as to his or her eligibility for assistance;

b)   any decision of a local housing authority as to what duty (if any) is owed to him or her and anyone found to be homeless or threatened with homelessness;

c)   any decision of a local housing authority to notify another authority of a local connection.

The Housing Act 1996 required that reasonable preference be given by local authorities to the six categories of people indicated below:

- people occupying insanitary or overcrowded housing or otherwise living in unsatisfactory housing conditions

- people occupying housing accommodation that is temporary or occupied on insecure terms

- families with dependent children

- families consisting of, or including someone, expecting a child

- households consisting of, or including someone with, a particular need for settled accommodation on medical or welfare grounds

- households whose social or economic circumstances are such that they have difficulty in securing settled accommodation.

In 1998, the Labour government set itself the target of reducing those sleeping rough by two-thirds by 2002.

The Rough Sleepers Unit set up the government provided £96m over a three year period to tackle homelessness. Initially this money was for the London area but has since been extended to other towns and cities. However, it must be noted here that in addition to the funding provided by central government, large amounts are spent by local authorities in discharging their statutory duties to homeless people. An average of £15,500 per household per year is spent on dealing with the homeless (this is considerably more than providing a new council home).

The government in 1998 published a report entitled *Bringing Britain Together : a National Strategy for Neighbourhood Renewal*. This report identifies that there are 4,000 council estates and 44 districts suffering from high concentrations of deprivation. The Report urges the fostering of partnerships between local people and providers of housing and other services. The government has allocated £800 million to the programme known as *New Deal for Communities*.

Many homeless people are unemployed and one of the government's initiatives is this New Deal for Communities. The aim of the New Deal is for councils to tackle social exclusion through drawing together regeneration and housing schemes and to involve residents, police and health services in transforming communities plagued by crime, unemployment and drug problems.

The government's priorities are

- getting people to work;
- getting places to work by dealing with issues like housing management and anti-social behaviour;
- building a future for young people;
- access to services such as banks and shops;
- making the government work better.

The first of the money is being spread between 17 deprived neighbourhoods across England in Liverpool, Manchester, Newcastle upon Tyne, Middlesbrough, Nottingham, Leicester, Birmingham, Sandwell, Kingston upon Hull and Brighton and Hove, and Hackney, Tower Hamlets and Southwark in London.

More areas will be able to bid for funding in future years.

In 2000, local authorities in England made a total of 251,500 decisions on applications for housing from households eligible under the homelessness provisions. Of this number 111,500 households met the criteria.

The Children Act 1989 places a duty on Social Services Departments of local authorities to provide accommodation for young people.

The Homelessness Act 2002 strengthens the safety net for homeless people and changed the framework for letting local authority homes and promoted choice. It required local authorities to take a more strategic approach to tackling and preventing homelessness; local authorities are required to produce homelessness strategies. These must include plans for:

- preventing homelessness;
- making sure there is enough accommodation for people who are, or may become, homeless;
- making sure there is enough support for people who are, or may become, homeless and to prevent homelessness recurring.

The Act abolished the duty of local authorities to maintain a housing register. However, local authorities must have allocation schemes. Now allocations can only be made to eligible persons. Local authorities must still accord 'reasonable preference' to persons in housing need; the homeless, those in unsanitary, overcrowded or otherwise unsuitable housing, those with a need to move based on medical or welfare reasons and those who need to move to a particular area where failure to move would cause hardship to themselves or others. Additional preference may be given to those who also have 'urgent housing needs'.

The Act

- removes the current 'two-year duty' to provide settled accommodation and giving local authorities an ongoing responsibility to provide settled accommodation for unintentionally homeless households in priority need;

- abolishes the duty on local authorities to consider whether other suitable accommodation is available before they can secure accommodation;

- restricts the circumstances in which an offer of an assured shorthold tenancy in the private rented sector constitutes a discharge of duty;

- introduces a new power (but not a duty) for authorities to secure accommodation for homeless applicants who are not in priority need and strengthening duties on advice and assistance;

- giving Councils the freedom to use their own properties as short-term accommodation for homeless people for as long as necessary, until a settled home becomes available.

Under a Statutory Order the government has also extended the groups of people to have a priority need for housing. These groups are:

- 16 and 17 year olds;

- care leavers aged 18–21;

- people vulnerable because they have fled violence;

- people assessed as vulnerable because of an institutionalised background such as former prisoners.

The changes to the legal framework for allocating and letting local authority homes is intended to give councils more flexibility over their allocation schemes and to encourage them to give more choice to people seeking housing. These changes are summarised below:

- councils no longer have to have a housing register although they can, if they wish. In practice most authorities have retained some kind of list of people who apply for housing;

- councils have to publish a policy which explains how they let their homes and whether they will offer a choice of accommodation;

- everyone has the right to apply for available homes – unless they are in an ineligible category, for example, 'persons from abroad' who are not allowed to go on the housing register;

- councils are able to treat other individual applicants as ineligible if they have been guilty of unacceptable behaviour serious enough to make them unacceptable as a tenant;

- councils have to consider all applications for housing – except from ineligible people – and are not able to exclude particular groups;

- everyone (except ineligible people) who needs housing, or who needs to move to a particular area, is entitled to get reasonable preference for a home;

- people who live outside a local area will be able to apply for housing in that area, although the council will be able to take into account whether an applicant has a local connection;

- local authorities will have to provide free help for anyone making an application that needs it.

The Act introduced a new provision that a person is not eligible for assistance if he is a person from abroad who is ineligible for housing assistance. A person who is subject to immigration control within the meaning of the Asylum and Immigration Act 1996 is not eligible for housing assistance.

Similarly an asylum seeker or a dependent of an asylum seeker is ineligible for housing assistance. For this purpose a dependent means a person who is the spouse or a child of his under the age of eighteen and who has neither a right of abode in the United Kingdom nor indefinitely under the Immigration Act 1971 to enter or remain in the United Kingdom.

Asylum-seekers

Fifteen years ago, at the end of the cold war, you could have been forgiven for predicting a rapid decline in asylum applications. For almost 40 years, only small numbers of people, predominantly those fleeing Communism, applied for asylum in the UK. However, the collapse of superpower politics resulted in a global economic and political upheaval, which has meant an explosion in people wishing to migrate to the West. Migration has been fuelled by modern mass communications, which have allowed those living in poorer countries access to information about opportunities in the West. This, together with ethnic conflicts in every region, has rapidly transformed global migration. The result has been a rapid increase in the numbers of applications for asylum for both genuine and economic reasons.

A refugee is a person who owing to a well-founded fear of being persecuted for reasons of race, religion, nationality, membership of a particular social group or political opinion, is outside the country of his nationality and unable, or owing to such fear is unwilling, to avail himself of the protection of that country. The Asylum and Immigration Act 1996:

- provided that a person from abroad subject to immigration control was not eligible for housing assistance from a local authority; the only duty which arose if that person does not have the right to abode within the UK is the provision of temporary accommodation;

- the measures introduced by the Act were intended to remove access to public resources to thousands of households who entered UK seeking sanctuary, but who had received no decision about their future residence status.

As a result of the Immigration and Asylum Act 1999, asylum seekers have been excluded from the mainstream welfare and housing system in this country. Unlike other homeless families, they cannot approach the local homeless persons unit for assistance, they cannot apply for social housing through the local housing register and they cannot find their own accommodation because they are not entitled to housing benefit. Instead they must apply to the Home Office for housing via the National Asylum Support Service (NASS).

Detention is illegal unless deportation is imminent. Under Article 6 of the European Convention on Human Rights 'everyone is entitled to a fair and public hearing within a reasonable time by an independent and impartial tribunal established by law'. This means that once an appeal is lodged, deportation ceases to be 'imminent' and the applicant must be released from detention. This can then enable the applicant to benefit from Article 8 of the European Convention which states "everyone has the right to respect for his private and family life".

It should be mentioned here that nationals of the EU and the European Economic Area (which includes the EU plus Norway, Iceland and Liechtenstein) have the right to reside in the UK providing that they are working or able to support themselves financially. Other overseas nationals who wish to reside in the UK must obtain Home Office acceptance. The number of acceptances in recent years is as follows:

1982	4,223
1999	96,000
2000	124,000
2001	213,000

This figure is expected to continue to rise on government estimates to over 4m by 2023. This growth is roughly four times the population of Birmingham.

In recent years most asylum seekers have come from Iraq, Iran and Afghanistan, areas that have seen escalations of internal conflict and in the case of Iraq, a war with the West.

There are certain things that can perhaps be done now:

● settle people in areas with community support;

● avoid difficult to let estates where communities are already under pressure and refugees will stand out;

● give support;

● relieve pressure on agencies near ports of entry;

● give refugees a right to earn their own living;

It must be remembered that local authorities are obliged to provide food, warmth and shelter to destitute people under the National Assistance Act 1948. This Act requires social services departments of local authorities to help 'people who are aged, infirm or through other circumstances require care and attention'.

There have been four Asylum and Immigration Acts in the last 12 years. Many Ministers are concerned that the numbers must be rigidly controlled and are urging renegotiating the European Convention on Human Rights.

Supporting People

A new government initiative known as Supporting People came into effect in April 2003. This is a new and radical approach to providing housing and support services which will, for the first time, put funding on a firm and secure footing.

The Supporting People programme endeavours to raise the quality and effectiveness of support services, offering vulnerable individuals the opportunity to enjoy a more independent lifestyle within the community. By 'vulnerable' we mean older people, women with learning difficulties who are experiencing violence, rough sleepers, ex-offenders and those with alcohol or drug problems.

Under the programme local authorities have to assess the needs of such people in their area ensuring that appropriate and efficient services are provided.

The Programme is very much partnership based between local authority housing, social services, health, probation and providers of supported housing. Local authorities now have a single pot of money, solely for expenditure on support services, required by vulnerable people.

The Programme will:

- help older people to receive the help they need to live independently in sheltered housing or in their own home thus saving the costs of institutional care;

- assisting young homeless and rough sleepers prepare to settle in a new home and learn basic skills;

- enhance the quality of life of people with learning difficulties or mental health problems by making it possible for them to live in the community;

- provide community support for ex-offenders;

- provide specialist support for women experiencing domestic violence.

Socioeconomic Status

Earlier, we noted that the National Census provides a classification of households by 'socioeconomic status'. We have seen what a household is, but what does 'socioeconomic status' mean?

Various scales have been devised to give a precise definition of socioeconomic grouping for research. Classification is by the current or former occupation of the head of the household.

Table 2.3: Social grading

The National Statistics Socio-economic Classification Analytic Classes
1 Higher managerial and professional occupations
    1.1   Large employers and higher managerial occupations
    1.2   Higher professional occupations
2 Lower managerial and professional occupations
3 Intermediate occupations
4 Small employers and own account workers
5 Lower supervisory and technical occupations
6 Semi-routine occupations
7 Routine occupations
8 Never worked and long-term unemployed

Such scales are unsatisfactory for several reasons:

(a) Married women are classified by their husband's occupation rather than their own.

(b) There are often marked lifestyle differences within the occupational groups.

(c) The grading system can vary slightly between different market research agencies.

The Dependent Population

A term often used in the context of population statistics is 'dependent': this describes somebody who does not earn a living but has to depend on someone else. In broad terms this means the population over retirement age together with the population under working age form the dependent population.

There are two points to note about this definition.

●   Just because somebody is actually dependent on someone else (such as a disabled person aged between 20 and 60), it does not mean that they are technically classified as dependent for statistical purposes.

●   Even though many elderly people receive pensions or have private means and are not actually dependent on any other individual, they are nevertheless classified as dependent for statistical purposes.

There are 6.8m people of working age with long term or work limiting disabilities of whom just over a half were economically active. It is worth noting here that in 2002 there were 27.3m people of working age in employment in the UK, the highest since records began in 1959.

Economically inactive population

There are 7.9m people in the UK who are classified as economically inactive. This means that they are of working age but for a variety of reasons either are not looking for paid work or not available to start work.

Immigration

An immigrant is internationally defined as 'someone who, having lived abroad for at least 12 months, declares an intention to reside in the United Kingdom for at least 12 months'.

Immigration is often subdivided into primary and secondary immigration.

●   **Primary immigration** refers to the admission and settlement of heads of households in their own right.

●   **Secondary immigration** refers to the admission and settlement of those dependent on heads of households (mainly wives and children). It also refers to the admission and settlement of dependants (such as parents and grandparents) of those already resident in the UK.

Marriage and Divorce

Marriage

There has been considerable social change in England and indeed across Europe in the last few decades in the experience and social attitude to marriage. Marriage was fashionable in the 1960s despite the 'flower power' era and so called 'permissive age'. Nowadays, many people choose to cohabit before marriage, sometimes as a 'trial' and others as an alternative to marriage. 60% of men and women aged between 35 and 39 when they married for the first time had cohabited with their future partner. Currently there are 1.5m cohabiting couples in England and Wales; this number is expected to double by 2024. Cohabiting is just as common before second marriages take place.

The number of first marriages in the UK in 2002 was 179,000; this is less than half the number in the peak year of 1970 (390,000). More than 40% of any marriages in 2002 were remarriages.

The average age of women in England and Wales marrying for the first time in 2002 was 27 and for men was 29 compared to 23 and 27 respectively in 1961.

For those who had been divorced, the median age for remarriage was 37 for women and 41 for men.

Table 2.4: Average age at first marriage: by sex, EU comparison, 1961 and 1998

	1961		1998	
	Males	**Females**	**Males**	**Females**
Denmark	25.7	22.8	31.7	29.4
Sweden	26.6	23.8	31.7	29.3
Greece	29.2	25.2	30.3	26.5
Italy	28.5	24.7	30.0	27.1
Irish Republic	30.8	27.6	30.0	28.2
Netherlands	26.4	24.1	30.0	27.6
Germany	25.4	23.4	29.5	26.9
Finland	25.8	23.6	29.5	27.5
France	25.6	23.0	29.6	27.6
Spain	28.8	26.1	29.4	27.4
Luxembourg	26.9	25.4	29.6	27.2
Austria	26.5	23.8	29.2	26.7
England and Wales	25.6	23.1	29.1	27.0
Belgium	25.0	22.8	27.8	25.7
Portugal	26.9	24.8	27.1	25.1
EU average	26.7	24.1	29.6	27.3

Source: Eurostat

Divorce

Those who do marry now have a 40% chance of getting a divorce; the number of divorces peaked in 1993 at 180,000 in the UK. There were 159,000 divorces in the UK in 2002. The United Kingdom has the highest divorce rate in the European Community (almost twice the average).

Legal changes in the last 30 years or so have made it easier to get a divorce as well as allowing couples to divorce earlier in marriage. The Divorce Reform Act 1969 introduced a single ground for divorce that of irretrievable breakdown which could be established by proving one or more of certain facts – adultery, desertion, separation with or without consent, unreasonable behaviour or mental cruelty. This came into effect in 1971. As a result of this easing of divorce legislation, the number of divorces has increased and similarly the number of remarriages. The Matrimonial and Family Proceedings Act 1984, which reduced the minimum period after marriage before a petition for divorce could be filed, also increased the number of divorces (couples can now file for divorce after their first wedding anniversary whereas previously they had to have been married for three years).

In 2001, 9% of divorces in the United Kingdom were of marriages that had lasted under three years, compared with only 2% in 1981 (see Table 2.5).

You need to consider the children of divorces. Seven in ten children affected by divorce are aged ten years or under and around one in four children were under five years old. Various studies show that people who experience parental divorce are more likely to form partnerships at a younger age than those whose parents did not divorce.

Teenage marriages are more likely to break down than those later in life.

There are an increasing number of step families being created. This can affect children. Such family types may be formed when lone parents, whether single, separated or widowed from new partnerships.

Whilst we are looking at divorce we also need to look at pensions. You may wonder why pensions at this stage when we are looking at divorce. A pension can be the largest asset owned by a couple and is often worth more than the family home. Under the Pensions Act 1995, a court can 'earmark' all or part of a pension from a former spouse but money cannot be paid until the planholder retires. So the longer the planholder continues to work and not draw on the plan, the longer the former spouse has to wait for money.

The Welfare Reform Pensions Act 2001 now provides for pension sharing or pension splitting in the case of a divorce.

Table 2.5: Divorce: by duration of marriage

United Kingdom %	1961	1971	1981	1991	2001
0-2 years	1	1	2	9	9
3-4 years	10	12	19	14	13
5-9 years	31	31	29	27	28
10-14 years	23	19	20	18	18
15-19 years	14	13	13	13	12
20-24 years		10	9	10	9
25-29 years	21	6	5	5	6
30 years and over		9	5	4	5
All divorces (=100%) (thousands)	27.0	79.2	155.6	171.1	161

Source: Social Trends

Table 2.6: Adults moving house after break-up of marriage or cohabitation: by tenure before and after move, 1991–2001

Great Britain	Tenure after separation			Percentages
	Owner-occupied	Rented from social sector	Rented privately	All movers
Tenure before separation				
Males				
Owner-occupied	47	5	48	100
Rented from social sector	33	52	15	100
Rented privately	33	9	58	100
All tenures	40	17	43	100
Females				
Owner-occupied	49	13	38	100
Rented from social sector	6	65	29	100
Rented privately	55	19	26	100
All tenures	42	25	33	100

Sources: Social Trends

2.4 Major Demographic Changes and Forecasts

The UK will face major demographic changes over the forthcoming decade. We shall now examine these.

Total Population

The latest population census for the United Kingdom was carried out in April 2001. *Social Trends* shows that the population in 2001 was 59.8 million people. This is the 20th largest in the world. It is interesting to note here that the world's population exceeded 6bn people in 2001 – this is an increase of over 3.5bn over the previous 50 years.

It may be interesting to ponder for a while on earlier population figures extracted from the censuses 1801, 1851 and 1901. The undermentioned population figures show the drastic increase in population.

1801 – 8,893,000

1851 – 17,928,000

1901 – 38,237,000

Table 2.7: UK Population (past and projected future totals)

Year	Population (millions)
1961	52.8
1971	55.9
1981	56.4
1991	57.8
2001	59.8
2025	65.0 (projected)
2040	66.0 (projected)

Source: Social Trends

Table 2.8: Population of the United Kingdom

United Kingdom				Thousands				
	1901	1951	1961	1971	1981	1991	2001	2021	2025
England	30,515	41,159	43,561	46,412	46,821	48,208	49,997	54,262	55,013
Wales	2,013	2,599	2,635	2,740	2,813	2,891	2,946	3,067	3,085
Scotland	4,472	5,096	5,184	5,236	5,180	5,107	5,115	4,973	4,926
N Ireland	1,237	1,371	1,427	1,540	1,538	1,601	1,698	1,803	1,813
UK	38,237	50,225	52,807	55,928	56,352	57,808	59,756	64,105	64,836

Source: Social Trends

The population of the United Kingdom increased by 56% between 1901 and 2001 to reach 59.8 million (Tables 2.7 and 2.8). During this period the population of England increased by 64%.

The rate at which population changes depends on the net natural change (that is, the difference between the number of births and deaths) and the net effect of people migrating to and from this country.

Put simply, it would appear that there is likely to be an increasing demand for housing, although the rate of this increase will gradually reduce to a low level by the middle of the 21st century.

In the summer of 2003, the government unveiled plans for 300,000 new homes which could cover vast swathes of the south east. The scheme is on top of a commitment to build 1.1m houses across the region by 2016, bringing the total to a staggering 1.4m.

Total Population by Sex

The male/female ratio of the total population is complicated by two factors:

- More boys than girls are born, so there are more young men than young women.

- On the other hand, more men than women die each year, so that women outnumber men from about the age of 40. In Britain, the average life expectancy is currently 75 years for a man and 80 years for a woman. These figures have shown a considerable improvement from those of a hundred years ago – 45.5 years for a man and 48 years for a woman (1901).

Table 2.9 shows the population by age since 1901 with projections through to 2021.

Although the numbers of young males and older females will increase a little more quickly than the numbers of young females and older males, the male/female ratios will not change very significantly in the foreseeable future. There are not, therefore, any significant housing conclusions to draw from the male/female population statistics but there certainly are conclusions to be drawn from the age of people.

Total Population by Age

You need to be aware that the proportion of people aged 80 or over in the population is projected to more than double between now and 2051 from just under 4% to just over 9%. Concern has been expressed by politicians recently on the increasing proportion of the population over pensionable age, largely due to the increased share of national budgets that pensions will take and the increasing cost of health care for the elderly.

Table 2.9: Population: by age: 2001

United Kingdom   Percentages

	Under 16	16-24	25-34	35-44	45-54	55-64	65-74	75 and over
Mid-year estimates								
1901	34	20	16	12	9	6	3	1
1931	26	18	16	13	12	9	5	2
1991	21	14	16	14	12	10	8	5
2001	21	11	16	15	13	10	8	6
Mid-year projections								
2011	18	12	13	15	15	12	9	6
2025	18	10	13	13	13	14	10	9

Source: Social Trends

The implications of these predictions for housing are not hard to see.

- As the number of older people goes up, the demand for smaller houses suitably designed for older people will also increase.

- Because 159,000 couples divorce each year, the demand for more (and smaller) units of accommodation may also increase, although some allowance should presumably be made for remarriage.

Table 2.10: Population Breakdown: England 2001

Age group and numbers in thousands of people

0–14	15–29	30–44	45–64	65
4,747	4,626	5,502	4,693	3,292
4,522	4,625	5,645	5,785	5,747

Source: Office of the Deputy Prime Minister

Total Population by Geographical Area

The key to where the population is increasing and where it is decreasing lies in a simple division of the country into urban (metropolitan) areas and rural (non-metropolitan) areas.

Broadly speaking, between 1971 and 2001 the population in non-metropolitan areas increased and the population in metropolitan areas decreased, reflecting the movement of people from urban to rural areas. There is a slight trend now, however, for people to move back into metropolitan areas. In the future, lower population growth is predicted for the non-metropolitan areas of southern England and the Midlands, while the metropolitan areas should stop losing population. However, in northern England, Scotland and Wales the trend of increasing population in the non-metropolitan areas is expected to continue, with a corresponding decrease in metropolitan populations.

Once again, the significance for housing of these demographic forecasts is not hard to see. The predictions show roughly where the future of housebuilding lies. In particular, they reveal that there is likely to be a rising demand for housing in the rural areas outside southern England and the Midlands. There is also likely to be a continuing demand for housing in the urban areas within these regions: a reminder that the problems of inner cities are not going to go away, which is something we shall consider in Unit 10.

2.5   Changes and Forecasts in Particular Groups

So far we have looked at the broad demographic picture, taking the population as a whole. In order that we can consider the likely future demands on housing, we need to look at smaller categories within the population. In particular, we should examine demographic changes and forecasts relating to:

- the homeless;

- the elderly;

- lone-person and single parent families;

- ethnic minorities;

- disabled persons;

- single people;

- mentally ill/handicapped persons;

- women at risk;

- the movement of industry and how it affects the distribution of the population.

The Homeless

We looked at the term 'homeless' earlier in this unit. Let us have a brief look at the background to the current legislation and other issues around homelessness.

Illness can lead to homelessness and homelessness itself brings an increased risk to health and many exacerbate health problems. In addition homelessness is associated with unhealthy behaviour such as alcohol or substance abuse together with a high risk of violence. It is difficult for homeless people to register with GPs; hence homeless people make greater use of Accident and Emergency Departments of hospitals than the general population.

In some parts of the country local health agencies provide specialist services, including special GPs, outreach teams for street homeless people, mobile clinics and health care services in hotels/hostels and day centres.

Homeless people, with a whole family sharing one room, in bed and breakfast accommodation often feel that they are imprisoned between four walls. They share washing and cooking facilities with strangers. Parents worry about the irreversible damage caused to their children by ill health and lack of space for the children to develop. The effects can be long-lasting.

Families living in bed and breakfast accommodation represent one of the most disturbing examples of social exclusion. In a report *More than a Roof – a report into Tackling Homelessness* the government set out its approach to tackling homelessness and in it the government has set a target that by 31 March 2004, no family with children will be placed in bed and breakfast accommodation, except in an emergency and then for no more than six weeks. Following the report, the government set up the Homelessness Directorate and has made £200m of funding available to help local authorities be innovative, proactive and effective in ceasing to use bed and breakfast accommodation and to reduce rough sleeping and prevent homelessness.

In a report by Nacro *Women Behind Bars – A Positive Agenda for Women Prisoners' Resettlement* it shows that four out of ten women prisoners expect to be homeless on release. Women in prison often lose their home, job and ties with their children, the report says. Yet homelessness, lack of money for basic needs and loss of family support all jeopardise women's chances of leading stable and crime free lives after release.

The report suggests that local authorities should undertake homelessness assessments on women prisoners prior to release.

Female ex-offenders have different housing needs to their male counterparts, particularly mothers trying to reunite their families. A safe and permanent home can make a significant difference not only to their own lives but also their children's.

Prior to the 1977 legislation, the only statutory duty applying directly to the homeless was sesction 21 (i) of the National Assistance Act 1948. It required that Social Services 'provide temporary accommodation for those in urgent need, need arising in circumstances which could not reasonably have been foreseen ...'

Although there was a dramatic rise in the level of homelessness following the Rent Act 1957, little was done by the government until the issue in 1966 of government circular 20/66 by the Ministry of Housing, forerunner to the Department of the Environment, Transport and the Regions, which recommended minimum standards for hostels and more sensitive treatment of the homeless. This followed widespread public concern in the wake of Jeremy Sandford's television play *Cathy Come Home*. This television play produced in 1966 is regarded as one of the most influential plays ever produced. At the time 25% of the population tuned in to watch it. The play portrays the devastation in a young family's life ground down by poverty and a draconian and bureaucratic welfare system. Blurring the distinction between documentary and fiction, the film made a lasting impression on those who watched it. It pricked the nation's conscience and showed cracks in the welfare state. Questions were asked in Parliament the very next day and it boosted a public awareness of the situation. The following week Shelter, the national campaign for the homeless was launched.

Although first shown in 1966, it has been shown on television many times since and is now available on DVD.

When *Cathy Come Home* was first shown, there were 12,500 people including children in emergency accommodation for the homeless. Nearly forty years on the situation is far worse. At the time of *Cathy Come Home*, it was rare to see people sleeping out on the street; now it is commonplace. Emergency accommodation in bed-and-breakfast hotels is an improvement on the old workhouses but a hotel room suitable for one or two people on holiday is no place to bring up a family. During an evening, amid a sea of beds and boxes and suitcases containing the families' possessions, Dad may typically be watching television, Mum cooking up on an illegal electric ring, baby crawling around creating havoc (as they do!) and daughter trying to do her homework.

Walk along any street in Britain at any time of the day now, you will see the homeless, men and women of all ages huddled in drafty recesses. There are the old homeless and the young who are drawn to the cities and end up begging and alienated. In London alone the Salvation Army estimates that there are 75,000 homeless – the equivalent of the population of Cheltenham. All the time the number is swollen by the discharge of mental patients, the decrease in low-cost housing stock and the change in rules affecting benefit for young people (referred to later in this unit under Housing Benefits).

In 1967 Crisis at Christmas began because of concern about the single homeless. It was renamed Crisis in 1989 to reflect its year-round operations.

In 1968, the Seebohm Committee on the Social Services recommended that local authority housing departments should be responsible for dealing with the homeless. This was endorsed in 1969 by the Central Housing Advisory Committee. In 1971 the government published two studies: one by Greave on London and one by Glastonbury on Wales and the south-west of England. Both reports contained alarming statistics on the escalating evidence of homelessness.

Charities had for some time campaigned for legislation to assist the homeless before Lord Ross, then a Liberal MP, sponsored the Housing (Homeless Persons) Act in 1977. Many of them felt that the Act did not go far enough, however it did make the following provisions:

- required the housing authority to satisfy itself as to whether the applicant was homeless or threatened with homelessness;

- required the housing authority to give advice and assistance to applicants;

- provided that if an applicant had connection in another local authority's area then that authority must deal with the matter, although provision was also made for the first authority to provide temporary accommodation while the issue was being sorted out;

- provided that a housing authority must notify any applicant requiring help of its decision in writing and, if unfavourable, of the reasons for it.

Housing

Homelessness has continued to grow since the Housing (Homeless Persons) Act was passed in 1977.

The majority of households accepted as homeless become homeless for the following reasons:

- breakdown of relationship with partner;
- loss of rented or tied accommodation;
- parents no longer able/willing to accommodate;
- other relatives/friends no longer able/willing to accommodate;
- mortgage default or rent arrears.

Many housing authorities provide temporary accommodation for people presenting themselves homeless; costs vary throughout the country and it is quite common for London Boroughs to pay in excess of £100 per night per household. This is currently costing the London authorities in the region of £400 million per annum.

Local housing authorities are required to provide a 24-hour service of assistance for those claiming to be homeless. In a case in October 1988, Lord Justice May and Mr Justice Kennedy found that the London Borough of Camden was in breach of its statutory duty by providing only a restricted service (during office hours) for the homeless.

You should note here that local housing authorities are required to assist persons who are homeless, but this does not mean that they must provide permanent accommodation. However, in practice many do because of the high costs of bed-and-breakfast accommodation, referred to earlier. In *Pulhofer v London Borough of Hillingdon* (1986), now a well-cited case on the homeless, Pulhofer appealed against the decision by Hillingdon council that they were not homeless because the Pulhofer family had been provided with accommodation at a guesthouse. The family had a single room at a guesthouse with no private cooking or washing facilities. Cooking facilities and three bathrooms were shared at the guesthouse and in total there were 36 people at the guesthouse. The House of Lords dismissed the appeal and stated that 'the Act (Housing (Homeless Persons) Act 1977) was an Act to assist persons who are homeless, not an Act to provide them with homes.'

The Act was amended by the Housing and Planning Act 1986 and required local authorities to have regard to the accommodation in which people were living. Hostel accommodation was regarded as satisfactory.

In the *Pulhofer* case, in determining whether it is reasonable for an applicant to continue to occupy accommodation, a local authority may have regard 'to the general circumstances prevailing in relation to housing in the district of the local authority to whom he has applied.

You should note that in *R v South Herefordshire District Council ex p Miles* (1983), it was held that a rat-infested hut just 10 feet x 20 feet with no mains services occupied by a couple and their two children was not unreasonable, but remember that this case was decided before the Housing (Homeless Persons) Act 1977 was amended by the Housing and Planning Act 1986.

In a recent Department of the Environment, Transport and the Regions report, it was noted that the majority of households accepted as homeless had no earned income: only 20% were in some form of employment (including part-time) and 10% were in receipt of retirement benefits. In addition, 80% were households with dependent children or were pregnant women.

Official figures on homelessness do not include those who are roofless. Such people do not, as a rule, complete census returns. Remember that the Census forms are both delivered and collected from people's front doors! Sources such as the Salvation Army and Shelter say approximately 10,000 people sleep rough each night in London and a further 2,000 in cities such Bristol, Leeds and Birmingham.

Homeless people can fall into various categories:

- those without a roof over their heads that live in parks, doorways, barns or sleep rough generally;

- those in homeless accommodation (insecure accommodation) such as bed and breakfast accommodation, short stay hostels, hotels, squatting or short-life housing;

- those about to be released from prison, care, hospital or armed forces;

- those sharing accommodation where relationships are intolerable, eg violence, abuse or family breakdown;

- those sharing involuntary, eg women living with violent partners.

When we refer to the homeless, it must be remembered that there are homeless in rural areas as well as in inner city areas. Often we tend to think of the homeless as those people who sleep in cardboard boxes or sleeping bags on the Strand, Victoria Street or the Embankment. Back in the 1990s at least 150 people slept rough in London's Lincoln Inn Fields until the area was fenced off by the local authority.

Research carried out by the School for Advanced Urban Studies and the Rural Development Commission shows the numbers of homeless in deep rural areas has tripled in recent years.

Crisis

Crisis at Christmas was set up in 1967 to help the homeless on the streets; 36 years later the number sleeping rough has trebled.

A report published by Crisis (whose name has changed to make the public aware of the plight of the homeless at all times, not just at Christmas) reveals some startling facts. The report entitled *Sick to Death of Homelessness*, draws attention to the fact that 617 people died in one year as a direct result of 'sleeping on the streets'. The author Simon Keys, stresses that homeless people are:

150 times more likely to be fatally assaulted

34 times more likely to commit suicide

8 times more likely to be killed in an accident

3 times more likely to die of pneumonia or hypothermia.

Similar reports show similar statistics. In 2002 in London 79 people died living on the streets. A more recent report *Out of the Shadows* shows that tuberculosis is 25 times more prevalent among single homeless people than the general population. A further report emphasized that the average age of homeless persons at the time of their death was 42 compared with the national average of 76.

Funding for bringing back into use empty flats above shops has been made available known as LOTS (Living over the Shops). The government accepts that this was not a cheap way to produce homes. The scheme in some circles is known as FOTS (Flats Over The Shops).

It is interesting to note that under the Local Government Finance Act 1992, local authorities can obtain a County Court 'Charging Order' against a defaulter's home which can be enforced by a sale for those who fall behind with their Council Tax. Such debtors would probably be considered intentionally homeless and thus denied alternative housing by their local authority.

Sir George Young moved from being Housing Minister in July 1994 to become Financial Secretary to the Treasury. One of the last acts as Housing Minister was a proposal to replace the right of homeless persons to have permanent accommodation with one whereby the local authority had a duty to find the homeless temporary accommodation for 12 months and not necessarily local authority accommodation. The intention was to stop queue jumping above others on the Councils' waiting lists.

At the Conservative Party Conference at Blackpool in 1993, Sir George Young said 'We must ask ourselves whether the signals sent out by this legislation sit comfortably with the values we share; with the self-reliant society we want to improve. How do we explain to the young couple who want to wait for a home before they start a family that they cannot be rehoused ahead of the unmarried teenager expecting her first, probably unplanned, child? How do we explain to parents that if children stay at home they may have a long wait before they are rehoused? But if they evict their children they may go the top of the queue and get secure accommodation? What signal about family responsibility does that send out?'

Sir George Young's comments were followed by a government consultation paper *Access to Local Authority and Housing Association Tenancies* issued early in 1994 and covering three major areas of proposed reform:

(i)   the reform of the homelessness legislation;

(ii) a new approach to the allocation of housing resources by local authorities and housing associations;

(iii) making the best use of the private rented sector.

The proposals referred to above and embodied in the Housing Act 1996 changed the definition of homelessness to exclude anyone with access to 'suitable accommodation'. Local authorities now allocate permanent housing to people on their waiting list. Furthermore local authorities must allocate tenancies in their own housing stock and nominations to housing associations only to applicants on their waiting list. Local authorities' allocation policies have to be in accordance with the Office of the Deputy Prime Minister's regulations to ensure fairness and consistency.

It shows the former government's clear intention was to rely on the private sector to house the homeless. The effect of their actions, however, created a 'revolving door' with temporary lets for two years being followed by homelessness reapplications – such a system particularly affected the education of schoolchildren who would be frequently changing schools etc. Local authorities had to review individual cases of homelessness after two years.

The government is committed nationally to a radically new approach to tackling rough sleeping through its Rough Sleepers Initiative. This is an approach which aims to 'break the cycle' by helping people off the streets and offering them a fresh start. This approach had a clear target of reducing the number of people sleeping rough to a third of its current level by 2002 and ideally to as near to zero as soon as possible. The 2002 target was achieved. A budget of £145 million has been provided for the Rough Sleepers Initiative for the first three years.

We need to consider ways in which the causes of homelessness can be alleviated. Briefly these can be summarized as follows:

- counselling for debt, social and family crisis;

- better support through the benefit system;

- increase in the supply of social housing;

- more effective mortgage and rent arrears control;

- sensitive, helpful and accessible debt advice;

- greater use of non-possession debt-recovery devices;

- wider availability of mortgage rescue schemes;

- operation of flexible tenure, when people cannot afford to pay a mortgage;

- higher level of employment and less dependency;

- more effective credit risk assessment and relevant lending limits;

- greater use of crisis insurance.

Homelessness is not about a lack of housing; it is often a manifestation of a life course involving bad health, crime, drug dependency, no job and family disruption. Homelessness is not victimhood either; the ways forward are often about empowering individuals to find themselves, find work, friends, a passage into a more settled lifestyle.

Table 2.11: Homeless households in priority need accepted by local authorities by region 2000

	Total acceptances	Acceptances per 1,000 households
North East	5,130	4.7
North West	13,110	4.6
Yorkshire and the Humber	8,950	4.2
East Midlands	7,280	4.2
West Midlands	13,700	6.3
East	9,410	4.2
London	28,610	9.2
South East	14,310	4.3
South West	11,050	5.3
England	111,550	5.4

Source: Social Trends

Social Exclusion Unit

Social exclusion is what can happen when individuals or areas suffer from the combination of linked problems such as unemployment, poor skills, low incomes, poor housing, high crime environment, bad health and family breakdown.

The Social Exclusion Unit was set up by the government in 1997 and forms part of the government's strategic approach to tackling social exclusion. Dealing with social exclusion is one of the government's priorities in terms of spending and budgets. Its purpose is to devise and implement policies to prevent social exclusion. It is recognised that (i) children in poor and overcrowded houses are disadvantaged during their school years (ii) poor housing harbours crime and anti social behaviour.

Issues facing teenage parents, rough sleepers, deprived neighbourhoods and young people at risk of social exclusion are complex and interconnected.

Since the setting up of the Social Exclusion Unit the following has happened:

- there are more than two thirds fewer people sleeping rough on the streets than there were in 1998;

- the number of children excluded from school fell by over one third by 1999/2000;

- conception rates among teenagers are falling significantly – a 7% drop among under 16s in 1999;

- 15% more teenage parents are now in education, training or employment than in 1994;

- the Connexions Service has helped 17,180 young people identified as not being in education, training or employment to settle successfully into a job, training or full-time education;

- Neighbourhood Management pilots, where a single team or person is put in charge of a neighbourhood, are running in 20 areas under a £45m programme;

- the £900m Neighbourhood Renewal Fund has been set up for the 88 most deprived areas to tack deprivation and improve social services;

- the new £450m Children's Fund which will provide funding for local services to prevent young people from being socially excluded.

The Elderly

The number of people aged 65 and over continues to rise. Whereas to reach 100 was rare at one time, now it is becoming commonplace. In 2002 there were 3,000 new centenarians (ten times more than in 1960). By 2030, it is estimated that there will be 36,000 centenarians each year.

23% of the population are over state pension age (females 60 and over and males 65 and over). This is an 18% increase in last 30 years. Similarly over three times as many people over the age of 90 than 30 years ago. The proportion of people over 65 years of age is projected to increase to 24% by the year 2051. As one gets older one becomes less healthy. 40% of those over 60 suffer from a limiting long-term illness; 50% of those over 85 have some form of dementia (this lasts on average eight years).

The trend towards earlier retirement makes no sense when we are living so much longer and remaining healthy. Many people retiring in their fifties will spend more time as pensioners than they did at work. Indeed the government has expressed concern over the effect that the increase in the number of state pensioners will have on the national budget and as to how health care institutions will cope.

The age at which men and women receive state pension is to be equalized to 65; this will be phased in after 10 years starting in April 2010. Women born before 6.4.50 will be unaffected, while the pensionable age for those born between 6.4.50 and 5.3.55 will gradually increase. All women born on or after 6.3.55 will become eligible to receive state pension at age 65.

One of the questions faced by people when they retire is whether they should stay in their present house (whose size or layout they may no longer be able to manage) or whether they should move house. Whatever they decide, there will be implications for housing.

For the elderly, independence and dignity are most important. However, it must be realized that as they are able to do less, they are likely to spend longer in their homes. In addition, many old people are unable to continue to cook or clean and may even have trouble keeping themselves clean; such people turn to the social services department of local authorities for help from carers and meals on wheels.

The use of the various personal services by elderly people in the United Kingdom increases with age. While 9% of people aged 65 – 69 received help from a local authority home help or home care worker in 2001, the proportion is much higher for people aged 85 and over, and is 30%.

The frailer one becomes, the more need there is to watch other people enjoy life through their activities. Good views from windows help, as do landscaped gardens.

Every day 315 people need long-term care for the first time. If a person has assets of over £19,500 (and, of course, properties will be) then they do not qualify for help with care home fees. 40,000 houses each year are sold to fund care costs.

In 2000, local authorities provided 398,000 households with home help and home care; much of this was provided by independent sector providers (private sector plus the voluntary sector) who were commissioned to carry out the care by local authorities. It must be remembered that there is now recognition and awareness of the work undertaken by informal carers, ie individuals who provide care for family members, friends or others in the community.

In order to combat age discrimination in employment, the government intend to let people work until they are 70. The government consider that the talents and experience of older people, who want to continue working, should not be lost. The government have emphasised that the proposed default age of 70 is not a national compulsory retirement age; people would still be free to retire at any age.

Many politicians (of all political persuasions) and many people consider that all workers have the right to retire with dignity and a decent pension at 65 or earlier if they wish.

The main benefit for older people is the retirement pension which is received by around 7.4m people. Older people may also receive other benefits – 2.5m receive sickness and disability benefits and 627,000 are in receipt of non-disabled income support to boost their low incomes.

The Care Standards Act 2000 was a very controversial piece of legislation and did in fact inflict immense harm on the elderly in residential and nursing homes. Many homes were required to close because they did not meet the new stringent standards. These standards included the width of doors in care homes to the number of lifts and baths. Within three years, 2,400 homes had closed and 50,000 bed spaces were lost.

The government did a u-turn in 2003 and removed the stringent standards and stated that although such standards were important "they should not mean good local care homes having to close".

Under the non-binding new rules, every care home will have to state whether it meets the standards, "letting those who are choosing homes make an informed decision for themselves". Rules governing staff training will remain mandatory and be enforced by inspectors.

The English House Conditions Survey 2001 indicates that retired households tend to have the most living space ($58m^2$ per person), even when compared with other small households. Whilst this additional space assists when children and grandchildren visit, such homes can be more expensive to maintain and heat for those with modest retirement income and savings.

Design features which should benefit the elderly include:

- one-level accommodation with no steps;

- wide access and wide circulation areas;

- ample room for wheelchairs or for the use of walking sticks or frames;

- knobs, handles and switches which are easy to see, easy to operate and easy to grasp with just one hand;

- rails to assist mobility;

- easy plumbing fittings in bathroom, w.c. and kitchen;

- a high level of heating and insulation to prevent cold and draughts*;

- a high level of illumination and use of contrasting colours for changes of direction, level or surface;

- alarm systems;

- spyholes in front door,

- landscaped garden

- good views from windows

- telephones.

*As from 1999 a payment of £100 (since increased to £200) is made to every household over pensionable age for a winter fuel bonus. Ironically this is paid even if living overseas!

Back in 1983 the then Department of the Environment published *Housing for the Elderly*. This suggested various initiatives to help the housing problems of the elderly:

● For those who preferred to stay where they were, suggested initiatives were:

- assistance with improvements to their present home;

- assistance with repairs to such items as roofs, walls and foundations;

- assistance with improvements to heating and insulation;

- agencies and advice services to implement the above;

- financial support from the then Department of Social Security often by way of a loan and a legal charge placed on the property;

- alarm systems

- wardens

- good neighbour services.

● For those who preferred to move to a new house, suggested initiatives were:

- shared ownership schemes for the elderly (in conjunction with housing associations);

- shared ownership (see Unit 9);

- schemes whereby local authorities moved the elderly near to their younger relatives.

The new government in February 1998 announced a £5 million boost to schemes that help elderly and disabled people to stay in their houses. The boost was a considerable increase in funding for home improvement agencies, which help to carry out adaptations and improvements for poor, elderly and disabled people.

Later in the course we shall look at the schemes referred to above and how the grants scheme assists the elderly, especially the more frail. Only 700,000 of the over-65s have opted for sheltered accommodation with help on hand to tackle day-to-day emergencies. Of that total, less than a fifth have actually bought their own home. The great majority of over-65s rely on local authorities and specialist housing associations.

Better healthcare is helping people live longer. Changing social patterns have meant that the traditional way of dealing with old age – care by younger relatives – is waning. Research shows that fewer people are now willing to care for highly dependent parents or grandparents and that nursing care has become politically acceptable. Much of the sector is funded in some form by the tax payer either through local authority funding or direct funding from the government.

As we can see, the very old need homes with special adaptations to help them to cope and often those over the age of 65 need smaller houses. This is because it is more difficult, and more expensive, to maintain larger houses.

Nevertheless, recent research has shown that only 30% of men and women above retirement age, who were living in their own three-bedroomed (or larger) homes, thought that they had too many rooms. This statistic is of somewhat dubious value for various reasons, not least because of the well-known reluctance of older people to move.

In London, the quality of the houses owned by many elderly people leaves something to be desired. The research also revealed:

- dwellings in need of improvement (often with obsolete kitchens or an outside w.c.);
- houses that were costly to heat because of poor insulation;
- elderly people often on low income and with limited financial resources to carry out repairs and improvements;
- houses inconveniently situated: away from bus or train routes, or from shops or relatives.

The point to bear in mind is that there are problems at present with housing for the elderly. This is demonstrated by the research on housing stock putting forward some suggested solutions. However, the demographic forecasts reveal that in the future these problems are likely to get worse simply because the number of elderly people increasing.

One-person and Single-parent Households

One in five families is now headed by a single parent (it was one in 13 in 1971). Nearly 40% of single mothers have never married; there is also a growth in never-married lone fathers. Just over one in eight people lived alone in 2002.

In general, one-person and single-parent households require smaller houses than larger households; obviously they need less space. In addition, a single adult often cannot afford accommodation of a size comparable with that which two (or more) adults could buy or rent on their combined incomes. It follows that if the number of one-person and single-parent households increases, then there will be a greater demand for smaller dwellings.

We would, of course, expect an increase in the numbers of one-person and single-parent households simply because the population level as a whole is rising. What would be more significant would be an increase in the proportion of these households, within the total number of households. Why should this be the case? Because such an increase would indicate a switch from family-sized accommodation to smaller accommodation.

In fact, the latest statistics show an increase in the population of one-person and single-parent households. As one might suppose, the increase in the number of one-person households is largely brought about by the increasing numbers of elderly people. As we saw earlier the number of elderly is predicted to continue increasing. The rising trend is not due entirely to the elderly living longer but also to more single young people living on their own.

As we have seen, another of the factors that explain the increase in the number of single-parent households is divorce.

Once again, demography gives some indication as to the future of housing, since the increase in one-person and single-parent households will necessitate the provision of smaller houses in which to live.

Ethnic Minorities

Currently one in fourteen people in the United Kingdom are from ethnic minorities. Members of ethnic minority groups were present in the U.K in small numbers before the Second World War. The numbers increased significantly after that war and this growth was initiated by large scale immigration from the countries of the New Commonwealth following the passing of the British Nationality Act 1948.

What can be seen by Table 2.12 is that certain groups have double the number of children under 16. However, in contrast the white group had the highest proportion of people aged 65 and over (16% compared to Pakistani/Bangladeshi and Chinese groups). The percentage of elderly Asian groups will increase with time.

At first sight it might not be obvious why the presence of ethnic minorities has any implications for housing. Why should an Asian family, for example, have different housing requirements from any other family? The answer is that the implications are not so much for the type of housing required as for the ways in which it is provided.

Ethnic minorities have problems in obtaining local authority housing, mainly because they lack knowledge of the local authority housing system. Often they have large families, whereas local authorities do not have many large dwellings for rent. As a result, ethnic minorities tend to live in the less desirable local authority accommodation.

The English House Conditions Survey 2001 indicates that ethnic minority households tend to have the least living space with Pakistani and Bangladeshi households averaging only 22m^2 per person. 27% of the ethnic minority households are nearly three times more likely to live in poor neighbourhoods than white households.

Many local authorities insist on a residential qualification period before allocating dwellings to applicants; indeed the longer an applicant has been living in the area, the higher the points allocated to that applicant, which then gives them priority over others. In this way ethnic groups could fare less favourably than others.

There may also be language problems, for example where an old person's mother tongue is a language other than English. In recent years, leaflets produced by government departments and by many local councils have been translated into a number of ethnic languages.

Table 2.12: Percentage of people born in the UK by ethnic group and age 2000/01

Great Britain	Percentages				
	Under 16	16–34	35–64	65 and over	All ages millions
White	20	25	39	16	54.0
Black Caribbean	23	27	40	10	0.6
Black African	33	35	30	2	0.4
Other Black groups	52	29	17	–	0.3
All black groups	34	30	31	5	1.4
Indian	23	31	38	7	1.0
Bangladeshi	39	36	21	4	0.4
Pakistani	36	36	24	4	0.8
All Pakistani/ Bangladeshi	37	36	23	4	1.0
Chinese	19	38	38	4	0.1
Other groups	30	34	33	3	0.8
None of the above	32	33	32	3	0.7

Source: Social Trends

There is no indication that the numbers in the ethnic minority groups are going to increase significantly (other than through the natural rise in population). Certainly there is no reason to believe that immigration is going to expand in the foreseeable future. On the other hand, the ethnic minorities are not likely to get any smaller and their housing problems (mainly caused by communication problems) are going to remain.

You should be aware that the government published a White Paper in 1975 called *Race Relations and Housing*. Although it is unnecessary for you to know its recommendations in detail, you should bear in mind its statement that:

... as a fundamental aspect of housing policy, there should be no ethnic, racial, religious or class discrimination in the formulation or the application of housing policies and practices.

In this connection, it is worth noting that back in 1984 the London Borough of Newham was the first local authority to successfully gain possession against one of its tenants on grounds of racial harassment. In the case, action was taken against a mother with four children, two of whom were accused of racial abuse, drawing graffiti and threatening violence against an Asian family. The possession order was granted under 'nuisance' grounds for possession, in Schedule 4 of the Housing Act 1980 (now consolidated into the Housing Act 1985). There have been numerous similar cases since.

Local housing authorities were both praised and criticized in the Stephen Lawrence Inquiry Report by Sir William Macpherson in 1999.

The Report acknowledged that there was evidence of good practice, including up-to-date tenancy conditions and the prompt application of legislation to deal with racist tenants. However the Report stressed that too often housing departments were seen to be slow and bureaucratic in their response to racist behaviour.

In the report it was stated that 'housing is not immune from institutional racism'. The recommendations of the report were:

- definition of a 'racist incident' should be one which is perceived to be racist by the victim;

- racist incidents should be reportable to agencies other than the police 24 hours a day;

- information on racial incidents and crime should be made available to all agencies:

- systems should be in place to access local contacts within minority   communities;

- consider joint racism awareness training with agencies including police;

- local initiatives aimed at addressing racism should be supported;

- performance indicators needed concerning recording, prosecution etc.

The Race Relations Act 1976 states that it is unlawful for a person, in relation to premises of which he has the power to dispose, to discriminate against another:

(a)   in the terms on which the premises are offered; or

(b)   by refusing his application for the premises; or

(c)   in the treatment of him in relation to any waiting list for accommodation.

Furthermore, it is unlawful for a person, in relation to premises managed by him, to discriminate against a person occupying:

(a)   in the way he affords him access to any benefits or facilities; or by refusing or deliberately omitting to afford him access to them; or

(b) by evicting him or subjecting him to other detriment.

In spite of the legislation quoted above, ethnic minorities are still discriminated against:

- accommodation bureaux have received and acted upon instructions from landlords/ landladies not to let property to anyone with a non-European background.

- some local authorities have allocated poorer housing to ethnic minorities than to United Kingdom white people even though their circumstances were similar.

The Commission for Racial Equality issued a Code of Practice for Housing in 1991.

The Code deals with the problems of racial harassment and suggests approaches which can be adopted for victim support, acting against perpetrators and working with tenants, staff and other agencies.

There is a need for:

(i) keeping and monitoring ethnic records and taking action;

(ii) training of staff;

(iii) positive action policies where the number of ethnic minorities are under-represented among tenants and applicants for accommodation;

(iv) employment of ethnic staff;

(v) eradicating communication and language difficulties;

(vi) adoption of fair housing policies.

An interesting government report was published in 2001 entitled *Addressing the Housing Needs of Black and Minority Ethnic People*. This report gave a snapshot view of the main housing related problems faced by black and ethnic minority groups:

- over-representation in unfit properties and run-down areas;

- some groups (particularly some Asian groups) were less likely to be in social housing. This could be because of a preference for owner occupation; or an inability of local authorities and registered social landlords to reach out to black and minority ethnic groups;

- under-utilisation of supported housing services because of lack of awareness or inappropriateness of the services available; services needed to take cultural and religious sensitivities into account in their design and communicate these to target audiences;

- racial harassment;

- homeless applicants, including those from black and minority ethnic groups, often ended up with the worst social housing.

Under the *Race Relations Amendment Act 2000* public bodies have a legal duty to tackle unlawful discrimination and promote good relations between persons of different races. This duty applies to local authorities, Government Departments and a wide range of public bodies, including the Housing Corporation.

Disabled Persons

A government survey *The Prevalence of Disability among Adults* shows that one in ten of the population has difficulty in getting about. Six million adults in the United Kingdom have a significant impairment and one in seven households includes someone with a disability. There are 4.2m adults with mobility difficulties; furthermore just 2% of adults use wheelchairs at some stage. Only 17% of disabled people are actually born with a disability; 23% are disabled due to accidents – half of which are work-related. Almost 70% of economically active disabled people become disabled during their working lives. The greatest concentration is among the elderly (over 70% of the disabled are over 60 years of age).

Sheltered accommodation has become one of the major ways of providing housing which is designed to meet the needs of the disabled. Typically, there will be communal facilities such as a common room and communal laundry, plus support through an alarm system linked to a resident warden.

Let us look at what we mean by disability and look at some of the legislation around this subject. Disability can be defined as the loss or limitation of opportunity owing to social, physical or attitudinal barriers.

The National Assistance Act 1948 defines disabled people as 'persons who are blind, deaf or dumb or suffer from mental disorder of any description and other persons who are substantially and permanently handicapped by illness, injury or congenital deformity or such other disabilities as may be prescribed ...'

The Act imposes on local authorities the need to gather information on the number of disabled persons in their areas and to inform such people of the assistance available to them.

Housing authorities are required by the Chronically Sick and Disabled Persons Act 1970 to have regard to the special needs of disabled persons. The Housing Grants, Construction and Regeneration Act 1996 states that a person can be regarded as disabled if

a)   his sight, hearing or speech is substantially impaired;

b)   he has a mental disorder or impairment of any kind; or

c)   he is physically substantially disabled by illness, injury, impairment present since birth, or otherwise.

Following pressure from anti-discriminatory groups, various M.P.s tried unsuccessfully to introduce Private Members Bills to tackle the problems faced by disabled people. In July 1994, the Conservative government published a Consultation Document *Government Measures to Tackle Discrimination Against Disabled People* and a White Paper followed *Ending discrimination against disabled people*. This resulted in the passing of the Disability Discrimination Act 1995.

The Disability Discrimination Act 1995 received the Royal Assent on 8 November 1995. The preamble to the Act says it is 'an Act to make it unlawful to discriminate against disabled persons in connection with employment, the provision of goods, facilities and services or the disposal or management of premises; to make provision about the employment of disabled persons; and to establish a National Disability Council'.

The Act defines disability as a physical, sensory or mental impairment which has, or has in the past, had substantial and long-term adverse effect on a person's ability to carry out normal day-to-day activities.

The Act makes it unlawful to discriminate against a disabled person in connection with the sale, letting and management of premises, e.g by refusing to rent or sell a dwelling to a disabled person or by offering the dwelling on worse terms than the dwelling would be offered to others. Enforcement is by way of complaint to a county court and the remedies available are those available in the High Court. There is no upper limit on compensation, although there is a power to set an upper limit on the damages which may be awarded for injury to feelings.

Let us look at wheelchair and mobility housing.

- **wheelchair housing** is probably appropriate for about 2% of the disabled. Wheelchair housing means houses adapted for people who are confined to a wheelchair for the whole of the daytime;

- **mobility housing** is appropriate for about 15% of the disabled. Mobility housing means houses are adapted, but not to the extent of wheelchair houses, because the disabled persons are able to use crutches or walking frames. In mobility houses:

  - entrances need ramps;

  - it should, as far as possible, be easy to move around within the dwelling;

  - the bathroom, wc, kitchen and at least one bedroom should be at entrance level;

  - there should be adequate handles and grab rails;

  - there should be plenty of opportunity for those who cannot be physically active themselves to gain pleasure from observing the physical activity of others;

  - there should be good levels of both daytime and night-time lighting, to cater for those with failing eyesight. The use of contrasting colours may also be helpful.

The elderly and disabled who need extra heating suffered particularly after the introduction of VAT on fuel on 1 April 1994. VAT was fixed at 8% and was due to be increased to 17½% in April 1995. Fierce opposition and lobbying forced the government to change its mind on the further increase. The current VAT rate on heating fuel is 5%. Age Concern has estimated that an extra 10,000 elderly and disabled people have died each year as a result of the introduction of VAT.

Studies show that mortality rises by 7% for each 1°C drop in temperature. The difference between summer and winter temperatures results in a rise in blood pressure which increases the risk of heart attack by 21% and a stroke by 34%.

Building Regulations (covered in Unit 13) were amended in October 1998 to make features such as wider doorways and staircases, level floors and ground-floor toilets compulsory. The aim of the changes is to enable disabled people to approach and enter a building and move around it more easily. Homes now are defined as life-time homes and as such suitable for young and old alike; this reduces the need to move later in life as one becomes more frail.

Sick and disabled people receive help in the form of cash benefits. In 2002 more than 3.1m people were in receipt of such benefits for sickness, disability or both. The main benefits are incapacity benefit (which replaced invalidity benefit and unlike its predecessor is withdrawn when claimants reach retirement age), and severe disablement allowance for sickness and disability allowance.

Disabled Facilities Grants

Social Services and Health Authorities can assist with home adaptations such as stair-lifts, showers and wheelchair ramps.

Single People

For those young people who either go on to further education (for example, at universities) or leave home in search of employment and independence, there is always the difficulty of finding suitable accommodation at a reasonable price. For nearly all of them, it is a question of renting accommodation. Few local authorities provide accommodation for single people and so it is necessary for these young people to turn to private landlords or the housing association movement for help. Very few have the opportunity to purchase dwellings because of their low incomes, and thus they are unable to gain a place on the ladder of home-ownership.

Mentally Ill or Handicapped Persons

People who are mentally ill need the help of relatives and friends, and this assistance can often best be given in their own homes. Handicapped people need similar design features in their dwellings to those listed earlier in this unit, in the section above for the elderly.

Unfortunately, many mentally ill people actually live on the streets of large towns and cities. Some hostel places are available for the mentally ill together with community-based psychiatric teams being able to make contact with homeless mentally ill people. The number of mentally ill people living on the streets in London is disputed; the government estimate the figure to be in the range 300–500, whereas the mental health charity SANE considers the figure to be nearer 5,000.

Fuel Poverty

Fuel poverty is an age old problem and although the worst aspects are a thing of the past, it still exists. Each year there are cases of elderly people forced to live in a single room because they cannot afford to heat the rest of their house. This invariably results in excess deaths during the winter months in England. Currently there are 30,000 excess deaths each winter in England.

Excess winter mortality data refers to the difference between the number of deaths which occur in the winter months and those that happen in the summer months. Seasonal factors such as influenza and respiratory infections which are transmitted much more successfully during the winter months are to blame for part of the difference in the mortality rate but the effect of the cold, for example, in exacerbating circulatory diseases also contributes to these additional deaths.

If we compare winter deaths with those in other countries such as Sweden and Norway where the winters are much colder, the number of excess deaths in those countries is less than half of those in the UK. The fact that countries with much more severe winters than the UK experience comparatively low variations of mortality across the seasons suggests that poor housing standards and comparatively low incomes are crucial factors. Schemes exist to improve homes in England by offering insulation and central heating packages to fuel-poor households.

Care in the Community

The government published a White Paper in November 1989, *Caring for People*, which encouraged elderly and disabled people to remain in their own homes with the support, if necessary, of suitable services. Grant aid is available for works within the home under the Housing Grants, Construction and Regeneration Act 1996, in the form of Disabled Facilities Grants.

The White Paper has the effect of putting the more frail elderly person into sheltered accommodation or a residential home. As from April 1993 the Social Services Departments of local authorities have been responsible for assessing what help should be given to people who need community care services and for making the necessary arrangements. For some, home helps and meals on wheels may be the answer; for others it might be sheltered accommodation, residential care or a nursing home. These points are laid down in the National Health Service and Community Care Act 1990.

The intention of the legislation was to close all remaining mental health institutions (except for acute and secure units) by 1995. This target was met.

The problems faced by organizations in providing suitable accommodation for the mentally ill include:

(i)   lack of capital resources to build or purchase the necessary properties;

(ii) lack of revenue funding to ensure the proper and effective management of the accommodation once completed and therefore insufficient funds to provide appropriate care and support for residents;

(iii) difficulties with local communities' attitudes in accepting the mentally ill within their bounds;

(iv) lack of experience in meeting such profound needs through the voluntary sector and within a community setting;

(v) lack of experienced staff in the voluntary sector;

(vi) difficulties in gaining planning consents for schemes designed to help those with special needs;

(vii) already stretched community health and social services care facilities;

(viii) in many areas the only housing on offer is in unpopular and rundown districts which make people feel isolated and unsafe;

(ix) the narrow reach of community care assessment and cutbacks in housing benefit leave many without access to support services.

(x) many people have difficulty getting their needs recognized.

The legislation gave local authorities the responsibility to house people leaving mental institutions. However, the support system to help mentally ill tenants maintain their tenancies is inadequate. Many find themselves unable to cope with everyday life and the demands of being a responsible tenant after months or years in institutions.

The Care in the Community policy has reduced institutional care and further increased the need for suitable housing.

Women at Risk

It remains a sad fact that many women are battered by their husbands or partners. In their flight from their homes they turn to friends for shelter. The local authorities assist some women under the Housing Act 1996; very often local authorities provide accommodation in a women's refuge. Over the longer term, these battered women are normally unable to purchase properties and must therefore depend on local authorities or housing associations for rented accommodation.

Domestic violence is the crime least likely to be reported to the police. Domestic violence is not just slaps, cuts and bruises. It can involve sexual and emotional abuse leaving the victim feeling miserable and worthless.

One in four women experience domestic violence at some time in their lives; it accounts for 25% of all violent crimes reported to the police. Chillingly, two women die every week through domestic violence. 50,000 women and children, who flee their homes every year, being able to find a safe place to stay is vital. Untangling the physical and emotional damage inflicted by domestic violence is a daunting task and needs effective partnership working between police, social services, the voluntary sector and housing providers.

People fleeing domestic violence account for 16% of all homeless acceptances by local housing authorities and, if their accommodation and support needs are not adequately met, then the likelihood of the victim returning to the perpetrator is high – repeat homelessness is a very real risk for these women.

On average a woman puts up with 35 assaults before making a complaint to the police, even then half of all complaints are dropped before the case appears in court. Many women cannot face the thought of sitting in the courtroom giving evidence against a violent partner.

New legislation is expected to be passed in late 2003/early 2004 under the Domestic Violence Bill which is designed to make it easier for the battered partner (usually a woman) to escape the attacker. An extra £7m is expected to be provided for temporary refuges, although the aim is for women to stay in their own homes.

Child protection

Some 35,000 children are currently on child protection registers in England. These registers are for children who have more serious problems and are considered to be at risk of abuse. A plan is devised by the local authority to protect the child. The children remain at home.

2.6 First-time Buyers

So far, we have looked at the more vulnerable groups as far as housing accommodation is concerned. A group we have not yet considered is first-time buyers. For these people, it is necessary in nearly all cases to obtain a mortgage. Let us look at what a mortgage is.

Mortgages

A mortgage may be defined as a conveyance of land or an assignment of chattels as a security for the payment of a debt or the discharge of some other obligation for which it is given.

Mortgages are frequently granted by financial institutions other than building societies, such as banks, insurance companies and local authorities. Building societies and banks facing competition on mortgages offer various types such as endowment mortgages, fixed mortgages and low-start mortgages.

An outline of the present mortgage system is as follows. Firstly, somebody decides to buy a house, for £150,000 say. The prospective purchaser (**mortgagor**) then applies to a building society or bank (**mortgagee**) for a mortgage. In other words, the society or bank will provide most of the £150,000. Some building societies and banks will lend the whole of the purchase price (a 100% mortgage); others will lend up to, say, 95% of the purchase price. However, all financial institutions will take into account the income of the purchasers, because there is no point in lending £150,000 to a purchaser who cannot afford the repayments.

Suppose that the purchaser receives a mortgage for £125,000. Under a normal repayment mortgage, he will start off paying a monthly amount depending on interest rates prevailing at the time. In the early years of the mortgage, much of this payment is taken up paying the interest on the loan. As time goes by, more and more of the monthly repayment goes towards paying back the £125,000 capital sum. At the end of the mortgage period (usually 25 years), the £125,000 plus interest will have been repaid and the owner-occupier will own his house outright.

The problem with an ordinary mortgage is that it does not match up with the normal income structure of the mortgagor. Most mortgagors start off on a relatively low income, but move up the income ladder as time goes on with increments added to the salary and the prospect of promotion. In our example the mortgagor might be paying £500 per month out of a monthly salary of £1,800 during the early years, whereas towards the end of the mortgage period he might be paying the £500 out of a monthly salary of £3,500. Instead of paying the same proportion of his or her salary throughout the mortgage, the mortgagor has to find a larger amount at a time when he or she can least afford it and a relatively small amount when he is better off. Clearly the structure of a mortgage and the usual income structure are out of step.

In times of inflation, the problem is even easier to see. Salaries and wages will spiral upwards to keep up with inflation, but the mortgage repayments should stay roughly the same (although they will, of course, vary with the prevailing rates of interest). Considering our example, the payment of £500 a month might be a ridiculously low figure in 25 years, if inflation has reduced the purchasing power of the pound.

One way around this mortgage/income structure anomaly is for building societies or banks to grant low-start mortgages. The idea behind them is simply that a mortgagor should repay less in the early part of the mortgage period (when he is earning less), and more at the tail-end of the mortgage (when he is better able to afford it). Most mortgages are now this type.

Mortgage interest tax relief

Interest payable on a mortgage was subject to tax relief until April 2000. Phasing out tax relief has shown savings for the government of £1.9 billion in 1998/99 and £2.0 billion in 1999/2000.

Arrears and repossessions

After the housing slump or the late 1980s/early 1990s together with the economic recession, many people fell into arrears with their repayments resulting in many thousands of dwellings being taken into possession by the mortgages.

The period 1991 to 1994 saw a dramatic increase in the numbers of properties taken into possession. The reasons for this vast increase were as follows:

- the recession in the housing market;

- high interest rates 1989/90;

- the increase in unemployment.

Mortgage rescue schemes were introduced which provided a possible solution by offering a rescue service for people who were in difficulties with their mortgages and at risk of losing their homes. Direct payments of social security are now made to financial institutions. The schemes operate by transferring the form of tenure from ownership to renting or shared ownership (see Unit 9) doing so from a housing association; those 'tenants' who qualify can claim housing benefits to meet their housing costs.

All major building societies and banks have participated in schemes working with housing associations and offering them loans at low interest rates. The benefits for mortgagors are:

- their debts are cleared with financial institutions and possibly other debts if enough equity is raised;
- they can keep their own home;
- they do not become homeless;
- they do not have to move to another property which might be less desirable;
- they may have an option to repurchase the property in the future;
- housing benefit makes it possible to meet part or all of the housing costs;
- shared ownership is possible;
- sales into a market in recession are avoided.

The benefits for mortgagees are that:

- outstanding debts are cleared;
- interest charges stop running at an early stage;
- repossession is avoided;
- disposal costs for building societies or banks are lowered;
- a higher price can be obtained from a housing association than from an auction.

The problems with mortgage rescue schemes for housing associations are that:

- considerable staff time is consumed;
- 'pepper-potting' of properties (scattering) occurs, leading to high management costs for housing associations;
- applicants with second mortgages are not eligible;
- it is difficult to set affordable rents and at the same time meet debt costs;
- sales into a market in recession are avoided.

Negative Equity

In Unit 1 we saw how there has been greater aspiration for home-ownership over the last 23 years. Tenants were encouraged into marginal home-ownership through incentives such as the right to buy.

The collapse of the housing market in late 1980s caused problems for owner occupiers, and in particular, for first-time house owners who purchased their homes during that period. For the first time since the 1950s nominal house prices fell. This has introduced the term 'negative equity trap'. This describes the situation in which the outstanding mortgage debt is more than the current nominal value of the home despite the drop in interest rates over the last few years. Fortunately with the recent increase in house prices, the number of people in the negative equity trap has gone. In 1992 there were 1.2m in this position.

Owners with negative equity found it difficult to move because they were unable to redeem their existing mortgages, although some building societies and banks implemented mortgage rescue schemes whereby borrowers trapped in negative equity could transfer their existing mortgage, including the element of negative equity, from their existing property to a new home on the same or a lower value.

Owners are now actively encouraged to rely on mortgage protection insurance policies rather than income support in the event of sickness and redundancies. Income support is not payable for the first nine months. The Conservative government was embarrassed to note that people claiming under such policies were liable to be taxed their highest rate on the 'income' from their claims. Pressure was put upon the government by both backbenchers and Council of Mortgage Lenders to change the law. Some 2 million home owners with mortgages were affected. Consequently the then Chancellor of the Exchequer, Kenneth Clarke, rushed through emergency legislation to remove the threat of taxing home owners' mortgage insurance policies.

In 2003, the government announced that they were considering extending the delaying the payment of income support for the mortgage interest payments for 14 months. This is another example of owners being encouraged to rely on mortgage protection policies.

Insurance cover is also available. It is possible to pay only for accident and sickness or only for redundancy. Policies normally pay out for twelve months, although no payments are usually made for the first two or three months. Self-employed people and contract workers find it more difficult to get cover. Some policies actually require that the self-employed declare themselves bankrupt before they pay out.

Housing Benefits

Housing Benefit is means-tested and aimed at tenants on lowest incomes. It covers rent rebates for council tenants and rent allowances for housing association tenants and private sector tenants. It does not cover home owners who, if on low income, may get help through the income support system but only after the first nine months out of work.

Means-tested assistance has been available since 1972 (following the passing of the Housing (Finance) Act that year); Housing Benefit itself was introduced in 1982. Housing Benefit was introduced following the Social Security and Housing Benefits Act 1982 since amended by the Social Security Act 1986.

Claimants are now assessed on the basis of the income support means-test and if a claimant's income is less than what is known as the "applicable amount", then Housing Benefit is paid in respect of 100% of eligible costs. Anyone with a capital of more than £16,000 cannot get Housing Benefit. The applicable amount for a claimant is the official measure of the amount that people in different circumstances need to meet basic living conditions so local authorities do not have to pay the full amount if the accommodation is considered too large or the rent too high.

Housing Benefit is really a form of social security but it is administered by local authorities. All applicable amounts for rent rebates are met in full by the Exchequer and 95% of the benefits for private sector tenants are met. Help towards the cost of administration is given.

Housing Benefit is extremely complex to administer and the level of fraud is extremely high costing the tax payers hundreds of millions of pounds.

Amazingly enough those on low incomes who try to improve themselves are caught in a poverty trap whereby immediately their income rises above a basic level, they lose 97p of each additional £1 of income!

Housing benefit is sometimes known as rent rebates or rent allowances. It is assessed, administered and paid by local authorities. It is governed by the Social Security Administration Act 1992 and the Social Security Contributions and Benefits Act 1992.

Housing benefit helps with housing costs on many different types of accommodation such as furnished or unfurnished flats, bedsits, rented houses or hostels or lodgings, provided rent is paid to a landlord. It does not apply to those people purchasing their dwellings.

Housing benefit cannot be claimed if a tenant lives in the same dwelling as the landlord and the landlord is a close relative of the tenant or partner.

If a council tenant makes a successful application for housing benefit, then a reduction is made in the rent payable. An allowance is paid to a housing association or private landlord tenant who makes a successful application for housing benefit.

Since January 1996, local authorities must ensure that for private rented accommodation, the size is right for the applicant; the local authority will only pay a portion of the rent if the rent is too high.

From October 1996, the maximum rent to be used in the calculation of housing benefit for the *single* under-25s is based on the average rent in the area for single-roomed accommodation with the shared use of toilet and kitchen facilities. This does *not* apply to:

- a tenant of a registered social landlord;
- a tenant under 22 who has been subject to a care order or was provided with accommodation by the council under the Children Act 1989;
- a tenant who is severely disabled;
- a tenant who has one or more non-dependants residing with him.

The rent level used to determine housing benefit is assessed by rent officers, officials of the Inland Revenue. If the local authority or claimant is dissatisfied with the market rent determination, a request can be made for re-determination by an experienced rent officer from an adjoining or different registration area.

2.7 Migration of Industry

In a British Market Research Bureau study commissioned by the Building Societies Association, it was discovered that when moving house:

- 50% of people move less than three miles;

- fewer than one in ten move more than 100 miles;

- the average distance moved by adults in the UK is 19.9 miles.

The reason why most people move house is to obtain a bigger and better home; however, people also move in pursuit of employment.

In Great Britain, the labour force numbers some 27 million people, or 45% of the total population. If a company moves, or a company starts up at a new location, then many people in the labour force will move house and a large proportion of these will also take their families with them. Nowadays more and more businesses are moving away from the cities, taking advantage of lower costs and the attractive sites which many non-central areas provide. The number of people migrating after their employment is therefore likely to increase in the future.

This connection between migration and rising employment has two implications for housing:

- The housebuilding industry will need to take note of where the demand for houses is likely to move to. Once a business – or several businesses – have moved to an area, then that area is likely to be developed more rapidly (with an attendant rise in land and house prices).

- Those in public sector housing will look for more help in moving.

In April 1981, the government set up the **National Mobility Scheme**. This was a voluntary scheme with most public housing authorities involved. Those people who had the promise of a job in a new area or who had other social needs to move (for example, a relative who needed help and support because he or she is old and permanently ill) could obtain help to move. Local authorities made 1% of their relets available to those who applied for accommodation under the scheme.

The following year (April 1982) saw the introduction of the **Tenants' Exchange Scheme**, whereby council tenants could exchange their dwellings with other council tenants. The administration of the scheme was taken over by the National Mobility office in 1984.

Other schemes to assist with mobility have been LAMS (London Area Mobility Scheme) and HALP (Housing Association Liaison Project). The government decided to merge all these in 1990 and grant 100% government funding for a trial period of three years. These schemes were merged under the title of HOMES; this stands for the Housing Organizations' Mobility and Exchange Services. This was set up in April 1991 and amalgamated the earlier mobility schemes thus ensuring greater efficiency, reduced administration and simplicity of operation for both housing staff and tenants.

It is a company limited by guarantee and supported by the office of Deputy Prime Minister.

At first HOMES was divided into four sections:

LA HOMES which was originally concerned with people needing to move from one local authority area to another through the National Mobility Scheme. The scheme allowed people to

- move to be near employment

- move to look after a sick relative or bring a sick relative nearer

- move away from an area to avoid domestic violence and harassment

LB HOMES which dealt with London-wide moves among London Borough applicants through the HOMES Across London Scheme and the HOMES Move-On Scheme for single people in temporary hostel accommodation.

HA HOMES which assisted tenants of housing associations, co-operatives and other voluntary sector landlords to move through the HA Pool HOMESWAP.

The first three schemes above are now amalgamated into a single nomination scheme which can be used by both landlords and tenants and is known as the HOMES Mobility Scheme.

This scheme assists local authorities, housing associations or co-operative tenants who need to move. To be eligible a tenant:

- must be taking a job opportunity which is too far away to travel to every day;

- must need to be closer to relatives or friends so that they can give or receive support;

- must be experiencing domestic violence;

- must have justifiable health reasons to move.

In order to assist mobility, predefined targets were set. For housing associations this was set at 4% of their net lettings; for local authorities the targets are set at 2% of their net lettings.

HOMESWAP enables tenants to move from area to area with less fuss than is possible for owner occupiers with the minimum of official involvement. Exchanging properties enables the best use to be made of housing and people are able to move into housing more appropriate to their needs.

HOMESWAP relies on a computer database system designed to give interested tenants details of prospective swaps into the area they wish to move to. No charge is made for this service. The HOMESWAP Scheme provides up to five prospective exchange partners in their chosen area.

HOMES services are now available on the web. At the time of writing the text (Summer 2003) 45,000 applicants had already registered for an exchange under HOMESWAP on the Internet whereby contact is made with people in other parts of the country who have exactly the property they need. It must be stressed here that there is still a telephone support service for those without access to the Internet. People registered on the system will still receive automatic six-weekly matching letters from HOMES and be able to do their searching using the HOMESWAP lists displayed in housing offices and, in some areas, public libraries.

There is a further scheme known as Mutual Exchanges, which is for two or more tenants to 'swap' their properties within one local authority area.

For this scheme to operate, the tenant completes a housing transfer mutual exchange form. The details are circulated to other tenants interested in wishing to swap their properties.

It is necessary to have the agreement of the local authority (ie the landlord) otherwise the tenants would still be responsible for 'original' rents.

Local authorities agree to mutual exchanges providing tenants are not in rent arrears. Local authorities will also check the condition of the dwelling (known as a pre-void inspection) to ensure that no damage has been done to it.

Local authorities will not allow either substantial overcrowding or under-occupation to occur as a result of the transfer. Similarly if the exchange resulted in a property specially designed or adapted for a disabled person or an elderly person being occupied by someone without similar needs, then the local authority would prevent the transfer.

There is no limit to the number of times a tenant can complete a mutual exchange.

Summary

In this unit we have looked at how demography can help the development of housing, by predicting changes in the size and composition of the population.

We have considered some of the available statistics and the known trends, both for the population in general and for certain minority groups such as the homeless, the elderly, one-parent families or first-time buyers.

3

HOUSING REPORTS

Objectives

After studying this unit, you should be able to:

- explain the need for housing reports;
- write detailed notes on each of the three main reports, namely Tudor Walters, Dudley and Parker Morris;
- define 'standard amenities';
- summarize the current fitness standards;
- explain the need for building regulations.

3.1   Introduction

The purpose of publishing national reports on housing standards has subtly changed over the years. The first report was concerned with maintaining an adequate standard of housing. It set out to determine what the standard should be, so that new dwellings could provide adequate living conditions. To a certain extent this is still true of more recent reports. However, the emphasis has changed slightly.

The content of reports and the recommendations made tend to be much more technical nowadays, as a result of the increased sophistication in house construction techniques. The reports also indicate more what the housing market wants rather than what it needs. Building adequate dwellings is no longer a problem for modern technology, but building the standard and type of dwelling desired by potential housebuyers is still something of a hit-and-miss affair.

Up to the time of the First World War, the provision of housing was not seen as a social service. Dwellings were provided by speculators for purchase or rent. Naturally, they only provided houses built to a standard which the populace could afford and two factors meant that there was little opportunity for standards to improve. Firstly, higher standards would mean higher construction costs and therefore higher rents, and because the speculative housebuilder could see that nobody could pay higher rents, the housebuilder did not attempt the higher standard.

Secondly, at that time local and central governments did not concern themselves with housing standards, even though they had the power to do so. Instead they concentrated on minimum levels of sanitation and on avoiding unfit housing. We shall look at this further in the next unit when we consider relevant legislation relating to housing. There was nothing to compel higher standards from housebuilders.

After the First World War, there was a serious housing shortage – of good-quality homes in particular. The greatly increased cost of building and rate of interest on capital meant that speculative builders found it unprofitable to operate, particularly in providing dwellings for the working classes. There was a demand for 'homes for heroes' returning from the war. Local authorities were to become the main providers of housing for rent; they were given subsidies for the first time to build houses and housing was to be regarded as a social service. Here was an obvious opportunity to do something about the standard (as well as the number) of houses. One of the immediate results was the commissioning of the first government report on housing standards: the Tudor Walters report.

3.2   The Tudor Walters Report

Two architects, named Raymond Unwin and Barry Parker, worked in establishing the first Garden City at Letchworth, Hertfordshire, in 1904. Unwin went on to become the leading influence behind the design and layout proposals contained in the Tudor Walters report which provided the basic architecural framework for the development of inter-war municipal housing. He was bitterly opposed to the high-density housing which had been seen in the latter part of the 19th century.

The Local Government Board set up a Committee in July 1917 'to consider questions of building construction ... of dwellings for the working classes'. This was under the chairmanship of Sir John Tudor Walters, MP. The objects of the Report were to 'profoundly influence the general standards of housing in this country and to encourage the building of houses of such quality that they would remain above the acceptable minimum standards for at least 60 years'.

The Tudor Walters Report was published in 1918. Its full title was the *Report of the Committee to Consider Questions of Building Construction with the Provision of Dwellings for the Working Classes*. The fact that the working classes is mentioned explicitly in this title is another indication that housing was rapidly being seen as a social service.

The report made four main recommendations:

●   that houses should be built rather than flats; 12 houses to the acre should be built in towns and 8 houses to the acre in the country;

●   on the composition of houses to be built: each house should contain:

     -     three bedrooms;

     -     a living room (and a parlour in larger dwellings);

- a separate kitchen;

- if possible, a separate bathroom fitted with hot and cold water (alternatively, hot and cold water should be provided in the scullery);

- a bath (though not necessarily in a bathroom).

● on the size of houses to be built: a three-bedroomed, non-parlour type house should be 855 sq. ft and a parlour type house 1055 sq. ft. These sizes were exclusive of fuel and other stores.

● houses should have a wider frontage as this provided more air, light and garden space.

The Report stressed that careful design was a better way of saving money than lowering standards. However, at this time most local authorities lacked experience in design and construction, consequently they needed guidance.

Following publication of the Tudor Walters Report, the Local Government Board in 1919 issued a Housing Manual detailing advice to local authorities as to the terms on which government grants would be available. This Manual adapted the principles of Tudor Walters but increased the space recommendations to 900sq ft for three-bedroom non-parlour houses and 1080 sq ft for parlour types. Internal wcs were to be provided in new houses and a bath had to be either in a bathroom or the scullery.

At the time the standards were considered high. These high standards were reflected in high rents and restricted access to council housing to skilled manual workers only as they were the only ones who could afford the rents.

In the period between the wars, standards of housebuilding were based on the Tudor Walters recommendations, representing a significant improvement in housing conditions. But, by the late 1930s, pressure on housing began to grow again and standards were subsequently lowered. A report in 1936 revealed that there were severe problems of overcrowding in north-east England and in the London area.

3.3   The Dudley Report

Just before the Second World War public opinion was sought as to what housing the public wanted. This *Enquiry into People's Homes* showed that people wanted a separate 'sitting room' and a bathroom – the bathroom not to be downstairs or in the scullery. There was strong support for a wash-hand basin in bathrooms. Better kitchens were also required.

The government turned its attention to housing again, but was distracted by the advent of the Second World War in 1939.

After the war an opportunity existed to improve the standard of housing once again, because during the war many, many thousands of houses had been either damaged or destroyed by enemy action.

Recommendations for post-war standards of accommodation and design were made by a subcommittee of the then Central Housing Advisory Committee.

In 1944, the subcommittee published its report (which came to be known as the Dudley Report after its chairman, Lord Dudley). The Report followed the same basic approach as Tudor Walters and framed its recommendations about house design in terms of minimum room sizes and adequate circulation space. The main recommendation of the Report was the 'minimum standard' house would be built at a density of 16 to the acre instead of 12 in towns. The floor space of these three-bedroom houses was 900 sq ft.

The Report concluded that there was an increasing need for more two-bedroomed houses in view of smaller family size.

The main recommendations were subsequently incorporated into a *Housing Manual*, published in 1944 by the then Ministry of Health and issued to local authorities to use as a guide. Recommendations from the Dudley Report which were included in the manual were that houses should have:

- increased floor space for bedrooms;

- hot water supply to bath, sink and wash-basin;

- heated linen cupboards;

- a second wc;

- fitted cupboards;

- extra lighting and power points.

The report formed its recommendations about house design in terms of minimum room sizes and adequate circulation space. Central government was thus able to raise standards and exert its influence over local authorities, but at the same time leave them a free hand to have their own schemes designed within the given framework.

The recommended minimum of 900 sq ft for a three-bedroomed house was well exceeded during the period of the Labour government up to 1951; indeed, the council houses of the 1940s remain the most spacious council houses ever built.

3.4   Housing Manuals

Housing manuals were published in the period 1949-1953, together with supplements in 1952 and 1953. In 1951 the Conservatives came to power partly on a manifesto promise to build 300,000 houses a year (Labour had promised only 200,000). This steep production target was met, but only at the expense of housing standards. A manual *Houses*, published in 1952 by the then Ministry of Housing and Local Government, reduced space standards as part of an economy drive but encouraged separate dwellings.

More and more smaller houses were built, designed for four people rather than five. They included two-bedroomed houses and smaller three-bedroomed houses. These became known as 'Macmillan Houses' or 'People's Houses', because they were the direct result of the government's policy to push production at the expense of standards.

As well as an increase in the number of small houses, the facilities provided within a dwelling were cut. Local authorities were told (via the Housing Manuals) to economize not only with the design of a home, but also with the services and equipment to be installed in it. Perhaps the most significant of these cuts was that a second w.c. (which up until then had been mandatory in larger houses) was no longer required.

3.5 The Parker Morris Report

By 1960, it was again apparent that pressures on housing were increasing, this time because living standards had risen dramatically; it was time for housing standards to catch up. The Central Housing Advisory Committee at the time set up another subcommittee (this time chaired by Sir Parker Morris) to:

> ... consider the standards of design and equipment applicable to family dwellings and other forms of residential accommodation, whether provided by public authorities or by private enterprise, and to make recommendations.

The Parker Morris Report (more properly called *Homes for Today and Tomorrow*) was published in 1961 and is regarded as one of the most influential reports on housing. The report was realistic and practical and exerted enormous influence on design, particularly of council houses. The report took the increase in living standards since 1944 as the main reason for revising the specification of new housing. The committee criticized the Dudley Report standards and said:

> ... Houses are being built at the present time which not only are too small to provide adequately for family life but also are too small to hold the possessions in which so much of the new affluence is expressed.

The Report was written at a time when 1,000 families moved into a newly-finished house every working day, when one household in three possessed a car and four in every five a television. Nowadays there are 24m cars registered in the UK and 28% of people have access to two or more cars; this has doubled in just the last 20 years.

The main recommendations of the Parker Morris Report were:

- In general, more space should be provided in houses.
  - High priority should be given to providing houses with more floor space. Overall floor areas required as a minimum were stated to be 800 sq.ft. (74.32m^2) for a 4-person intermediate terrace house with two storeys and 910 sq.ft. (84.54m^2) for a 5-person intermediate terrace house, plus 50 sq.ft (4.65m^2) of general storage space in both cases. The theory was that larger houses were a good investment because they were more adaptable to future needs.

- Space should be provided in new houses for new household equipment, such as washing machines, refrigerators, etc.

- Kitchens should be large enough to enable the occupiers to take at least some meals there.

- In most dwellings, the w.c. should be situated in a room of its own (although in some smaller dwellings it could be placed in the bathroom).

● Estate design should be improved.

- Space should be provided for cars, on the basis of one for each household.

- Terraced houses should be set out in such a way that suitable access was available from one side to the other.

- The general appearance and layout of housing should be improved – for example by improving gardens and the external appearance of houses.

● Heating standards for houses should be set. The report recommended a minimum standard of 13°C for the kitchen and 18°C for living and dining areas, when the temperature outside was – 1°C.

● In general, housing standards should not be based purely on the number and size of rooms, as they had been in the past. They should be set instead in terms of 'the activity of the occupants'.

In the early 1960s, Great Britain had become an affluent society and by 1963

- 82% of households had a television set;

- 72% of households had a vacuum cleaner;

- 45% of households had a washing machine;

- 30% of households had a fridge.

The government obviously approved of the Parker Morris Report, even though implementing its recommendations would inevitably lead to higher housing costs and increased subsidy costs.

At first, local authorities were encouraged but not obliged to implement the new standards. Nevertheless, by 1965 half of the local authority houses were designed taking into account either the space standards, the heating standards, or both. Two years later the Housing Subsidies Act 1967 was passed, which provided that Parker Morris standards would be a necessary qualification for subsidies, although the relevant part of the Act did not come into force until 1 January 1969. It is worth bearing in mind that the Parker Morris standards were minimum standards; the idea was that, wherever possible, they should be exceeded. However, the government also guarded against the possibility of rocketing subsidies by applying a cost yardstick. The cost yardstick set the maximum cost of dwellings for which Exchequer subsidies would be paid for any local authority scheme.

The Parker Morris standards and the complementary housing cost yardstick remained in force until 1981, when both were terminated under the Local Government, Planning and Land Act 1980. To replace them, central government instituted a system whereby most of the responsibilities for housing were given to local authorities. Local authorities now had to demonstrate 'value for money' in their housing programmes, which were submitted to the then Department of the Environment only for an overall view. Local housing authorities decided what standards and cost provide the best value for money.

Since Parker Morris standards were abandoned, both local authorities' and housing associations' standards have declined particularly with regard to space.

The Housing Corporation issued new design guidance in the early 1990s; this guidance is not mandatory and very few housing associations adhere to it.

3.6   Statutory Requirements

Other than the requirement for local authorities to show value for money in their housing programmes, there is surprisingly little legislation relating to the design of houses. The two main areas of legislation relating to design are:

● parts of the Housing Act 1985;

● parts of the Local Government and Housing Act 1989;

● delegated legislation in the form of local bye-laws (the Building Regulations) (see Unit 13).

Legslation on Provision of Amenities

We saw in Unit 1 the standard amenities set out in Section 508 of the Housing Act 1985. To recap these are:

- a fixed bath or shower (see notes 1 and 2);

- a hot and cold water supply at a fixed bath or shower (see notes 1 and 2);

- a wash-hand basin;

- a hot and cold water supply at a wash-hand basin;

- a sink;

- a hot and cold water supply at a sink;

- a water closet (see note 3).

  Notes:

1. a fixed bath or shower shall be in a bathroom, unless note 2 applies.

2. if it is not reasonably practicable for the fixed bath or shower to be in a bathroom but it is reasonably practicable for it to be provided with a hot and cold water supply, it need not be in a bathroom but may be in any part of the dwelling which is not a bedroom.

3.   a wc shall, if reasonably practicable, be in, and accessible from within, the dwelling or, where the dwelling is part of a larger building, in such a position in that building as to be readily accessible from the dwelling.

That is not to say that new houses cannot be built lacking standard amenities. Why not? Because the Building Regulations say so.

We also need to consider the fitness standard laid down in the Local Government and Housing Act 1989. Again, as we saw in Unit 1, this states that a dwelling is unfit unless it has:

- a piped water supply;

- a wash basin with hot and cold water;

- a fixed bath or shower and an internal w.c;

- drainage and sanitation facilities;

- facilities for cooking and food preparation, including a sink with hot and cold water and waste disposal facilities;

- adequate natural and satisfactory artificial lighting, heating and ventilation;

- substantially free from rising damp, penetrating damp and condensation.

In addition the dwelling must be structurally stable and in adequate repair.

The government announced in 1999 that it was re-examining the fitness standard with a view to allocating a points system on the severity of the 'unfitness' category. We referred to this in Unit 1.

Building Regulations

Local authorities have the power to make building bye-laws (a form of delegated legislation). Such bye-laws have been incorporated into the Building Regulations.

The Building Regulations set out in fairly general terms what should be provided in a house in terms of amenities, safety, construction standards and so forth, together with some technical detail on how construction should take place. They apply to both public-sector and private-sector builders, and local authorities have the power to enforce alterations or amendments to dwellings that do not comply in some way. Local authorities also have the power to relax the Regulations in specific instances, where they are obviously inappropriate.

The Building Regulations do not contain every single rule or standard in one enormous volume, but instead make frequent reference to relevant British Standards. In some areas, the Building Regulations may also operate in tandem with bye-laws which are peculiar to that particular local authority.

English House Conditions Survey 2001

We made reference to the English House Conditions Survey 2001 earlier in this text. It is worthy of note that this Survey shows that recent built dwellings are on average smaller and on smaller plots than older housing. The average size for a post-1980 home is 83m² compared to 88m² for those built before 1980. Nevertheless, the average amount of living space per person provided by homes has increased, largely as a consequence of a fall in household size.

The Survey shows that 94% of homes now have central or programmable heating; 76% have double glazing and 35% a second wc.

3.7   Future Reports on Housing

So, we can see that the last commissioned report on housing standards was carried out by the Parker Morris Committee in 1961, over 40 years ago. What are future housing reports likely to concentrate on? There is no way to be certain. Probable future concerns will be a mixture of social considerations and some of the more recent advances in housing technology. They could include:

-    attention to better insulation to reduce noise;

-    safety precautions in the siting of playgrounds;

-    maximum use of natural light;

-    providing efficient means of refuse disposal;

-    ample provision of storage space;

-    efficient and adequate lift facilities;

-    provision for accommodating leisure activities;

-    effective double-glazing, central heating systems and cavity wall insulation;

-    air conditioning;

-    CCTV.

Summary

In this short unit we have looked at the main reports that have influenced design standards over the years. You should remember that the main reports were:

●   the Tudor Walters Report;

- the Dudley Report;
- the Parker Morris Report;

and be able to make brief notes on each. We have also considered the legislation on the provision of amenities and the Building Regulations.

4

HISTORICAL BACKGROUND – DEVELOPMENT OF HOUSING POLICY

Objectives

After studying this unit, you should be able to:

- explain how pressures have prompted housing legislation;
- outline the provisions of the main pieces of housing legislation relating to your course;
- describe the effects of various pieces of housing legislation.

4.1   Introduction

From the first three units, you may feel that housing is a large and complicated topic. There is a mass of statistics relating to house building, population size and movements. On top of that, housing is subject to political and economic pressures which are difficult to quantify or predict. We have made a brief mention of some legislation in earlier units; but there is in fact a great deal of detailed legislation involved with housing.

The best way to see why such a complex situation has evolved is to look at how it evolved. In this unit we shall look at how reports and legislation have influenced the development of housing.

Your syllabus requires you to know only about historical developments and legislation in housing since 1915. However, in order to understand the pressures on housing at that time, it is necessary to take a brief look at events well before 1915. Indeed, we can sensibly start at a time when there was no legislation affecting housing.

4.2   Early Pressures on Housing

Even before the Industrial Revolution in the late 1700s, there were problems with housing. In London, cramped and congested conditions already existed. These conditions were one of the main causes behind the Great Fire of London in 1666. From historical records, we know that John Farynor was baker to King Charles II. One evening in September 1666, he went to bed in his room above his bakery in Pudding Lane having forgotten to clamp down his bread ovens. Within hours 13,000 houses had been destroyed, 87 parish churches burned down and 300 acres blackened. Even shops built on London Bridge caught fire, causing sparks to start fires south of the Thames.

During the Industrial Revolution, more and more people were attracted to towns because that was where the new industries (and the jobs) were to be found. Not surprisingly, builders of the time sought to cash in on the increasing number of town-dwellers; they built small 'jerry-built' dwellings as quickly as they could. The builders were not particularly concerned with public health and so the new buildings only made conditions in towns more cramped and congested.

Local government had no interest or involvement in housing at the time. As a result, there were no curbs on the building of sub-standard dwellings. Their number continued to grow and, even today, they provide the basis of slum problems in many industrial towns and cities.

Housing became a public health issue as the industrialization sucked people from the countryside into the appalling slums in the cities. In 1832 there was a cholera epidemic which affected rich and poor alike. Furthermore, there was a violent outbreak of fever in Spitalfields in London in the winter of 1837. As far as housing is concerned, the importance of the epidemic is that in 1842 a report came to be written by Sir Edwin Chadwick, Secretary of the Poor Law Commissioners, called *The Report on the Sanitary Conditions of the Labouring Population*. This report expressed concern, based firmly on public health considerations, about the housing conditions of the poor.

We looked in Unit 2 at life expectancy. It is worthwhile pondering for a moment on life expectancy in the 1800s. At the time of Chadwick's Report there were epidemic diseases such as typhoid and cholera which had been caused by overcrowded and insanitary living conditions. Children were particularly affected.

For adults, the overcrowded, insanitary, confined and unventilated dwellings caused labourers to die from tuberculosis and respiratory complaints. Chadwick's Report showed average expectations of life in Wiltshire in 1840:

- Gentlemen and persons engaged in professions, and their families   50 years
- Farmers and their families   48 years
- Agricultural laboureres and their families   33 years

4.3   Early Legislation

Sir Edwin Chadwick's report became the basis for the first Act which attempted to influence housing: the Public Health Act 1848. Over the next 50 years came other acts which affected housing, culminating in the Housing of Working Classes Act of 1890; this is often referred to as the first true Housing Act.

Although legislation prior to 1915 is not part of the syllabus, you should have some idea of the acts passed before that date and what they were intended to achieve.

- **Public Health Act 1848**

  The purpose of this Act was to try to relieve the insanitary conditions of working-class housing. However, the provisions of the Act were not mandatory, so local authorities could not enforce any changes in housing conditions even when these were especially poor.

- **Labouring Classes Lodging Houses Act 1851 and Common Lodging Houses Act 1851**

  These two Acts, known as the Shaftesbury Acts, gave local authorities the power to build (and inspect) lodging houses for the labouring classes. They also laid down a minimum standard of cleanliness. It is these two Acts which mark the true beginning of housing legislation.

- **Nuisances Removal Act 1855**

  It was this Act which first introduced the now familiar phrase 'unfit for human habitation'.

- **Artisans' and Labourers' Dwellings Act 1868 (the Torrens Act)**

  This Act gave local authorities power to improve or demolish individual dwellings; it is therefore the first legislation concerned with slum clearance.

- **Artisans' and Labourers' Dwellings Improvement Act 1875 (the Cross Act)**

  This Act widened the slum-clearance powers of local authorities, by giving them the power to improve or demolish areas of insanitary dwellings (rather than just individual insanitary dwellings).

- **Public Health Act 1875**

    This Act made several important provisions:

    - it imposed a minimum standard of building construction;

    - it enabled sewers to be provided;

    - it gave authorities the power to regulate street layouts.

- **Housing of the Working Classes Act 1885**

  This Act made minor amendments to existing legislation.

- **Housing of the Working Classes Act 1890**

  This was mainly a consolidating Act, that is one which brings together various provisions of earlier Acts. It is usually regarded as being the first true Housing Act and we shall now look at it in more detail.

This early legislation was administered through a Central Board of Health.

Effects of the Housing of the Working Classes Act 1890

This Act was necessary because the earlier acts covered the position, inspection, improvement or demolition of dwellings in a rather complicated and confusing manner.

The main points contained in the Act gave the local authorities powers:

- for dealing with unfit houses;

- for clearing slum areas and carrying out improvement schemes;

- for providing houses, flats and lodging houses to be owned and managed by themselves;

- for acquiring land, by compulsion if necessary, for any of the above purposes.

The 1890 Act had both positive and negative influences on housing:

- On the positive side, local authorities were, albeit slowly, beginning to build dwellings; at last the provision of housing was beginning to be seen as a local authority responsibility. However, later government legislation (Local Government and Housing Act 1989) stated that local authorities should be providers of housing only as a last resort!

- The negative aspects were that tighter building controls tended to discourage private builders, and not all local authorities acted to reduce the resulting housing need.

In any case, the effectiveness of the Act was somewhat undermined by the rising cost of land and labour. The legislation of the day made no provision for government subsidies to local authorities or private builders and, in fact, subsidies for housing remained non-existent for another 30 years, as we shall see.

The powers conferred by the 1890 Act were amended and enlarged during the next 20 years. In 1909, the Housing and Town Planning Act was passed; this improved the law with regard to housing, introducing for the first time powers for dealing with town planning.

4.4   During the First World War

In spite of the growing legislation on housing, when the First World War began local authorities had built only 20,000 houses. In other words, almost all of the housing in existence in 1915 had been privately built.

However, we must not confuse privately built with privately owned. Although the majority of houses had been privately built, in 1915 less than 10% of households in Britain actually owned the houses in which they lived. About 90% rented housing from private landlords.

During the war the level of house building dropped (except in a few munition areas) and a shortage developed. Not surprisingly, landlords and bodies able to grant mortgages tried to exploit the situation by charging high rents and interest rates. Consequently, the government of the day stepped in with the first legislation controlling rents:

- **Rent and Mortgage Interest (War Restrictions) Act 1915**

  This Act was passed at a time when sharply rising rents caused discontent in areas where munitions were made for the war, particularly in Glasgow.

  The Act:

  - prevented landlords from profiteering and prohibited the increase of rents above the August 1914 figures (there was an exception to this where the rent included rates and an increase was allowed in respect of the rates element);

  - gave tenants some security against eviction;

  - prevented an increase in mortgage interest rates;

  - prevented the calling in of mortgages.

The Act was intended for the use as a wartime measure but became impossible to repeal later after the war during times of rapid inflation and acute housing shortage.

As the war came towards its end, it was recognized that there was a serious shortage of housing. Although nearly three-quarters of a million men died in the First World War, the birth rate was increasing and thus there was a demand for more housing; it was estimated at the end of the war that 800,000 new dwellings were needed.

Many of those who returned from the war, where they had lived in trenches, were forced to live in appalling conditions, sometimes sharing rooms with relatives or even living in wooden shacks, caravans and railway carriages, often without sanitation.

It was clear that a sizeable programme of housebuilding would have to be undertaken and that such a programme would be a sensible time to improve the standard of houses being built, especially for those who had served their country in the trenches abroad. The country would need to build 'homes fit for heroes to live in', as Walter Long (President of the Local Government Board) stated. The Prime Minister, David Lloyd George, stated 'our task is to make Britain a country to live in.' The government set about concentrating its resources on the planning of a post-war housing policy.

In 1917, the government created the **Ministry of Reconstruction** to oversee the planned growth in housebuilding. This was to be seen as the pivot of the post-war social policy providing large numbers of good-quality houses. The plan was dramatic, aiming to build something like 60,000 dwellings a year. New methods of financing and organizing housebuilding would be needed, because the methods in operation before the war would not be able to cope with such a huge task.

4.5   Between the Wars

It is important to realize that much of the legislation passed after the First World War was designed to stimulate housebuilding in one way or another. The first important inter-war legislation was passed in 1919.

It was recognized that the private housing market was unable to supply enough houses to meet the chronic shortages in reasonable condition at rents which the working classes could afford; hence the government had to intervene.

- **Housing and Town Planning Act (1919) (the Addison Act)**

  This Act was named after Dr Christopher Addison, President of the Local Government Board and later the first Minister of Health, who steered it through Parliament. It was one of the very few pieces of housing legislation to have the approval of all political parties. The overall objective of the Act was to build 500,000 houses within three years. It was an important Act for two reasons:

  - it made local authorities statutorily responsible for providing housing. They were required to survey the needs of their areas for houses within three months and they had to make and carry out plans for the houses needed with the approval of the Minister of Health.
  - for the first time, it provided an Exchequer subsidy for housebuilding.

  The response to the Addison Act, as far as the government was concerned, was a case of both good and bad news.

  - the good news was that the level of housebuilding soared. Some 176,000 houses were built under the Act. In fact there was serious concern that the building industry would not be able to cope.
  - the bad news was that the form of subsidy provided by the government proved unwise. It worked in such a way that the Exchequer bore the loss on all approved schemes except for the product of a 1d (one old penny) rate. This proved too expensive, and so two years later the scheme was replaced by another, based on a fixed sum per dwelling. By 1922 the housing programme was reducing.

  At first, the thought of the Government subsidizing local-authority building was not welcomed but gradually became acceptable.

  Although the Act allowed local authorities to begin large scale housing work after the First World War, it was usually the 'respectable poor' who were accommodated in these dwellings, with the poorest families still living in privately rented rooms.

  Prior to this legislation, as we have seen, there was virtually no council housing. There had been a handful of charitable trusts and model dwellings companies (fore-runners of the housing association movement) who had provided this type of accommodation for rent.

- **Housing Act 1923 (the Chamberlain Act)**

  This Act was designed to encourage private enterprise building and to apportion the cost of assisted housebuilding more fairly between the Exchequer and local authorities. In particular, the Act reduced the amount of subsidies previously available for local-authority housing and, for the first time, introduced a subsidy to builders for houses provided by private enterprise. The subsidies worked as follows:

- for general housing: the government paid £6 per house per year for 20 years either directly to the local authority or via the local authority to a private builder, in respect of each house built and with no requirement that there should be a rate fund contribution. (This was designed to limit municipal activity and to encourage builders, who could also claim subsidy on houses that reached certain minimum standards and were defined as for the working class. The emphasis was now on private enterprise building houses and not relying on local authorities).

- for slum clearance: the government paid a grant covering half of the annual loss incurred by a local authority.

The Act also enabled local authorities to lend money to guarantee building society advances on small houses and to lend working capital to builders of small houses.

- **Housing (Financial Provisions) Act 1924 (the Wheatley Act).**

This Act increased subsidies to local authorities in an effort to restore and increase the level of public (municipal) housebuilding. The government hoped to provide 1,500,000 houses in fifteen years.

- **Housing Act 1930 (the Greenwood Act)**

This was another unsuccessful government initiative, which attempted to stimulate the process of slum clearance, but it achieved little because the country was in the grip of an economic depression at the time. With the limited slum clearance, local authorities became landlords to poorer people who had been dispersed from their appalling homes and to assist them with the higher rents, rent rebates were introduced for those who could not afford the council rent. Rent rebates, however, were not popular with local authorities because it involved rather complicated administrative procedures. Furthermore, the payment of rent rebates was not mandatory on local authorities.

Towards the end of the inter-war period, there were three more important pieces of legislation.

- **Housing (Financial Provisions) Act 1933**

This Act abolished subsidies to local authorities for 'general needs' council housing, although subsidies still existed for specialized housebuilding. It had the effect of opening the door for private building for owner-occupation and is one of the reasons why building societies grew so rapidly in the 1930s.

- **Housing Act 1935**

This Act was aimed at the problem of overcrowding (and is sometimes referred to as the Overcrowding Act); it defined overcrowding and made local authorities responsible for dealing with the problem. Local authorities were required to undertake a full inspection in all areas to ascertain the extent of overcrowding. The Act also altered the rules for local authority housing accounts, making rent rebate schemes more practicable and attractive. This Act also set up the Central Housing Advisory Committee which was referred to in Unit 3.

A survey of overcrowding, undertaken in 1936, revealed that, out of nine million inspected, 341,554 houses in England and Wales were overcrowded. This means that 3.8% of all the houses were overcrowded, and in some areas the figure was as high as 20%.

● **The Housing Act 1936**

This was another consolidating Act, ie one that brings together various provisions of earlier Acts. Until 1957, it was known as the Principal Housing Act.

Between the two wars (1919–1939) a total of 4,998,000 houses were built as follows:

Private enterprise	3,886,000
Local authority	1,112,000

Effects of the Inter-war Legislation

Housing legislation between the wars affected three main areas:

● housing production;

● housing standards;

● the growth of building societies.

Housing production

House production in the inter-war period was slow to start but reached a peak in 1927-1928 when 239,000 houses were built, of which about half were built by local authorities and about half by private enterprise. More than half of the privately built houses were subsidized.

Between 1929 and 1933, the level of housebuilding dropped slightly. It rose again in the mid-1930s, when building costs and interest rates were low. In addition, the composition of housebuilding changed after the Housing (Financial Provisions) Act 1933: private enterprise now accounted for some 200,000 of the houses built each year. A total of between 325,000 and 347,000 houses were built in each of the five years up to 1939.

Housing standards

One of the reasons why housing legislation came into being initially was a growing social conscience over the country's standard of housing. Some improvements were made by legislation:

● the Housing Act 1923 made the provision of a bath a condition of subsidy.

● the Housing (Financial Provisions) Act 1924 laid down that the bath in subsidized houses should be in a bathroom.

However, housing standards in general were still poor. For example, a hot water supply was still the exception rather than the rule. During the 1930s, the economic depression forced housing standards to stay low, for the simple reason that tenants could not afford anything better. It was not until after the Second World War that legislation began to have a more noticeable effect on housing standards.

Growth of building societies

The early 1930s saw a period of low interest rates, low wages and low material costs; this resulted in a mass market for home ownership. However substantial deposits (around 25%) were required by building societies. We shall see shortly how mortgage terms were extended and it became possible for mortgagors to borrow more than 70-75% of the house value under the Housing (Financial) Provisions Act 1933.

At this time an average three bedroomed semi-detached house was about £650 to purchase (£1 per week on a mortgage); detached houses were in the region of £1,000 to purchase.

When subsidies to local authorities to build 'general needs' housing were abolished in 1933, the intention was to let private enterprise take over the building of private houses either for letting or for owner-occupation. From 1933, the role of public housing was meant to be confined to slum clearance and rehousing problems.

At the same time, building societies found that they had a tremendous surplus of money. They had survived the economic crisis of the early 1930s and they continued to attract new investment. The real income of those in employment was rising and investment in the building societies was also increasing rapidly.

In fact, one MP commented in 1939 that the Housing (Financial Provisions) Act 1933 was:

> ... placed on the Statute Book simply because the building societies were absolutely bursting with money for which they had no outlet, and it compelled local authorities to cease to build houses for the ordinary applicants, for one purpose only, namely in order that people might be driven into the hands of the building societies and called upon to purchase houses for themselves.

The combined effects of the Housing (Financial Provisions) Act 1933 and the amount of activity from the building societies were threefold:

- there was a dramatic rise in private enterprise housebuilding.

- most of the houses built were for owner-occupation, not letting. Home ownership by mortgage has remained a major factor in the housing market ever since.

- not only did the building societies expand, but they also proved themselves flexible and able to meet the new demands placed upon them. In particular, they altered their lending practices:

  - mortgage terms were extended from the usual 15-20 years to 21-25, or even 30 years.

- it became possible for mortgagors to borrow more than 70-75% of the house value. Perhaps the most common method was for insurance companies to guarantee the amount in excess of that lent by the building society.

Ways of reducing deposits were developed including the Builders' Pool scheme whereby the builder advanced cash to the building society to make up most of the difference between the mortgage and the valuation, thus limiting the purchaser's deposit to 5% or less.

4.6   *During the Second World War*

During the Second World War, housebuilding virtually ceased apart from dwellings for war workers. Unlike the First World War, enemy action took place in the United Kingdom during 1939 to 1945. As enemy action intensified, the shortage of homes became more apparent following serious damage and in many cases destruction by air raids. Some 475,000 homes were destroyed or made uninhabitable and a further 3.5 million houses suffered some war damage. This reduction and deterioration in the housing stock happened alongside a growth in the population as well as two million marriages between 1939 and 1945.

- **Rent and Mortgage Interest (War Restrictions) Act 1939**

  At the start of the war, this Act brought rents under control and provided security of tenure (in just the same way as the 1915 Act of the same name did, and for the same reasons).

Billeting for housing for those who had to move for war-time employment and evacuation (especially children from target areas) was used. Similarly requisitioning powers were used to utilize empty houses to overcome the housing shortages. Powers to undertake these functions were given to local authorities in the Housing (Temporary Provisions) Act 1944.

The same year saw the passing of the Housing (Temporary Accommodation) Act 1944. This Act provided for £150 million to be spent on the manufacture and erection of temporary homes. These were pre-fabricated bungalows. The first 'prefabs' were mainly two-bedroomed, factory-built bungalows and local authorities were able to rehouse in them those families whose dwellings had been destroyed by enemy action. Originally they were to be used for a maximum of ten years. Many remained until the late 1970s and even today some can be spotted in inner-city areas. Prefabs in Wake Green, Birmingham actually have Grade II Listed Buildings Status!

It is important to bear in mind that these three Acts were brought about by the war: if the war had not happened, the Acts would not have been needed. It would not be appropriate to call any of them true 'housing' acts.

However, there were a number of reports published during the war years. Probably the three most influential were the following:

- the Report of the Royal Commission on the Distribution of Industrial Population (the **Barlow Report**). This report had been commissioned before the war, but was eventually published in 1940. Its main recommendations were:

    - the further redevelopment of congested areas, particularly London;

    - the dispersal of both population and industry evenly across the country;

    - the establishment of a central planning authority.

- the final report of the Expert Committee on Compensation and Betterment (the **Uthwatt Report**). The main recommendations of this report, published in 1942, were:

    - that the state should hold the rights to develop underdeveloped land;

    - that methods should be instituted whereby the state could acquire for the community the enhanced value of the land.

- the Report of the Committee on the Utilization of Land in Rural Areas (the **Scott Report**). This report, also published in 1942, made a variety of recommendations on the development of rural areas, including the improvement of rural housing.

These three reports were regarded as something of a trilogy, pointing the way for the inevitable housing programmes which would have to be set up after the war. At the time, the country needed two million additional dwellings.

Two other reports had a direct influence on the building of post-war homes:

- the Interdepartmental Committee on House Construction (the **Burt Report**)

    This committee, which first reported in 1944, looked in general at existing and alternative methods of housing construction, bearing in mind the lack of various building materials immediately after the war. The committee remained in existence for some years and reported on standards of house construction in 1946 and again in 1948.

- Report on the Design of Dwellings (the **Dudley Report**)

    This report, also published in 1944, analysed how ordinary families utilized their housing space and made recommendations on minimum standards which were considerably higher than those of inter-war houses. It also laid stress on the close connection between housing and town planning. We looked at this in some detail in Unit 3.

4.7　After the Second World War, up to 1960

After the Second World War the emphasis was on addressing the housing shortage and political parties vied with each other to build new homes. Throughout the war years there had been a coalition government led by Churchill.

Then on 5 July 1945, the country went to the polls and threw out the man many had said had won the war and elected Clement Attlee as Prime Minister. The Labour government turned its attention from military to housing problems; it wanted to do something but did not have the means. The government also had to deal with industrial reconstruction, nationalization and welfare state programmes. In addition there was a shortage of materials coupled with a balance of payments problem. We saw earlier the extent of damage caused by enemy action; remedies were needed to rectify the housing shortage and alleviate the overcrowding problem of existing accommodation, much of which was unfit and needed to be demolished. Many houses had no running water, no electricity, no sanitation, toilets with no flush systems etc, many people used local public baths for washing. Clement Attlee encouraged a post-war social housing boom which aimed at meeting general needs and not just housing the poor.

In an endeavour to do something about the squalor, William Beveridge, a Civil Servant, engineered a new society: one whereby the state would provide for people's education and look after their health, care for the needy and ensure work for the fit. All this he said would be pointless unless each family could be rescued from the cramped slums and given a proper place to live. This was the introduction of a welfare state caring for people 'from the cradle to the grave'.

There was to be a system of social insurance with contributions from workers, employers and the state which would provide benefits for unemployment, sickness, pensions and everything from maternity to funeral grants. Family allowances would be paid to offset poverty and 'national assistance' provided to people who fell outside other benefits. A major vision of Beveridge was the creation of 'a national health service'.

Aneurin 'Nye' Bevan was put in charge of housing to rent. He said 'we must introduce in our modern villages and towns what was always a lovely feature of England and Welsh villages where the doctor, the grocer, the butcher and the farm labourer all lived in the same street. I believe that it is essential for the full life of the citizen to see that the living tapestry of a mixed community ...'. His first step was the presentation of a White Paper to Parliament called simply *Housing*. This was presented in March 1945 and represents an important landmark in the recent history of housing. It set out an ambitious programme of housing development, which can be summarized as follows:

- to provide a separate dwelling for each household;

- to speed up and finish pre-war slum clearance and deal with overcrowding;

- to make long-term, progressive improvements in housing conditions.

It was believed that something like 1.25 million dwellings would be needed to meet the first two objectives. To meet the third objective, it was clear that a continuous (and long-term) building programme would be needed. Because it was obviously impossible to provide such a large number of permanent dwellings quickly, the post-war period saw the continued building of 'prefabs'. In addition, there were numerous adaptations and conversions of older dwellings and repairs to those that had been war-damaged.

The government's aim was, however, to provide permanent dwellings, the target being 900,000 houses by 1951. In 1946 new, higher subsidies were introduced for council housing under the Housing (Financial Provisions) Act 1946. The level of housebuilding immediately increased. Once again, the building industry found itself hard pressed to cope. In the years 1949–1952, the production of houses stabilized at about 170,000 a year, all of which were built to the standards recommended in the Dudley Report.

New Towns

The *Housing* White Paper referred to above ensured that local authorities would be the main producers of social housing and this would be allocated by them in 'balanced' communities on the basis of housing needs.

Proposals were made by a New Towns Committee (the Reith Committee) set up in 1945 and in three separate reports it made recommendations for the implementation of proposals for new towns. The New Towns Act 1946 gave effect to most of the recommendations and provided for the establishment by the then Ministry of Town and Country Planning of government-financed and appointed development corporations for the development of new towns in an endeavour to relieve housing problems in different regions of the country.

The concept of new towns was not entirely novel. It owed much to the early ideas of Ebenezer Howard, a social pioneer of the late 19th century. The 1946 New Towns Act built on those ideas and was given added impetus by the Town and Country Planning Association. Under the Act, 22 new towns were built. The list includes some familiar names:

Table 4.1:New Towns

New town	Year declared as a new town
Stevenage	1946
Harlow	1947
Aycliffe	1947
Peterlee	1948
Welwyn Garden City	1948
Hatfield	1948
Basildon	1949
Bracknell	1949
Corby	1950
Skelmersdale	1962
Telford	1963
Runcorn	1964
Redditch	1964
Washington	1964
Milton Keynes	1967
Northampton	1968
Peterborough	1968

Table 4.1:New Towns *(continued)*	
Warrington	1968
Central Lancashire New Town	1970
which comprises: Preston,Chorley and	
Leyland	

The Act was updated and consolidated into the New Towns Act 1965. You should bear in mind, however, that the Local Government and Housing Act 1989 has since repealed this legislation and all the housing stock in these new towns has been transferred to local housing authorities or local housing associations.

Other Legislation

As well as increasing subsidies, the Labour government of the day sought to remove any class restrictions on the provision of housing. Until 1949, local authorities were able to allocate houses only to 'the working classes'. This term was not defined in the legislation and the rule was not strictly enforced. But however vague the statutory provision was, the government abolished it altogether in the Housing Act 1949. From that time, the intention was for local authorities to plan their housing programmes 'to meet the varied needs of the community', rather than catering only for the working classes. The Act also introduced improvement grants, payable at the discretion of local authorities to owner-occupiers and landlords, of 50% of the cost of approved works up to £600 (this was raised to £800 in 1952). A 'thirty-year' life period was required for dwellings and private landlords were empowered to raise their rents by 6% of their share of the costs.

You may wonder exactly what the role of the building societies was in this period immediately after the war. The answer is that their activities were very low key, devoted mainly to financing purchases of existing houses. Although the societies had emerged from the war with a tremendous surplus of funds, they were not able to help the house expansion programme because the Labour government preferred to use the local authority mechanism. In 1950, the first tower blocks were built under the control of the Labour government; this was at The Lawns, Harlow and was an eleven storey tower. The tower blocks were built with steel frames and bricks, and fire escapes in each block. Private enterprise in housing was strictly curtailed until 1952.

The former LCC estate at Roehampton in London was built between 1952 and 1958. This estate was built from pre-cast components, housing 9,500 people and was the largest estate in Europe. There were 25, eleven storey towers, five ten storey blocks, terraces of four storeys, terrace houses and slab block maisonettes.

The Labour government's target of building 900,000 houses by 1951 was not met and was one of the reasons for the party's defeat at the elections.

When the Conservatives took power in 1951, one of their election pledges had been to produce 300,000 homes a year. This Conservative administration, through its Minister of

Housing, Harold Macmillan, opposed the building of tower blocks. The Conservatives began their period of office by opposing much of Labour's welfare state; however, their opinions changed as more tower blocks were completed – these were seen as a vote-catcher. The Housing Act 1952 removed restrictions on private housebuilding and increased subsidies to local authority housebuilding yet again. Not surprisingly, levels of housebuilding surged upwards and this time building societies were able to use their accumulated funds to finance the private housing sector. It was from this time that owner-occupation became the dominant form of tenure in Britain. The promise by the Conservative government of 300,000 dwellings per annum was achieved by 1953.

Another White Paper was published in 1953, called *Housing – the Next Step*. This paper set the theme of Conservative government policy right up to 1964. It concentrated on five main issues:

- the encouragement of private enterprise;

- the encouragement of owner-occupation;

- the restoration of private renting, with provision to allow rent increases so that repairs could be carried out;

- slum clearance;

- the encouragement of repairs and improvements to existing stock.

There is no need for you to know in detail all the various pieces of legislation that were introduced to implement these objectives. The more important ones are summarized below:

● **Housing (Repairs and Rent) Act 1954**

This Act dealt with the problem of obsolescent houses through slum clearance and by encouraging improvement and repair.

● **Housing Subsidies Act 1956**

This Act revised subsidies on new buildings by local authorities and promoted redevelopment rather than 'general needs' construction. The subsidies were linked with storey height. Consequently the new subsidy scale was an incentive to local authorities to build high and the production of tower blocks increased rapidly, especially those of 15 storeys or more.

● **Housing Act 1957**

This was a consolidating Act which, until 1985, was known as the 'Principal Act'.

● **Rent Act 1957**

The intention behind this Act was that the better privately-owned houses should be freed from rent control, creating an incentive for the poorer houses to be repaired and improved (so that they too could escape rent control in their turn). The effects of the Act varied widely from place to place. The purpose of the Act was to revive the private rented sector. Generally speaking it failed in this and actually encouraged some landlords to exploit new tenants with high rents for poor accommodation. Also landlords such as Perec Rachman, a notorious landlord in north-west London, forcibly evicted existing tenants on low-rent agreements so that property could be rented out at a much higher new rent.

● **Landlord and Tenant (Temporary Provisions) Act 1958**

The purpose of this Act was to give security to tenants, made necessary because some landlords were again exploiting the housing shortage by evicting tenants (thereby obtaining vacant possession), or by charging extortionate rents. Such bullying tactics by landlords became known as 'Rachmanism' after Rachman (see above).

● **House Purchase and Housing Act 1959**

This Act encouraged the improvement of older houses.

- the government lent £100 million to the building society movement which, in return, made loans available on older (pre-1919) properties. This had the effect of encouraging owner-occupation.

- it also made mandatory grants available to owners (provided they met certain conditions), to enable them to install as standard amenities:

  - a fixed bath or shower;

  - a wash-hand basin;

  - a hot and cold water supply;

  - a water closet;

  - a ventilated food closet (i.e. satisfactory facilities for the storage of food).

Legislation and, perhaps more importantly, public awareness of control and local government activities within the sphere of housing had advanced a long way since the First World War. By the end of the 1950s, considerable attention was focused on housing. The 1950s were certainly boom years for housebuilders. However, the majority of poorer people were still untouched by the frenzy of building which the politicians were so proud of. By the end of the 1950s over three million families lived without bathrooms, two million families shared outside toilets and many had no internal running water. The period from 1960 to the present day has seen an even more intensive legislative interest in housing development, as we shall see in the next unit.

4.8 Other Influences on Housing

So far we have dealt almost exclusively with legislation designed to affect housing directly. Other factors, such as particular events, key individuals or reports, can also influence housing in a rather less direct fashion. Let us look at two of these, during the period we have covered:

- pioneers in housing management;

- garden cities.

Pioneers in Housing Management

No text on housing would be complete without at least a mention of Octavia Hill (1838–1912). She is widely acknowledged to be the originator of modern housing management methods. She campaigned to place controls on slum landlords who were making enormous profits cramming families into insanitary conditions. She strongly believed that housing should be provided by the private sector, not by local authorities, and also had the courage to put her ideas into practice. Her opinion that housing should not be provided by the public sector has not made much of a mark on history, but the efficient way in which she managed her own properties has. Many of her methods were introduced throughout the country, where they paved the way for housing management as we know it today.

Octavia Hill was born in Wisbech and was the daughter of a merchant who was associated with many radical liberal causes of the time. Her mother was the daughter of Dr Southwood Smith, a leading sanitary reformer. She was associated from an early age with social reform and did much to improve the conditions in which poor people lived in London.

Following the illness of her father when she was only a teenager and the collapse of the family business, the family moved to London. Octavia Hill had to work for money for the family (unlike most Victorian philanthropists).

Although her desire had always been to be an artist, she found herself working in a toy-making workroom for poor children and experienced at first hand their atrocious living conditions. This led to her campaign to improve the houses in which the poor lived. Assisted by John Ruskin she obtained houses in Marylebone, improved them and let them out to families and endeavoured to prove that if a landlord's duties were carried out in a businesslike way, it would be possible to provide reasonable conditions and yet make a reasonable return on the investment. She collected the rents herself and in this way got to know the tenants and encouraged them to take a pride in their homes.

Eviction was threatened if arrears of rent were incurred or if the tenants did not meet Octavia Hill's standards. She provided areas for children to play (and a supervisor to organize their games) and also, wherever possible, some open spaces.

Although her ideas are well over 100 years old, there has been much that can be linked in with modern day views, eg:

a)   improving older dwellings rather than building new;

b)   concern for people:

    (i)   in poor housing conditions, and

    (ii)   without homes,

c)   increasing numbers of poorer people in rented accommodation.

In later life, Octavia Hill went on to become one of the founder members of the National Trust.

Perhaps unexpectedly, some employers proved themselves pioneers in the housing field. These were enlightened industrialists who realized that healthier, well-housed employees were far happier and, more importantly, extremely productive. The majority of employers in the late 19th century built houses for their employees as quickly and cheaply as possible, if they built them at all. But some employers were more enterprising and possessed more foresight. They built 'model' estates or villages in which to house their employees. Quite apart from general humanitarian grounds, of course, these employers realized that employees would work more efficiently in more attractive working and living conditions. Probably the best known of these model estates are:

Estate	Originators
Port Sunlight	Viscount Leverhulme
Bourneville	George and Richard Cadbury
Aintree	Sir William Hartley
Hull	Reckitt
Saltaire	Sir Titus Salt

Garden Cities

We referred briefly to Garden Cities when we looked at the Tudor Walters Report earlier. Let us look now in a little more depth.

In 1902, Ebenezer Howard published a book called *Garden Cities of Tomorrow* in which he proposed the creation of self-contained new towns. His idea was that the town should be built in a way that it could be planned and developed to benefit everyone. The town would be surrounded by rural 'green belts' for recreation and agriculture. In short, the concept of a garden city was a town where people could work, live and spend their recreational time without any need to go elsewhere.

Ebenezer Howard put these proposals into practice when Letchworth Garden City was formed in 1903. This was a successful project relying mainly on private capital and private housing with very little local authority provision at first. It was followed by the creation of Welwyn Garden City in 1919. Perhaps more importantly, the idea of a garden city caught the imagination of those working in housing, with the result that a Garden Cities Association was formed. Eventually this was renamed the Town and Country Planning Association, and it still exists today.

Summary

This rather daunting unit has attempted to describe the pressures that have prompted housing legislation and to examine some of its effects.

Legislation has probably been the single most important influence upon housing. In the next unit, we shall examine legislation from the 1960s onwards and look at other important influences on housing.

Table 4.2: Summary of housing legislation

YEAR	ACT
1848	**Public Health Act**
1851	Labouring Classes Lodging Houses Act
1851	Common Lodging Houses Act
1855	Nuisances Removal Act
1868	Artisans' and Labourers' Dwellings Act
1875	Artisans' and Labourers' Dwellings Improvement Act
1875	**Public Health Act**
1885	Housing of the Working Classes Act
1890	**Housing of the Working Classes Act**
1915	**Rent and Mortgage Interest (War Restrictions) Act**
1919	**Housing and Town Planning Act**
1923	**Housing Act**
1924	Housing (Financial Provisions) Act
1930	**Housing Act**
1933	Housing (Financial Provisions) Act
1935	Housing Act
1936	Housing Act
1939	**Rent and Mortgage Interest (War Restrictions) Act**
1944	Housing(Temporary Accommodation)
1944	Housing (Temporary Provisions) Act
1946	Housing (Financial Provisions) Act
1946	**New Towns Act**
1949	**Housing Act**
1952	Housing Act
1954	Housing (Repairs and Rent) Act
1956	Housing Subsidies Act
1957	**Housing Act**
1957	Rent Act
1958	Landlord and Tenant (Temporary Provisions) Act
1959	**House Purchase and Housing Act**

5

HOUSING – THE 1960s ONWARDS

Objectives

After studying this unit, you should be able to:

- outline the provisions of the main pieces of housing legislation during this period relating to your course;

- describe the effects of various pieces of housing legislation;

- state the recommendations of the Duke of Edinburgh's report.

5.1   Introduction

We have so far looked at legislation and influences from the 1800s up to 1960. In this unit we shall look at the legislation from the 1960s onwards. This study text was published in 2003. We shall also look at other influences on housing during this period.

5.2   Legislation in the 1960s

In 1960, a White Paper called *Housing in England and Wales* predicted that most local authorities would complete their slum clearance programmes by 1965, but that new problems caused by dispossessed families would be created. The government's aim in the White Paper was 'to secure that there will be houses for sale and houses for rent in sufficient numbers to keep pace with the rising demand of a prospering society. As real incomes go up, more and more of this need, both for sale and to rent, should be met by private enterprise'. Local authority housing was to be for those who could 'neither afford to buy or pay economic rents'.

The Housing Act 1961 widened the scope of Exchequer subsidies in yet another attempt to stimulate housebuilding, by dividing available grants up into two levels (of £8 and £24 paid over 60 years) and linking them to the local authority housing revenue account; the exact details of how it worked are beyond the scope of your syllabus. Another important provision of the 1961 Act was the creation of a £25 million fund, out of which payments could be made to housing associations who provided 'cost rent' (or low rent) housing.

Two years later, almost the same cycle of events was repeated. A White Paper called *Housing* was published in 1963, stating that urgent action was required to deal with slums and obsolescent housing and to produce new dwellings with an emphasis on improving areas. The White Paper also commented that industrialized housebuilding held some advantages over traditional methods. The Conservative Housing Minister at the time, Keith Joseph, actively encouraged authorities to build high-density, high-rise system-built flats in urban areas.

During 1963, Birmingham City Council had wanted a dramatic acceleration of its house building programme and together with Bryants (a local builder) it embarked on a programme of system-built tower blocks. Some such blocks had been put up elsewhere in the country. They were cheap, fast to erect but definitely not up to the established standard for local authority housing. Within five years Bryants had dealt with £25 million worth of contracts for such building with Birmingham alone.

By 1964, promises of more and better housing by the Conservatives were not enough to revive flagging enthusiasm for its policies generally and, in the election that followed, the Labour Party returned to power with Harold Wilson as its leader.

Richard Crosman, the Labour Housing Minister, said that 'factory-built houses can be just as good as a production line car and once you get the thing going at the factory you come off jolly fast!'

The Housing Act was introduced in 1964. This Act was the first to mention 'area improvements'; it granted powers to local authorities for the compulsory improvement of dwellings to provide standard amenities in improvement areas. It was also this legislation that created the Housing Corporation with £100 million of government capital to help housing associations.

System-built tower blocks were erected throughout the country; the slum clearance programme advanced to make way, room and space for system-built developments. This created a succession of problems in due course and was certainly not what Bevan had envisaged earlier. People by now were reluctant to move to these tower blocks; they preferred ground-floor squalor to high-rise anonymity.

The same year saw the introduction of the Protection from Eviction Act 1964, which aimed to prevent evictions of tenants as had been highlighted in the Rachman era following the passing of the Rent Act 1957.

The Labour government's intentions with regard to housing had been set out in a White Paper, *The Housing Programme 1965-1970*. This provided for 500,000 new homes (both public and private sector) per annum, at the same time undertaking a programme of slum clearance. This target was not achieved, however, because of:

-    financial problems, which led to the devaluation of the pound in 1967;

- higher interest rates;

- economic climate generally.

In the following year, the Rent Act 1965 introduced the concept of 'fair rents', fixed by independent rent officers.

In 1967 there were two pieces of legislation that we should briefly refer to. First the Leasehold Reform Act 1967, which gave most holders of long leases on houses the right to have them extended for a further 50 years, or even to acquire the freehold. Secondly, the Housing Subsidies Act 1967, which introduced a new, more generous, subsidy system to local authorities in dealing with their housing programmes. The Act also introduced an option mortgage scheme which, from April 1968, gave house purchasers the choice of receiving normal tax relief at the time or taking advantage of a scheme whereby they received a subsidized mortgage rate of 2% below the current building society rate with a 'floor' limit of 4% This was to assist lower-income owner-occupiers. This scheme no longer exists.

In 1968, the Rent Act 1968 was introduced which consolidated earlier legislation.

A further White Paper, called *Old Houses into New Homes*, was published in 1968. Seeing that the government could not implement its programme of new building, it stressed that dwellings were important and should be improved rather than allowed to deteriorate and eventually be demolished. The previous year, the National House Condition Survey showed that there were 1.8 million houses unfit for human habitation in England and Wales.

The Housing Act 1969 resulted from this White Paper. The Act introduced various forms of grant designed to make house improvements a more attractive option. For the first time, grants were available for improvement of neighbourhood amenities in improvement areas (such as playgrounds for children, or rest areas for the elderly). The Act introduced the concept of General Improvement Areas – these were areas of higher graded pre-1919 (predominantly private sector) houses in need of modernization or in danger of deterioration. (General Improvement Areas have now been superseded by Housing Renewal Areas, under the Local Government and Housing Act 1989. General Improvement Area status ceased to exist on 31 March 1991.) General Improvement Areas are covered in more depth in Unit 10.

5.3   Legislation in the 1970s

The Conservative Party came to power in 1970 and passed the Housing Act 1971, which made some minor amendments to the Housing Act 1969.

In 1972, under the Housing (Finance) Act 1972, considerable changes were made to the system of housing subsidies. Part of the Act was very controversial: local authorities lost the power to charge 'reasonable rents' (as laid down in the Housing Act 1957), instead they were obliged to charge 'fair rents' (as laid down in the Rent Act 1968) and tenants were able to apply for rent rebates. Effectively this made rent rebate schemes mandatory.

Housing

The 1972 Act made provisions for certain housing association subsidies and in return the housing associations were required to charge rents according to the 'fair rents' principle.

As with local authority tenants, housing association tenants were able to claim rent allowances. Note here that housing association tenants could not receive rent rebates because these were administered by local authorities for local-authority tenants only. Similarly rent allowances were made available to private tenants living in unfurnished accommodation.

In 1973, there were two White Papers on housing; these were *Widening the Choice: The Next Steps in Housing* and *Better Homes: The Next Priorities*. The White Papers proposed what were called Housing Action Areas. These were groups of predominantly private sector houses, generally 300-500 in total, although no maxima or minima were detailed in the legislation. These dwellings were mainly in rundown areas where there was social deprivation. Smaller Housing Action Areas were also declared, the smallest being one with just eight houses! The idea was that these residential areas would be seen as entities where both houses and the environment could be improved; the policy was clearly established in favour of rehabilitation of older property and not redevelopment. (The concept of Housing Action Areas has been replaced – as have General Improvement Areas – by Housing Renewal Areas, under the Local Government and Housing Act 1989. Housing Action Area status ceased to exist on 31 March 1991.) Like General Improvement Areas, Housing Action Areas are covered in more depth in Unit 10.

After these White Papers were published in 1973, there was a change of government and Harold Wilson led the Labour Party to victory in 1974. Surprisingly enough, much of the White Paper was adopted by the incoming Labour Party and the Housing Act 1974 was passed with considerable support for most parts of it from all the major political parties. The Act contained four main points of particular importance:

- it gave the Housing Corporation greater powers to make loans to housing associations.

- it set up a new system of financial aid for housing associations, called the Housing Association Grant (HAG). Other grants were revenue deficit grant, management deficit grant and hostel deficit grant; such grants enabled the housing association movement to contribute significantly to the work of rehabilitation in inner cities.

- local authorities were more strictly controlled by the Act when it came to spending on the conversion, repair or improvement of a property, particularly in the private sector – although they were also actively encouraged to give grants for the improvement of dwellings.

- it introduced the concept of Housing Action Areas.

The Housing Rents and Subsidies Act 1975 was a short Act, but it nevertheless made three important provisions:

- it repealed the controversial part of the Housing (Finance) Act 1972, concerning fair rents and reinstated reasonable rents for local authorities;

- it provided for loan sanctions where authorities found themselves overspending in excess of a maximum of 10% above the operative yardstick;

- it altered the subsidy system yet again.

The New Towns (Amendment) Act 1976 was designed to enable rented dwellings and associated property to be transferred from New Town Development Corporations and the Commission for New Towns to the appropirtate district councils.

In 1977, the Housing (Homeless Persons) Act was passed. While the principles and purpose of the Act are beyond reproach, it still generated considerable controversy because it placed great pressure on those local authorities whose catchment areas were more likely to contain 'homeless' persons. Put simply, a local authority was obliged to give advice and assistance to anyone applying under the Act. Those local authorities in an international airport/seaport catchment area were more likely to have far more applicants than a local authority in the depths of the countryside.

The Housing (Homeless Persons) Act 1977 was consolidated into the Housing Act 1985. The Housing Act 1996 repealed the earlier homeless legislation although much of the original legislation is embodied in it. Further homeless legislation was encompassed in the Homelessness Act 2002. The homeless legislation was covered in Unit 2. Have a look at this again to remind yourself.

Another Act specifically designed to ensure that those in need could be helped was the Protection from Eviction Act 1977. It focussed on unscrupulous landlords who might try to evict tenants without going through the proper legal procedures: for example, by cutting off tenants' water, electricity or gas. Such tactics are known as 'harassment' and, under the Act, landlords convicted could be jailed or fined or both (under a later piece of legislation, landlords can also have damages awarded against them).

The following year saw the passing of the Home Purchase and Housing Corporation Guarantee Act 1978. This Act tried to stimulate the numbers of first-time buyers through a specific subsidy and an interest-free loan scheme. The scheme involved planned savings to qualify for benefit and provide a bonus of up to £110 and a loan of £600 which was interest-free for five years. However, the attempt was not particularly successful because it was restricted to properties of relatively low market value. Very few purchasers opted for this scheme: for example, in 1987-1988 only 2,580 people took advantage of the scheme out of one million people who took out mortgages in the same period.

The scheme has since been abolished under the Local Government and Housing Act 1989.

5.4   Legislation in the 1980s

One factor which no doubt contributed to the low number of first-time housebuyers was that the country was feeling the bite of an economic depression and a high level of inflation. Many prospective first-time buyers could not afford to get into the property market, even taking into account the available financial aid. The depression affected housing in another, more direct fashion as well. Public spending was restricted, so that there was less money available for building houses in the public sector. One consequence of this policy was the 'right to buy' concept. This first appeared in the Housing Act 1980 and launched housing into the 1980s with something of a bang.

If we go back to 1979, the Conservative government came into power and almost immediately enacted its housing proposals in the Housing Act 1980. This is a very significant piece of legislation, mainly for the 'right to buy' idea which it introduced. However, it is important to remember that this was not the only provision made by the Act. Perhaps the best way to illustrate this fact is to quote the preamble (the short paragraph at the start of an Act, stating what the Act is going to do).

●   Preamble to the Housing Act 1980

> *An Act to give security of tenure, and the right to buy their homes, to tenants of local authorities and other bodies; to make other provision with respect to those and other tenants; to amend the law about housing finance in the public sector; to make other provision with respect to housing; to restrict the discretion of the court in making orders for possession of land; and for connected purposes. (8 August 1980)*

As is often the case, the preamble is a very general statement: specific provisions are left to the body of the Act itself. You should note at this stage the following points in the Housing Act 1980.

Tenants' Charter

Security of tenure was provided for local authority and housing association tenants. The right to succession by a spouse or family member was given on the death of a tenant. Tenants were also able to improve their homes and apply for improvement grants (although in reality very few ever did).

Tenants were given the right to take lodgers or sublet, provided that the landlord agreed.

Public sector landlords had to publish rules and procedures for allocation, transfer or exchange of tenancies; furthermore, local authorities had to establish machinery for consultation with tenants. Tenants had the right of access to their personal property files.

Deficit Subsidy

A new deficit subsidy system was introduced, whereby the government stated what level of increases it expected local authorities to make for its housing. The amount of exchequer subsidy granted was dependant upon the increases made by local authorities. If a local authority decided not to increase its rents but transfer money from the rate fund, the government would then claw back monies from the rate support grant made to the local authority.

Assured Tenancies/Shorthold Tenancies

Assured and shorthold tenancies were introduced for private sector tenants. We shall look in detail at these types of tenancies in Unit 8.

Right to buy

Secure tenants of local housing authorities and certain housing associations were given the right to buy their dwellings at discounts of 33.33% after three years, rising to 50% after 20 years of tenancy. We shall look at the Right to Buy in greater detail in Unit 9 because the 'right to buy' has proved to be a popular topic with examiners.

The Local Government, Planning and Land Act 1980 set up Urban Development Corporations in certain stress areas.

The Acquisition of Land Act 1981 deals with compulsory purchase. There are three main stages:

(i)   the compulsory purchase order is made when the common seal of the acquiring authority is affixed to it.

(ii)   the appropriate Secretary of State places an endorsement on the compulsory purchase order itself.

(iii)   the order comes into effect when notice of the fact of confirmation is given to the local press.

The compulsory purchase order is operative from the date when this notice appears by virtue of the Compulsory Purchase Act 1965; the order will lapse unless the power which it confers is exercised within three years of the order coming into effect.

The Housing and Building Control Act 1984 increased the discounts available to tenants purchasing property under the right to buy and allowed tenants of charitable housing associations to buy property on the same basis as other public sector tenants. The Act also introduced a right for tenants to purchase a shared ownership in their property.

Many council tenants have exercised their right to buy under the Housing Act 1980. Many were advised against it because it was already widely known that some of the dwellings being sold, in particular those with pre-cast reinforced concrete frames, were giving cause for concern. However, lenders were happy enough, at a time when real competition for mortgage business was developing, because the discounts gave adequate protection for the loan. Consequently few buyers thought it worthwhile getting their homes surveyed.

Shortly after the first council house sales were made the Building Research Establishment reported that structural components in Airey houses were weakened by corrosion. The houses were structurally unsound and proved impossible to sell on to others. Emergency assistance was provided to the owners of Airey houses in 1982. More faults were discovered on many other houses which had been sold from the public sector into the private sector and the government panicked and rushed through the Housing Defects Act 1984. The government feared that the right to buy would be discredited by the growing wave of resentment arising from owners left with unmortgageable properties that were uneconomic to repair.

Under the Housing Defects Act for a ten-year period (1 December 1984 to 30 November 1994) owners of such properties could require the local authority to purchase the dwellings back at 95% of their defect-free market value and payment of all legal fees. Remember these dwellings had been sold at between a half and a third of the price; hence the absurd situation was that owners of such dwellings made a good profit by selling back to the local authority which had sold the dwelling in the first place – a waste of scarce public resources.

Alternatively if owners did not wish to sell then they were entitled to a reinstatement grant of 90% (or in cases of financial hardship 100%) of:

- the estimated expenditure to be incurred, or

- the actual expenditure incurred, or

- the expenditure limit in force,

whichever was the least.

During the ten-year period some 10,500 defective houses were sold back to the Councils and £280 million paid to owners as reinstatement grants.

Three consolidating Acts were passed in 1985.

● The Housing Associations Act 1985, as its name implies, consolidated earlier legislation relating to housing associations.

● The Landlord and Tenant Act 1985 consolidated various miscellaneous provisions relating to both landlords and tenants.

● Undoubtedly the most important of the consolidating Acts was the Housing Act 1985. This comprises 625 sections and consolidated all of the housing legislation other than that contained in the two Acts above. It is applicable only to England and Wales.

The Housing and Planning Act 1986:

● introduced grants for new forms of housing management, such as tenants' co-operatives and for the training of housing officers from ethnic minorities;

● introduced a common parts grant for the repair or improvement work to the common parts of a building containing flats (this is covered in Unit 11);

● amended the right-to-buy legislation for flats and maisonettes with regard to discounts (certain other amendments to the right to buy were introduced and these are covered in more depth in Unit 9).

In June 1987, the Conservatives were returned to power for their third consecutive term. Their manifesto stated that they intended to:

- promote the spread of home ownership, largely by:

    - keeping the present system of mortgage interest tax relief; and

    - targeting improvement grants to the less well-off (under the existing systems at the time, the rich often qualified for grants as easily as the poor);

- attract new private investment into rented housing, by:

    - extending the system of assured tenancies; and

    - developing a system of short-term tenancies which would enable house owners to let their homes while, for example, they went abroad for a short period;

- create new Housing Action Trusts to take over council housing (in other words, to 'privatize' council housing estates);

- change the structure of local authority housing accounts;

- give tenants the right to form co-operatives (rather like mini housing associations) with their own budgets and management; and

- strengthen the legislation relating to harassment by landlords.

In September 1987, the government published a new White Paper entitled *Housing: the Government's Proposals* which set out the government's proposals for reforming housing legislation. The four principal aims were to:

- reverse the decline in rented housing and improve its quality;

- give council tenants the right to transfer to other landlords if they so desired;

- target monies to deal with the most acute problems; and

- continue to encourage the growth of owner-occupation.

Some of these intentions were incorporated into the Housing Act 1988; the others were included in the Local Government and Housing Act 1989. Later in the course we shall look in some detail at both these Acts, but the main points of both of them are detailed below.

- Housing Act 1988

    The main points of this legislation are as follows:

    - it established a new body, Housing for Wales (Tai Cymru), which took over the powers of the Housing Corporation in Wales;

    - it phased out Rent Acts by replacing fair rents with assured tenancies;

    - it amended the law relating to housing associations;

    - it established Housing Action Trusts (HATs). These are temporary organizations specially set up by the government to tackle major concentrations of run-down local authority housing in England, renovate it and pass it on to other forms of ownership and management. The primary objectives of HATs are to secure:

- the repair and improvement of the housing;

- its proper and effective management;

- greater diversity of tenure;

- improvement of social and housing conditions generally;

● approved landlords could now acquire either individual public sector properties or blocks of flats and maisonettes, thus substituting private for public involvement in housing and reinforcing the transfer of local authority housing to housing associations;

● the right to buy legislation was amended further;

● it dealt with the disposal of land and the application of capital money arising from the disposal;

● it introduced Tenants' Choice.

It is worthy of note here that Tenants' Choice and HATs were mechanisms to transfer ownership of council housing estates to other landlords. Under HATs, council housing stock was transferred to a government appointed board with funding for improvement works. HATs were bitterly opposed by tenants initially but eventually the first HAT was set up in Hull after the council had gained concessions from the government including the agreement that after completion, the tenants could transfer back to the council. A small number of HATs were created but these proved costly and the programme has since ceased. Tenants' Choice was abandoned shortly after being introduced.

The current way of transferring council properties is through voluntary transfers whereby local authorities can initiate the sale of all or part of their stock to another body with the approval of the tenants.

● Local Government and Housing Act 1989

This Act received the Royal Assent on 16 November 1989. It covers many points, the main ones being:

- it reforms the conduct of local government business;

- it revises the local authority capital finance;

- it provides a statutory framework for local authority interests in companies;

- it revises both housing revenue accounts and housing subsidies;

- it introduces a new framework for housing area renewal (housing renewal areas);

- it introduced a new system of grants for home improvement.

The pattern of housing expenditure has changed since the Conservative party came to power in 1979. Since April 1990, public housing has become increasingly self-financing and more expenditure comes from the tenants' pockets. This reverses the trend which began in the aftermath of the First World War with the Addison Act, which introduced the concept of Exchequer subsidy for public sector rented accommodation. We looked at this in Unit 1.

One important point to note here is that the government's intention under the Act was that local authorities should cease to provide housing, relying on housing associations and private and commercial landlords to be the future providers of rented housing. Thus local authorities had an 'enabling' role in encouraging other landlords to make provision.

Children Act 1989

This Act places a duty on Social Services departments to provide accommodation for young people in need.

5.5   Legislation in the 1990s

The Planning and Compensation Act 1991, gave new powers to enforce planning controls and gave owners, who lose their homes, compensation (market value of the home) together with home loss payments of 10% of the market value up to a maximum of £15,000. In September 2003, these amounts were revised and the maximum payment was increased from £15,000 to £31,000 and the minimum payment was increased from £1,500 to £3,100.

It should be noted here that compulsory purchase is an important tool in regenerating our towns and cities.

The Act detailed how capital receipts could be used. Twenty-five per cent of receipts from the disposal of dwelling houses sold under the Housing Act 1985 (mainly under the Right to Buy) and 50% of receipts from the sale of other buildings and land could be used. Housing Revenue Accounts were ring-fenced to stop transfers in either direction between the Housing Revenue Account and the General Rate Fund, which stopped council house rents being subsidized from the then Poll Tax Charge, General Account, or vice-versa.

In April 1992 the Conservatives were returned to power for their fourth consecutive term. Their manifesto for housing stated that:

● the right to buy would continue;

● mortgage tax relief would remain;

● a rent to mortgage scheme would be introduced nationwide;

● do-it-yourself shared ownership would be encouraged;

● a 'rent a room' scheme would be introduced with no tax being charged on rents received;

● homesteading schemes would continue;

Housing

- competitive tendering of housing management would be introduced;

- leaseholders would be able to purchase freehold or extend leases;

- more housing associations would be available to manage public sector dwellings;

- the programme of large-scale voluntary transfer of council properties to housing associations would continue but the limit on the number of properties transferred in a single batch would be reduced;

- Estate Action and Housing Action Trust programmes would continue, enabling tenants to take over and improve the worst estates;

- the existing right to repair would be improved and a right to improve would be introduced;

- an Ombudsman would be established for housing association tenants;

- a task force for bringing empty government properties back into use (either by selling or letting) would be established;

- a time limit would be set on land charge searches;

- a central property databank would be established which would expedite searches made at the Land Registry.

The Leasehold Reform, Housing and Urban Development Act 1993 became law on 20 July 1993. The Act covers various housing issues:

- there was a new right to collectively acquire the freehold from the landlord. This right applies to self-contained buildings of two or more flats and where at least two-thirds of the dwellings were leased by long leaseholders at a low rent (over 21 years).

  Similarly a leaseholder who had occupied a flat for three years (or a period amounting to three years within the previous ten) had the right to acquire a new lease on payment of a premium.

- amendments to the Housing Act 1985 and provision for the Rent to Mortgage Scheme.

- amendments to the provisions with regard to the Right to Buy.

  Local authorities were now enabled in the first instance to come to a judgment on right to buy exemptions. They could give a decision denying the right to buy for certain dwellings particularly suitable for the elderly (60 years or more) without reference to the Secretary of State for the Environment, although an appeal within 56 days is available.

  The right to a mortgage was abolished.

  The right to defer completion of a right to buy application was abolished.

  The right to a shared ownership lease was abolished.

- provides for a new Right to Repair Scheme for local authority secure tenants.

- gives the right to compensation for tenants' improvements. When improvements are carried out with the written consent of the local authority, compensation is paid when the tenancy ends.

- new rights and procedures for Housing Action Trusts (HATs) tenants to be consulted on a proposed disposal of stock by a HAT and to explicitly express the wish to return to the relevant authority.

- the Urban Regeneration Agency was established and its main objective was to secure the regeneration of certain land. The Urban Regeneration Agency was given powers of compulsory purchase.

These various housing issues are covered elsewhere in the study text and are linked with individual topics in the remaining units.

Government White Paper *Our Future Homes: Opportunity, Choices, Responsibility*

In June 1995 the government published a White Paper entitled *Our Future Homes: Opportunity, Choice, Responsibility*. The White Paper stressed that the aim of the government's housing policy was to ensure that a decent home was within the reach of every family.

The Conservative government put home ownership at the heart of its policies and acknowledged that negative equity had been suffered by many as a direct result of falling house prices. The government intended to do more for families who rented their homes by giving them wider choice and a better quality of life. The White Paper emphasized the three key terms of *Choice, Opportunites* and *Responsibility*: *Choice* by giving people a chance to choose in a free society; *Opportunites* by empowering people to make their own decisions; and *Responsibility* by accepting responsibility for the choices people made.

The main points of the White Paper are detailed below:

- support and expand home ownership.

- homeless families would lose their right to permanent housing to ensure social housing was allocated to those households with the best claim to it.

- housing association tenants would have the 'right to buy' their homes through a new Voluntary Purchase Grant, worth a discount of between £9,000 and £16,000 depending on location. Housing associations would be allowed to keep receipts for investment in new stock.

- social landlords would receive grants only if they allowed tenants to buy their homes.

- local housing companies would be established with the ability to borrow to finance repairs, improvements and redevelopment within affordable rent levels. They would be able to bid for housing association grant; the Housing Corporation would regulate rents and service standards. Council stock could be transferred to the local housing companies.

- no further cuts in mortgage interest tax relief would be made during the current session of Parliament

- private lettings would be boosted through housing investment trusts which would be exempt from Capital Gains Tax. These trusts would be formed because most financial institutions do not wish to own property directly. The trust would enable them to (i) buy and sell shares in housing without directly owning property and managing tenants and (ii) diversify their portfolios to reduce management costs.

- local authorities would have more powers to enforce fire regulations in housing in multiple occupation.

- mandatory repairs grants would be made discretionary. Grants for houses in multiple occupation (HMOs) would be limited. Help would be available for low-income homeowners whose homes were unfit (as defined in the Local Government and Housing Act 1989), the aim being to focus more funds and grants effectively, to improve peoples' quality of life and health and, in particular, to assist elderly and disabled people to stay in their homes through a new grant known as 'house repair assistance'.

- empty homes in the public sector would be reduced to 3% of the stock within 10 years.

- surplus government homes had to be sold within six months of becoming vacant.

- single parents would lose their priority on council waiting lists under the new homelessness rules. The White Paper stated that 'allocation schemes should reflect the underlying values of our society. They should balance specific housing needs against the needs to support married couples who take a responsible approach to family life'.

- half of all new homes must be built on 'brown field' sites where there were already housing developments; thus preventing encroachment into green field sites.

- new high-quality homes would be built through the government's Quality Initiative.

- the London Rough Sleepers Initiative would be extended beyond 1996.

- councils would be allowed to introduce probationary tenancies to combat anti-social behaviour.

- the Housing Association Ombudsman would become independent of the Housing Corporation and be given a statutory footing.

- to make use of partnerships and funding through the Single Regeneration Budget Challenge Fund.

- to improve energy efficiency in both private and social housing to meet the government targets for reducing CO_2 emissions.

Disability Discrimination Act 1995

We covered this Act in Unit 2 when we looked at housing for disabled persons. Please look back to refresh your memory.

The Housing Act 1996

The Housing Act 1996 received the Royal Assent on 24 July 1996 and enacted many of the proposals referred to above. The preamble to the Act states that it is an

> *Act to make provision about housing, including the provision about the social rented section, houses in multiple occupation, landlord and tenant matters, the administration of housing benefit, the conduct of tenants, the allocation of housing accommodation by local housing authorities and homelessness.*

The Act makes provision for local housing companies registered under the Companies Act 1985 to be social landlords alongside housing associations and local housing authorities. This is covered in Unit 7.

The Act enables tenants and other individuals to have complaints against social landlords investigated by a Housing Ombudsman.

Provision is made in the Act for local authorities to make registration schemes authorizing the authority to compile and maintain a register for their district for houses in multiple occupation. Where a local authority intends to make a Registration Scheme, it must publish notice of the scheme. A property must be registered under the scheme for five years and then renewed for further periods of five years. Reasonable fees must be set by the local authority, although the Secretary of State may specify the maximum.

Amendments were made to secure, assured and assured shorthold tenancies and these are covered in Unit 8. Similarly 'introductory tenancies' were introduced by the Act; this means local housing authorities or housing action trusts could provide for 'trial periods' for new tenants. These new tenancies are also covered in Unit 8.

The Act provides that local housing authorities may apply to the High Court or County Court for an injunction to deal with anti-social behaviour. This is covered in Unit 7.

Local authorities' allocation schemes for housing were revised by the Act. This is also covered in Unit 7.

Housing association grant (HAG) is replaced by social housing grant (SHG). This is also covered in Unit 7.

The Housing, Grants, Construction and Regeneration Act 1996 also received Royal Assent on 24 July 1996. The preamble to the Act states that it is

> *an Act to make provision for grants and other assistance for housing purposes and about action in relation to unfit housing ... to provide grants and other assistance for*

regeneration and development and in connection with clearance areas; to amend the provisions relating to home energy efficiency schemes; to make provision in connection with the dissolution of Urban Development Corporations, housing action trusts and the Commission for the New Towns; and for connected purposes.

This Act is covered in Units 10 and 11 in far more depth because grants and urban regeneration are popular questions with the examiners.

5.6 Labour Government

May 1997 saw the election of the Labour government under the leadership of Tony Blair. During its first term in office, no legislation was introduced by the Labour government. There were minor amendments to earlier legislation which were implemented by Statutory Instruments, such as allocation of social housing, changes to the limits on the discounts under the Right to Buy scheme and the release of some capital receipts.

The government has also announced that their intentions were to achieve by 2002 the following:

●   to cut the number of rough sleepers by two-thirds;

●   to cut the backlog of council house repairs by a quarter;

●   to improve 1.5 million council homes;

●   to complete 50 regeneration projects;

●   to ensure that 60% of new homes are on 'brown-field' sites.

The number of rough sleepers has been reduced by two thirds; work is continuing to meet the other achievements.

In April 2000, the government published a consultation entitled *Quality and Choice – a decent home for all.* The paper was the most comprehensive review of housing policy for over 20 years. The key points in this document were:

●   help for key workers to buy homes;

●   action against bad private landlords;

●   ten-year target to tackle repairs backlog (£19bn);

●   wider strategic role for councils;

●   wider choice for tenants including homeless people;

●   arms'-length companies as an option for council housing;

●   reforming social rents – rises held to inflation;

●   possible new single form of tenure;

- improving housing benefit;

- tackling other forms of housing-related social exclusion.

We have seen already the help provided for key workers under the Starter Home Initiative in Unit 1. Some of the other key points are picked up in more detail elsewhere in the text.

Let us look further at legislation some, at first sight, might not appear to be directly relevant to housing.

In its first Parliamentary session, the government tried to implement the Homes Bill 2001, but this failed due to lack of parliamentary time.

Human Rights Act 1998

This came into force in October 2000. For the very first time, basic rights and freedoms every citizen has come to expect, from freedom from torture and slavery to the right of a fair trial are now enshrined in English legislation.

The Act is based on the rights and freedoms found in the 1949 European Convention of Human Rights.

Article 8 contains the phrase 'everyone has the right to respect for … his home'. Already this is raising questions such as whether the homeless are guaranteed a home, a landlord cannot evict someone etc. Various cases have been through the courts and it is worthy of note that it appears that the everyday relationship between landlords and their secure tenants has changed very little. This is because social housing is one of those regimes where everything is written down in statute and the courts have, therefore, been extremely cautious about what they would consider to be treading on the toes of the legislature and introduce changes without Parliament first making those changes.

Many of the cases have revolved around anti-social behaviour. The underlying causes of anti-social behaviour are complex, with the perpetrators often likely to have mental health problems or some other special needs and to be living in some degree of poverty.

Commonhold and Leasehold Reform Act 2002

This gives leasehold tenants power over the management of their flats and makes it easier for them to obtain longer leases. It protects against unreasonable charges for administration and improvements.

The Act also extends the jurisdiction of Leasehold Valuation Tribunals and provides better access to a low-cost network of dedicated tribunals.

Homelessness Act 2002

This Act was originally part of the Homes Bill 2001. It is intended to give more protection and support to the thousands of rough sleepers and the 'invisible homeless' people throughout the country. While most of the Act deals with amendments to the Housing Act 1996, the government has placed a new duty on local authorities to carry out regular homelessness reviews and develop a strategy within a year.

The Homelessness Act 2002 strengthens the safety net for homeless people and changed the framework for letting local authority homes and promoted choice. It required local authorities to take a more strategic approach to tackling and preventing homelessness; local authorities are required to produce homelessness strategies. These must include plans for:

- preventing homelessness;

- making sure there is enough accommodation for people who are, or may become, homeless;

- making sure there is enough support for people who are, or may become, homeless and to prevent homelessness recurring.

The Act abolished the duty of local authorities to maintain a housing register. However, local authorities must have allocation schemes. Now allocations can only be made to eligible persons. Local authorities must still accord 'reasonable preference' to persons in housing need; the homeless, those in unsanitary, overcrowded or otherwise unsuitable housing, those with a need to move based on medical or welfare reasons and those who need to move to a particular area where failure to move would cause hardship to themselves or others. Additional preference may be given to those who also have 'urgent housing needs'.

The Act

- removes the current 'two-year duty' to provide settled accommodation and giving local authorities an ongoing responsibility to provide settled accommodation for unintentionally homeless households in priority need;

- abolishes the duty on local authorities to consider whether other suitable accommodation is available before they can secure accommodation;

- restricts the circumstances in which an offer of an assured shorthold tenancy in the private rented sector constitutes a discharge of duty;

- introduces a new power (but not a duty) for authorities to secure accommodation for homeless applicants who are not in priority need and strengthening duties on advice and assistance;

- giving Councils the freedom to use their own properties as short-term accommodation for homeless people for as long as necessary, until a settled home becomes available.

Under a Statutory Order the government has also extended the groups of people to have a priority need for housing. These groups are:

- 16 and 17 year olds;

- care leavers aged 18–21;

- people vulnerable because they have fled violence;

- people assessed as vulnerable because of an institutionalised background such as former prisoners.

The changes to the legal framework for allocating and letting local authority homes is intended to give councils more flexibility over their allocation schemes and to encourage them to give more choice to people seeking housing. These changes are summarised below:

- councils no longer have to have a housing register although they can, if they wish. In practice most authorities have retained some kind of list of people who apply for housing;

- councils have to publish a policy which explains how they let their homes and whether they will offer a choice of accommodation;

- everyone has the right to apply for available homes – unless they are in an ineligible category, for example, 'persons from abroad' who are not allowed to go on the housing register;

- councils are able to treat other individual applicants as ineligible if they have been guilty of unacceptable behaviour serious enough to make them unacceptable as a tenant;

- councils have to consider all applications for housing – except from ineligible people – and are not able to exclude particular groups;

- everyone (except ineligible people) who needs housing, or who needs to move to a particular area, is entitled to get reasonable preference for a home;

- people who live outside a local area will be able to apply for housing in that area, although the council will be able to take into account whether an applicant has a local connection;

- local authorities will have to provide free help for anyone making an application that needs it.

Housing Bill 2003

At the time of writing this study text (summer 2003), a draft housing bill was published for consultation.

The draft bill sets out specific legislation in five main areas:

- replacing the existing housing fitness standard with the evidence-based Housing Health and Safety Rating System (HHSRS) as a more effective basis for enforcement against unacceptable housing conditions;

- improving the controls on Houses in Multiple Occupation (HMOs), including a mandatory national licensing scheme, to tackle poor physical and management standards;

- giving local authorities powers to license all landlords in areas of low housing demand or similar areas where the growth and poor management of the private rented sector frustrates efforts to create sustainable communities;

- requiring anyone marketing a home to assemble a home information pack so that the information needed by buyers and sellers is available when the property is marketed and abortive costs on the buyer are reduced;

- modernising the Right to Buy scheme by tackling profiteering and emphasising purchasers' responsibilities so that it contributes more effectively to the supply of affordable housing.

The government is also considering reforming housing finance by:

- an overhaul of the housing revenue account (HRA) and making it 'user-friendly' to provide clear and helpful information for both councils and tenants;

- a new resource account which will show the value of assets, cost of capital tied up and expenditure to maintain them

    - taking expenditure on rent rebates away from HRA;

    - introducing a new major repairs allowance;

    - the need for business plans.

5.7   Other Influences on Housing

In the previous unit, we looked at the influences of Octavia Hill and others involved in housing during that period. Let us now look at a report that was published in 1985.

Report on the Inquiry into British Housing

The Inquiry into British Housing was carried out by a committee organized by the National Federation of Housing Associations, the forerunner of the National Housing Federation. The committee was chaired by the Duke of Edinburgh, who was president of the National Federation of Housing Associations, and its report (often referred to as the Duke of Edinburgh's Report) was published in July 1985.

The report had five main recommendations:

- existing forms of personal housing subsidies such as tax relief on mortgages was not justified and should be phased out and replaced by a 'needs-related' housing allowance. This 'needs-related' allowance would, the Report suggested, replace mortgage interest tax relief and housing benefit and would be extended to low-income owner-occupiers who continued to be a neglected group. This was, of course, a controversial suggestion and the least likely of all recommendations to be implemented. Indeed, the Conservative government had already stated that mortgage interest tax relief would not be abolished. However, this has now been phased out from April 2000 by the Labour government. Mortgage interest tax relief was dealt with in Unit 2.

- rents should be related to the capital value of the relevant property and owners encouraged to let vacant rooms. It was suggested that rents be four per cent of the current capital cost plus an allowance for repairs and maintainance; thus rents would give landlords a reasonable return but not be as high as an unregulated rent. It was anticipated that rents set on this basis would be sufficient to attract new capital investment into private renting.

- local authorities should adopt a more comprehensive approach to the housing function and should enforce housing standards more actively.

- housing conditions should be improved generally and especially in older areas and in the poorer council estates. The report made several recommendations under this heading of which perhaps the most important is that greater use should be made of area-based agency services.

- local authorities should be providers of housing only as last resort, ie local authorities should be 'enablers'.

The report stated specifically that its proposals formed a package and that they should be implemented as a whole rather than piecemeal. The Report stated that 'Our central recommendations hang together as a unity; they are not a checklist from which some parts and not others can be extracted'. Because of this insistence to treat as a total package, the government rejected the Report. Also the Conservative government of the day, under the leadership of Margaret Thatcher, were reluctant to phase out mortgage interest tax relief. In fact Margaret Thatcher remained committed to this and considered that mortgage interest tax relief should be retained right up to her departure in 1990. The Report criticized successive governments for making piecemeal decisions and failing to face up to the challenge of coherent, across-the-board reform. It also stated that homelessness, overcrowding and squalid housing conditions were not insuperable problems: they could be overcome by new building, renovation and better use of empty and under-used properties.

After the report was written in 1985, the Conservative government:

- restricted tax relief on mortgage interest to the basic rate of tax and lowered it to 15% in April 1995;

- introduced assured shorthold tenancies;

- introduced Housing Action Trusts;

- introduced a new 'fitness standard' with regards to dwellings;

- encouraged owners to let vacant rooms in properties.

After the report was published, there was a vast increase in homelessness, particularly in the numbers of young people sleeping rough. The nation's housing stock continued to deteriorate. The government had put the future of the local authority housing stock in jeopardy and the housing association movement was being encouraged to take over the local authorities' functions.

The Report was re-launched in June 1991, with some amendments mainly in an endeavour to reverse the decline in rented housing. Its release was again chaired by the Duke of Edinburgh. It re-emphasized points made in the earlier report and suggested tax incentives for landlords when renting dwellings. The proposal to withdraw tax relief gradually, if adopted, would have released about £7 billion per annum in 1991 which could have been used to meet the reforms suggested.

The new Report called for recognition that the ring-fencing of the housing revenue account had changed the relationship between housing and other local services. It argued that the logic of treating the landlord function as separate from other local authority accounts meant that the government should go one step further and treat local authority landlords in a similar way to independent housing associations. This would give the local authority freedom to raise private finance, secured against the value of its stock. Basically the idea here was to set up local housing companies. (Local housing companies are covered in more depth in Unit 6.)

When the Duke of Edinburgh announced the second report of the Inquiry into British Housing at the Institute of Housing Conference in Harrogate he commented: 'Most people in Britain are well housed but a substantial minority live in very poor conditions or are homeless. Clearly all is not well with housing in Britain and I am certain that everyone would like to see a system of housing finance and provision that is simple, fair, effective and economically sustainable.'

In connection with his comments on housing finance, the Duke of Edinburgh's report suggested an end to the system whereby most local authorities received housing benefit payments for their tenants reduced by notional Housing Revenue Account surpluses. It had at last been recognized that housing benefit was a social security payment and not a housing subsidy. Private landlords and housing associations had already received rental income based on full payment of housing benefit and it was only local authorites that were penalized in this way. The Local Government and Housing Act 1989 implemented this suggestion and local authorities are no longer penalized by a reduction in their Housing Revenue Account.

Although many points in the two Reports have been addressed by successive governments; the 'whole package or nothing' approach was never adopted.

Summary

Once again this may have seemed a daunting unit. However, it has attempted to take you through the relevant legislation for the last 40 or so years and to examine some of its effects. Again, to help you through the maze of legislation, a list of housing legislation appears below. Those printed in bold type are more important for your studies.

Table 5.1: Summary of housing legislation

YEAR	ACT
1961	Housing Act
1964	Housing Act
1964	Protection from Eviction Act
1965	Rent Act
1967	Leasehold Reform Act
1967	Housing Subsidies Act
1968	Rent Act
1969	**Housing Act**
1971	Housing Act
1972	**Housing (Finance) Act**
1974	**Housing Act**
1975	**Housing Rents and Subsidies Act**
1976	The New Towns (Amendment) Act
1977	**Housing (Homeless Persons) Act**
1977	Protection from Eviction Act
1978	Home Purchase and Housing Act; Corporation Guarantee Act
1980	**Housing Act**
1984	Housing and Building Control Act
1984	Housing Defects Act
1985	**Housing Act** (Consolidating Act)
1985	**Housing Associations Act** (Consolidating Act)
1985	Landlord and Tenant Act
1986	**Housing and Planning Act**
1988	**Housing Act**
1989	**Local Government and Housing Act**
1993	**Leasehold Reform, Housing and Urban Development Act**
1996	**Housing Act**
1996	**Housing, Grants, Construction and Regeneration Act**
2002	**Homelessness Act**

6

PARTNERSHIP OF PUBLIC AND PRIVATE SECTORS

Objectives

After studying this unit, you should be able to:

- outline the reasons for increased owner-occupation;

- explain the problems for private investment in housing;

- explain the need for 'social housing';

- define a building society;

- outline the history of building societies;

- explain why building societies influence housing;

- explain the Private Finance Initiative;

- describe how local housing companies are formed.

6.1   Introduction

Housing today consists of a balance between private enterprise and public enterprise. It is the government that decides where that balance should be set, either by stimulating the private sector or by expanding the public sector. The Conservative government made no secret of its wish to shift it in the direction of private enterprise when it was in office, as we saw in the previous unit. The incoming Labour government has said that it wishes to see sustainable home ownership and good quality, efficiently run social and private rented sectors, offering choice.

Private Enterprise

Private enterprise is a term that can be applied in the context of both the building and the ownership of houses.

- Private enterprise in housebuilding means houses built by a private builder, using his own capital (and, no doubt, sold for his own eventual profit).

- Private enterprise in house ownership means houses privately-owned, even though the owner could be paying a mortgage. Private house ownership can be further divided into:

  - homes owned privately and lived in by the owners (owner-occupiers);

  - homes owned privately but rented out to tenants (private landlords);

  - a combination of the above, where the owner lives in one part of the home and lets out another to a tenant (resident landlord).

Public Enterprise

Public enterprise is also a term that can be used in two different contexts.

- Public enterprise in building means houses built by the public sector (mainly housing associations and local authorities), although usually private building firms are subcontracted to carry out the building work itself.

- Public enterprise in house ownership means houses owned by the public sector (again, usually local authorities, housing associations or local housing companies registered under the Housing Act 1996) and rented out to tenants (the local authority, housing association or local housing company as a public landlord).

Another term used in connection with housing is municipalization. A definition of **municipalization** might be 'the situation where central or local government takes over and administers the functioning of private landlords'.

6.2 Historical Background

As we saw in Unit 4, up until the late 1800s there was very little public enterprise in housing. Virtually all houses were privately built and privately rented and very few were owner-occupied. The 'private v. public' argument of the time was about whether there should be any public enterprise at all. There was a strong body of opinion which said that there should not. This was known as the 'laissez-faire' attitude.

As we have already seen, the provision of public housing started to grow at the end of the First World War. It was at this time that the provision of housing began to be seen as a social service and this idea continued to grow throughout the 20th century.

Nowadays the argument is about whether any public housing, which governments have recently been referring to as 'social housing', should be provided and, if so, how much. It is recognized that there will always be a level of social need for public housing but the question is: what exactly is the level of that need and can it be provided by private-sector funding? There is no simple answer to this question, although perhaps one way to consider it is to turn the argument around and ask: what is the level of desire to be an owner-occupier?

6.3   Home Ownership

It is fairly obvious that if more homes are owner-occupied, then the requirement for social housing will fall. Remember, we are talking here about the borderline between social and private housing. There will always be those who need social housing, just as there will always be those who expect to be owner-occupiers, but at the borderline, if more people own their houses, then there will be fewer people needing social housing. Private-sector renting can assist here; private rented housing has increased slightly due to both assured and assured shorthold tenancies. (Tenancies are covered in detail in Unit 8.)

We looked briefly at the current situation on tenure, including home ownership, in Unit 1. Let us see how there has been a dramatic rise since 1914:

Table 6.1: Percentage of total dwellings owner-occupied in England

1914	10%
1950	29%
1961	43%
1970	50%
1976	53%
1983	61%
1987	65%
1988	66%
1989	67%
1998	68%
2000	69%
2003	70%

How has this dramatic change come about? One of the main reasons is that more people want to become owner-occupiers. This is one of the social factors mentioned earlier, which are difficult to quantify and predict. Some of the more obvious reasons for wanting to be an owner-occupier are given below:

- **Status:** rightly or wrongly, people see themselves as higher up the social hierarchy if they are owner-occupiers.

- **Freedom:** an owner-occupier can do what he likes to his house (within the statutory planning permission, Building Regulations framework and any restrictive covenants there may be on the property) whereas tenants do not usually have this freedom of action.

- **Finances:** house ownership is generally seen as a sound financial investment, in that it is a hedge against inflation and the house itself can if necessary be used as collateral to raise a loan at a future date. However, during the recession of the late 1980s and early 1990s there was a drop in house prices. It must be remembered that the value of the house can go down as well as up. We discussed this earlier in the text. Trends in 2003 have shown that house prices have started to increase again and appear to be nearing a levelling off stage.

Of course, it is not enough that people should want to own houses. The economic climate has to be such that desires can be transformed into reality. During most of the period when house ownership rocketed, economic conditions were indeed favourable. Some of the more obvious economic and financial factors enabling the growth of home ownership are given below:

- **Income:** there has been a period of rising real income for those in work; most people receive increments on their salary scales; many receive bonuses.

- **Building societies and banks:** the building societies and banks have become a formidable force in granting mortgages.

- **Incentives to purchase:** there are statutory incentives for people to buy their homes which include:

    - the right to buy, which offers substantial discounts to prospective purchasers under the Housing Act 1980;

    - subsidy and loan schemes introduced by the Home Purchase and Housing Corporation Guarantee Act 1978 (since repealed by the Local Government and Housing Act 1989);

    - mortgage interest tax relief (although phased out from April 2000);

    - exemptions from capital gains tax;

    - various house renovation grants which have been available from local authorities since 1949 (many of these have now ceased);

    - transferrable discounts to local authority tenants to purchase other dwellings (Housing Act 1988);

    - shared ownership schemes (Housing and Building Control Act 1984);

    - the rent to mortgage scheme encourages council tenants who are unable to purchase under the right to buy arrangements (Leasehold Reform, Housing and Urban Development Act 1993);

    - tenants' incentive schemes whereby housing association tenants were encouraged to purchase properties in the owner-occupier sector and now replaced by Voluntary Purchase Grants;

    - inflation which amortized the housing debt 'painlessly';

    - new Homebuy scheme introduced in late 1999 (see Unit 9).

Similarly there are private incentives and probably the most important of these are those introduced by building societies, banks and other lenders to make mortgages more attractive: for example, low-cost mortgages or endowment mortgages. We looked at the various types of mortgages earlier in this text.

It is an interesting question as to how many of these economic and financial factors came about because people wanted to buy their homes and how many would have happened anyway, so that the assistance given to house purchase was merely coincidence. That sort of 'which came first?' question is more properly addressed in an economics text. We shall not pursue it any further here.

Today people have a strong desire to become owner-occupiers. However, it is increasingly difficult for first-time buyers to break into the housing market, because of the big capital investment required. In other words, in spite of incentives and other financial factors, houses are simply too expensive for first-time buyers. In addition there is an element of risk and insecurity in the current climate, although as stated earlier the situation appears to be improving now.

The Conservative government, through the then Department of the Environment, suggested six methods by which local housing authorities and housing associations could try to help first-time buyers.

They could:

- improve houses with a view to sale whereby local authorities and housing associations improve run-down properties and sell at a loss; the loss being met by the Department of the Environment (known as IFS – Improve for Sale);

- use local authority mortgage guarantee powers introduced under the Housing Act 1980;

- sell run-down properties which can be improved by the purchaser; this is known as 'homesteading' where interest is waived on a mortgage for up to five years and a grant provided towards improving the dwelling;

- build starter homes in partnership with private builders, on land owned by the local authority;

- offer shared ownership, to enable those on low incomes to participate in ownership by using part-owning and part-renting schemes;

- sell local authority land at subsidized prices to private builders, individuals or self-build groups for starter homes.

The Labour government introduced a new scheme in late 1999 known as 'Home Buy'. This is similar to shared ownership and the buyer is responsible for 75% of the purchase price and the remaining 25% is paid for by the equity loan which will be repayable on resale at 25% of the current value of the property.

In 1999, the government produced a Consultation Paper to speed up home buying and selling; the Consultation Paper was called *A Key to Easier Home Buying and Selling*. We looked at this scheme earlier but here we go into more depth.

The background to the consultation paper is that most people prefer home ownership. It is usually the biggest single purchase made (although a pension plan could well cost more). It is a stressful time purchasing a dwelling; it can also be a frustrating time and can cause misery when things are not straightforward. It can also cause financial loss if things go badly wrong.

It takes a considerable time to purchase a property and the prospective buyer often makes an offer based on little more than the estate agent's particulars and brief visit to property. There is always the fear of gazumping as well.

The proposals outlined in the Consultation Paper:

- ensure that buyers and sellers are better prepared with as much information as possible right from the start;
- simplify and speed up transaction process;
- help both buyer and seller feel more secure at an earlier stage that the transaction will go through;
- hope to achieve all this by voluntary means.

Briefly buyers will be given an information pack comprising:

- copy of title deeds;
- seller's replies to pre-contract enquiries;
- replies to standard search enquiries made of local authority;
- copies of consents relating to planning and building control;
- for new properties copies of warranties and guarantees;
- survey report on condition;
- draft contract.

For leasehold properties, the pack would also consist of:

- lease;
- most recent service charge accounts and receipts;
- insurance policy;
- current regulations made by landlord or management company;
- memorandum and articles of the landlord or management company.

There are advantages and disadvantages to such a scheme:

Advantages

- help buyer to commit to transaction;
- expedite matters;
- demonstrate seller's seriousness and discourage time wasters;

- make process less stressful;

- help seller decide on appropriate asking price;

- places buyer in better position with regard to price/condition of property etc;

Disadvantages

- additional costs;

- survey carried out at a particular time and accuracy of report cannot be guaranteed over a long period;

- may still need separate valuation;

- buyer may not be confident about neutrality or reliability of seller;

- legal complexity – under present arrangements it is the surveyor who is liable to the buyer who commissioned the survey.

This proposal formed part of the Homes Bill 2001 which did not progress because of lack of parliamentary time. It is now encompassed in the draft Housing Bill 2003.

6.4   Housebuilding

As long as there is a demand for private houses, and we have just seen that there is such a demand, then private builders will be willing to provide them. The level of activity in the private building industry is mainly governed by demand, but there are two other factors to note.

Firstly, until 1949 it was necessary to obtain a licence for every privately built house (a regulation which had been instituted by the Labour government just after the Second World War). This requirement was removed in 1949 and interest in building houses immediately increased. Secondly, VAT concessions are available to most private builders (in much the same way as there are tax concessions available to mortgagors). In this way, the Exchequer 'subsidizes' private builders. There is often political debate on this sensitive subject, but there is no doubt that the concessions serve to stimulate the building industry.

6.5   Problems for Private Investment in Housing

So far, we have been largely concerned with looking at why private enterprise plays such an important part in housing today. However, it is important to remember that there are risks inherent in any investment. Housing is no exception.

The main risks within the housing market apply to all forms of private investor including owner-occupiers, private landlords and builders.

- the housing market is unstable and diffuse. It lacks real organization. If prices slumped or costs soared uncontrollably, many private investors would be unable to cope and part of the system would collapse.

- house prices and rents can fluctuate violently. There is always the possibility of a general fall in house prices, which would benefit nobody in the private sector apart from first-time buyers or those trading down or selling houses which are empty. This was experienced in the late 1980s, early 1990s although, as stated earlier, house prices are now rising.

Another risk inherent in private enterprise, affecting owner-occupiers in particular, is that older houses can be difficult to sell, which means that the potential of the investment made in a house may not be realized.

There are also risks for private landlords.

- major repairs to the rented property may become necessary.

- competition from subsidized social sector lettings is always fierce, but if it were to increase it could drive the private landlord out of business.

- nowadays, a realistic rent on a property can be higher than the costs of paying a mortgage on an equivalent property, so that the private landlord could find himself out of business as owner-occupation increases. Currently, interest rates are the lowest for 53 years.

Since the deregulation of the private rented sector in 1988, residential letting has carried less risk and raised greater income for the landlord; home owners, unable to sell their homes, have rented them out instead. As mortgage interest tax relief has been phased out from April 2000, the tax incentive for owner occupation has been reduced, so private renting should become a more attractive form of tenure.

The Housing Act 1996 introduces a new concept in social housing. Local housing companies can be set up. They must be registered under the Companies Act 1985 and make provision in their memorandum of association for the provision, construction, improvement or management of houses to be kept available for letting or hostels. Local housing companies can acquire, construct, repair or improve housing. They can also convert houses. In addition they can deal with shared ownership.

The local housing company must be registered as a social landlord with the Housing Corporation. Local housing companies are dealt with in more detail later in this unit.

The Housing Corporation can make social housing grants to registered landlords, including local housing companies, in order that they can provide social housing. The Housing Corporation can make grants to registered social landlords in respect of any discounts given by them to tenants exercising the right to acquire their dwelling under the right to buy, rent to mortgage or by a purchase grant to housing association tenants.

Both local authorities and the Public Works Loans Commissioners can make grants or loans to social landlords.

The building society movement has backed the idea of local housing companies as bringing a ray of hope to thousands of council tenants. The building society movement claims that there was little alternative to using private finance to tackle disrepair in council stock; even the release of capital receipts would be inadequate to tackle the volume of repairs necessary.

6.6 Joint Initiatives

In the past, the government (and others) have complained that the private sector should have more of a social conscience and should be more involved in urban regeneration. This amounts to a direct appeal for more integration between the private and public housing sectors.

Building societies and banks have worked closely with local authorities and housing associations in providing funds. One of the first ventures involved two building societies, Halifax (which at the time was a building society) and Nationwide, who jointly launched Partnership Renewal of the Built Environment (PROBE).

The idea of PROBE was that resources should be invested by the private sector to help cure the more social problems, such as run-down council estates. Under PROBE, the two building societies provided an initial funding of £150 million and a building firm (Lovell Holdings Ltd) provided the workforce.

Further initiatives are funding local housing companies with a social housing grant under the Housing Act 1996.

6.7 Building Societies

We referred earlier in this unit to the rapid rise in owner-occupation since 1914. One of the main factors influencing this rapid growth has been the presence of the building societies. This is because the building societies are able to use their funds to grant mortgages to prospective housebuyers.

So what is a **building society**? A building society is formed wherever ten or more people get together and decide to carry out the business of a building society. The Building Societies Act 1986 defines a building society as:

> A society may be established under this Act if its purpose or principal purpose is that of raising, primarily by the subscriptions of the members, a stock or fund for making to them advances secured on land for their residential use.

In other words, if a group of people get together and decide to conduct a business as described by the Act, then that group can call itself a building society. The Act goes on to detail the rules and regulations which apply to building societies. It also describes the powers possessed by building societies.

Since the Building Societies Act 1986, the competition between building societies has been fierce coupled with the need for low-cost financial services. In order to withstand these competitive pressures and to maintain their market shares, building societies must continue to grow. However, the only way to grow is by merger, especially between those which are already a substantial size. There have been several examples of this. Similarly we have seen major building societies now converting to company/bank status.

Origins of Building Societies

Building societies came into being in the late 1700s. They began in much the same way as the definition of a building society suggests. Groups of people got together and pooled their money to enable them to purchase land and build houses. Once all the members of the society had a home, the society dissolved. For this reason, the early building societies were called 'terminating building societies'.

The terminating societies were building societies which really did build houses. However, as time went on the societies became more interested in the financial side of business: increasing their funds by raising money from people who wanted to invest, and then making housing finance available to others. In this way, the terminating societies gradually became permanent building societies (because the financial side of the business can carry on as long as houses – any houses – are being built and sold).

Building Societies Legislation

The Building Societies Act 1874 gave societies corporate existence; this means that, in law, a building society exists as a legal entity distinct from its members.

Since then there have been a number of Acts, in 1894, 1960, 1962, 1986 and 1997. For your syllabus you do not need to know about these in great detail. Perhaps the three most important points to bear in mind are that:

- the Building Societies Act 1962 consolidated earlier building societies legislation;

- the Building Societies Act 1986 repealed the whole of the 1962 Act and at the same time extended the powers of building societies;

- the Building Societies Act 1997 enables societies to pursue any activities provided for in its Memorandum, i.e the constitutional document which sets out the organization's objectives and powers, subject to certain restrictions. It is likely that building societies will seek to introduce new memoranda to reflect the wider powers regime.

The Powers of Building Societies

The main powers, and indeed the main purposes, of a building society are to:

- accept money from the public;

- pay interest on that money;

- allow withdrawals on demand or at short notice;

- make mortgage loans to people wishing to purchase property.

Until 1986 these were the only significant powers of a building society. However, the Building Societies Act 1986 made some significant changes:

- building societies were now allowed to own and develop land and property, which was really coming full-circle back to the old terminating societies.

- building societies could now provide various services which up until 1986 were the province of other organizations, such as banks, estate agents and solicitors. These services are:

    1. Money transmission services.

    2. Foreign exchange services.

    3. Making or receiving of payments as agents.

    4. Management as agents of mortgage investments.

    5. Management as agents of land.

    6. Arranging for the provision of services relating to the acquisition or disposal of investments, whether on behalf of the investor or the person providing the service.

    7. Establishment and management of personal equity plans.

    8. Arranging for the provision of credit, whether on behalf of the borrower or the person providing the credit, and providing services in connection with current loan agreements to the party providing the credit.

    9. Establishment and management of unit trust schemes for the provision of pensions.

    10. Establishment and, as regards the contributions and benefits, administration of pension schemes.

    11. Arranging for the provision of insurance of any description, whether on behalf of the persons effecting or the person providing the insurance.

    12. Giving advice as to insurance of any description.

    13. Estate agency services.

    14. Surveys and valuations of land.

    15. Conveyancing services.

The Effects of Building Societies on Housing

Imagine that building societies and, more recently, banks got together and decided not to grant mortgage loans in certain areas. What would happen to that area? It is not difficult to see. Without loans, people would not be able to afford to purchase houses in the area, so fewer people would move in and fewer improvements would be made to properties. Gradually, the area would become run-down and undesirable: a vicious circle, since it would appear to confirm the building societies' original decision not to lend in that area.

This cutting off of an area from building society or bank funds is known as **red lining**. It has been a much more important issue in the USA than in this country. However, it does serve to show how central building societies and, more recently, banks have become necessary to housing policy and housing developments in the UK. Without the building societies, a great number of people would be unable to afford property; the pattern of tenure across the country would be totally different, and probably the housebuilding industry would not be in the form we know today.

Because building societies exert a considerable influence on housing, it is not surprising that several suggestions have been made as to how they should exert that influence. Not only that, but successive governments have seen the effects of building societies and banks as an important political issue and have given various forms of assistance to these institutions.

Government Support for Building Societies and Banks

Government support may take various forms, as discussed below.

Indemnities to building societies and banks

Under Section 442 of the Housing Act 1985, a local authority may, in certain circumstances, make itself responsible for a mortgage should the mortgagor fail to pay (known as a default by the mortgagor).

The relevant part of Section 442 reads as follows:

A local authority, with the approval of the Secretary of State, may enter into agreements with:

    (a) a building society lending on the security of the house; or

    (b) a recognised body making a relevant advance on the security of a house, whereby, in the event of default by the mortgagor, and in the circumstances and subject to conditions specified in the agreement, the authority binds itself to indemnify the society or body in respect of the whole or part of the mortgagor's outstanding indebtedness and any loss or expense falling on the society or body in consequence of the mortgagor's default.

By making this provision in the Act, the position of the building societies or banks was strengthened by allowing them to make loans of higher risk. This also influences the structure of housing tenure across the country by encouraging more people to take out mortgages and become owner-occupiers.

Tax relief for building society and bank investors

Building societies and banks deduct tax from deposit interest paid by them at a rate of 20% unless the investor has registered to have the interest paid in full if, for example, he has no earned income. Building societies and banks account for this deduction directly to the Inland Revenue.

Only higher-rate taxpayers have any further tax liability on the interest received by them. Those who do not pay income tax at all will not easily be able to reclaim the tax deducted if they have not already registered for gross interest. However, the effect of this arrangement is that building societies and banks can often offer attractive rates of interest to those who have no earned income.

This additional tax support for building societies and banks affects housing indirectly. Giving tax relief to investors encourages more people to invest, which strengthens the position of both building societies and banks alike and makes more funds available for mortgage purposes. The result is that more people will take the opportunity to borrow and become owner-occupiers.

Stabilizing the Supply of Funds for Mortgages

One way in which building societies have been urged to use their influence on the housing market is to make some attempt to stabilize the supply of funds for mortgages. At present, the supply of funds can vary considerably from month to month, as explained by *Housing Policy* in 1977:

> *The flow of funds available to building societies for making loans comprises repayments of principal by mortgagors, interest due to investors that is credited to their accounts instead of being paid out to them and the excess of new money invested over withdrawals (net receipts). The first two are comparatively stable, but net receipts fluctuate widely.*
>
> *... building societies' net receipts from investors have proved very sensitive to changes in the balance between the interest rates offered by them and by their competitors. These competing rates have fluctuated sharply in recent years – by as much as 4% in three months. Building societies cannot match such oscillations. They can alter the rates offered to investors virtually overnight, but to increase the interest rates on some four million building society mortgages is a major administrative task, especially as under many (particularly older) mortgage deeds, one to three months' notice of an increase must be given. This lag adds to the cost to societies of raising their rate structure.*

The report goes on to say that:

> *The combination of the reluctance of societies to alter their interest rates substantially or frequently and of volatile interest rates in the economy as a whole has led to large variations in building societies' receipts and, consequently, in alternating mortgage feasts and famines, damaging to housebuyers, house-owners and housebuilders.*

You do not need to understand all the complex financial reasons behind the instability of the supply of mortgage funds. You just need to know that the problem exists and that the main cause is that the net receipts of building societies fluctuate widely.

Similarly, you do not need to know in detail all the possible methods of solving this problem, but you should bear in mind the strategy suggested in *Housing Policy* in 1977, which is still valid today:

> *Greater stability in the volume of mortgage lending can be achieved by development of the voluntary arrangements between the government and the building societies through the Joint Advisory Committee. The building societies should:*
>
> (a) *build up their stabilization funds to higher levels when possible;*
>
> (b) *keep their structure of interest rates paid to investors more in line with the market;*
>
> (c) *adopt a more flexible relationship between the rate paid by mortgagors and the rate paid to investors;*
>
> (d) *be prepared to raise short-term loans on the money market.*

6.8   The Changing Role of the Building Society and Banks

As we have seen, building societies and banks have a vested interest in housing. This may seem obvious, however there are many factors besides owner-occupation which must be taken into account. These include the quantity of the housing stock and the different forms of tenure which are available.

Earlier in the unit, we saw how the level of owner-occupation has been increasing. Currently, 70% of all dwellings are owner-occupied and it is estimated that when this figure reaches 75% the market will be saturated. With this in mind, societies and banks in particular must plan how best to diversify their activities within the United Kingdom housing markets.

For some time now, building societies and banks have been involved in more than just the provision of funds secured by mortgages to prospective house purchasers. The most common form of investment is through partnership schemes, whereby the building societies and banks provide finance for other organizations, such as housing associations. Currently building societies and banks undertake substantial lending to housing associations.

The advice of the societies on other housing matters has also been sought. One example was the Heseltine project, which investigated the problems of housing in inner city areas following the riots in Toxteth, Bristol and Southall in the late 1970s and early 1980s. Here they were asked to give their comments from a financial perspective. These comments helped to form the basis of the Building Societies Act 1986.

Background

Let us look at how the Building Societies Act 1986 came about. The Building Societies Act 1962 did not allow societies to become directly involved in housing, although by setting up separate bodies they managed to do so indirectly. The Abbey National, for example, established its own housing association in the 1970s. In the 1980s the Woolwich established Woolwich Homes (1983) Ltd, since superseded by Woolwich Homes Ltd.

Societies also teamed up with other housing organizations. The Nationwide and Halifax, for example, joined with Lovells in the Elm Village scheme which provided 50 houses at cost.

Involvement with local authorities has also increased, particularly since 1983. With council houses and flats being sold, local authorities were encouraged by the government to persuade tenants to obtain their loans from building societies. This was seen as an alternative to transferring their debt from that of rent to that of a mortgage within the books of the same local authority. Links were therefore established with various other housing organizations, and societies became more interested in housing matters generally and also more proficient.

Section 17 of the Building Societies Act 1986 allowed societies to adopt the power to hold and develop land as a commercial asset provided they had a qualifying asset holding of £100 million.

Legislation relating to other bodies has also been introduced, which permits far more co-operation between different organizations. For instance, the Housing and Planning Act 1986 allows local authorities to transfer ownership of land and to delegate certain management functions. The lifting of such legal constraints will enhance cooperation.

The Need for Caution

Building societies and indeed banks have one major difficulty which they must overcome. They need to ensure that projects are financially sound. Some will adopt a break-even policy, others will simply not enter into non-profit-making activities. It is doubtful whether any would be prepared to make a loss on new ventures when there were now stricter controls on building society finances. Changes in the economy and labour market have added to the uncertainty for people making long-term mortgage commitments. Finally the building societies are accountable to their members, who provide the majority of the funds, and will continue to do so. Mortgage lenders have an obvious interest in getting the balance of the market right. They both finance home ownership and invest billions in housing associations.

For these reasons, direct involvement in housing is cautious and is conducted via partnership schemes. Larger societies have already taken the plunge. Five main areas have caught societies' interest and various schemes have been developed to enhance them.

They are:

- the extension of owner-occupation;
- specialist housing projects;
- rented housing;
- urban renewal;

- rent to let initiative.

We shall now consider each of these.

Extending Owner-occupation

Rising house prices, particularly in the south of England, meant that many who would like to own their home could not. The building societies introduced shared ownership schemes to help these people.

Under shared ownership schemes, the society or housing association owns part of the property and the borrower owns the rest. The borrower pays interest and principal on the part that is owned and rent on the remaining portion. Normally a housing association, which may be owned by the society or completely unrelated, receives the mortgage from the society.

In the early 1990s the Nationwide Building Society, for example, raised £30 million to support rent and shared ownership schemes. Loans were be provided at a special rate of interest. This concept has since been extended to the equity mortgage scheme, which provides a means of co-ownership that does not require a grant or subsidy. The building society advances the full purchase price of the property, but retains an equity share in any capital appreciation. Typically, full interest is paid on only part of the loan, with little or no interest likely to be charged on the balance. The intention is that, as their incomes increase, borrowers will be able to buy out their building society's share.

Cost sale developments are another area in which building societies have become involved. Working in conjunction with housing associations, they have built and sold properties on a non-profit basis. The scheme is used for first-time buyers on low incomes, particularly in areas where prices are high.

The building societies and banks believe their future in the owner-occupation side of housing lies in providing 'one-stop shopping centres'. In other words, a building society or bank would be able to offer a prospective housebuyer (or seller) all the services they need under one roof.

- A number of building societies and banks have already acquired estate agents, although some have recently sold them;
- The larger societies, holding qualifying assets of £100 million or more, are able to offer insurance and related services.

Mortgagors are obliged, by the terms of their mortgage deeds, to keep their homes in good repair. A well-maintained property is likely to retain its value for the building society or bank, should possession and sale ever prove necessary, better than one which is not. In practice, many people do not maintain their properties particularly well. Building societies and banks could increase their already good reputation, help borrowers look after their houses and ensure that the housing stock is enhanced if they offered repair and maintenance facilities. They could provide the finance and make arrangements for work to be carried out.

Many building societies produce a number of publications and videos on the subject of home improvements. These give advice on home improvements generally, external and internal maintenance, energy conservation and safety in the home.

Specialist Housing Projects

Building societies and banks have been involved in specialist housing but this has been mainly confined to providing specialist housing for the elderly. The consensus is that this sector should be improved.

Rented Housing

Societies and banks have not been much involved with providing rented accommodation because the return on money invested is not high enough to support borrowing. However, they have seen a need to balance housing tenures, recognizing that home ownership is not always suitable for every individual.

Now that index-linked finance is available, societies have less need to worry from a financial point of view. Generally, however, it is felt that societies could become involved with renting mainly in conjunction with housing associations. Considerable funding has been made by building societies and banks to housing associations in connection with large-scale Voluntary Transfers (see Unit 7). Help has also been given for mixed funding schemes: the societies provide the finance and the housing associations provide the expertise.

Urban Renewal

Some societies and banks see themselves playing a social role in housing. Although urban renewal is a topic that has been discussed for many years, its critics suggest that its advocates had, in fact, contributed directly to urban decay by adopting 'red lining' policies (whereby they refused to lend on properties in inner cities). Whether or not this was true, societies are now playing an active role in the regeneration of urban areas and a good example of this involvement was PROBE. PROBE Ltd was a development agency formed between the Nationwide, Halifax and Lovells Ltd and operated throughout the country. Such organizations need to be large if they are to have the finance and the expertise needed for such projects.

Buy to Let Initiative

The increase in private rented accommodation coincided with the massive slump in the owner-occupied market in the late 1980s/early 1990s. Whereas previous landlords had taken the opportunity of selling properties onto the owner-occupied market when gaining vacant possession, this proved difficult at that time with falling prices. Many landlords held onto properties waiting for house prices to rise again.

To assist further the private rented sector, a new initiative was introduced, the Buy to Let Initiative.

This was set up by the Association of Residential Letting Agents (ARLA) and launched in September 1996, supported by leading mortgage lenders. It is an example of where mortgage lenders have reconsidered their lending strategy and is the biggest single initiative yet to revise and expand the private rented sector. The Buy to Let initiative:

- encourages renting by increasing the number of private landlords able to offer good-quality property and stops forcing people to purchase property when they are too young;

- has encouraged lenders to offer rates in line with standard mortgages for owner-occupiers rather than treating private landlords as part of the commercial sector;

- allows potential rent income to be taken into account for mortgage purposes;

- has brought new landlords into the private rented sector who want to buy another property as a medium- to long-term investment;

- has encouraged most landlord investors, particularly new ones, to use a letting agent to manage the property, although some lenders will allow landlords to conduct their own management;

- looks set for a rosy future as more and more lenders are gradually adding this type of product to their range.

Currently, it is estimated that 15% of all purchases in the South East are for the buy to let scheme. At the end of 2002, there were an estimated 275,000 buy-to-lets worth around £24.2bn. The recent rise in house prices has actually contributed to an increased demand for property to rent as young people save for a deposit to get on the property ladder.

6.9   Private Finance Initiative (PFI)

All existing local government expenditure is classified as public sector expenditure and as a result is counted against the Public Sector Borrowing Requirement (PSBR) – the measure of the debt requirement of central government to meet its proposed level of expenditure. Significant investment is still needed in key areas of local government activity such as housing, education, environment and social services.

Private Finance Initiative (PFI) was launched in 1992 with the aim of improving the quality and quantity of the nation's capital stock by harnessing the private sector's management expertise and resources, and encouraging closer relationship between public and private sectors.

PFI is a programme whereby public sector projects are provided by the private sector in a contractual partnership usually using a 'DBFO' or Design, Build, Finance and Operate contract. The purpose of PFI is to enable investment without impacting the PSBR. To qualify, schemes have to be shown to transfer risk to the private sector and provide value for money to the public sector.

PFI for refurbishment and redevelopment of council housing is favoured by the government to enable local authorities to realistically use it as an option for large-scale regeneration. The essential character of PFI is that a private sector organization provides a service to the public sector and in return for access to an income stream for a fixed period, assumes a major part of the risk – e.g financing, achieving development timescales, variations in the costs of works and services, penalties for poor performance against the specification.

A good example of PFI is the Dartford Crossing which has been financed by the private sector and the public sector making payments under a concession agreement for their ongoing use and maintenance.

PFI has increased considerably recently after a period of reluctance by the private sector.

Let us look closer at Housing PFI. Projects include the refurbishment of existing social housing together with the provision of associated services. In return the private sector receives payment linked to its performance in meeting agreed standards of provision.

The local authority will sign a contract with a private sector 'Operator', usually known as a 'Special Purpose Vehicle', which will typically last 30 years. Over the first part of this contract, usually three to five years, the Operator will refurbish the homes. During this period and for the full length of the contract the Operator will provide certain services, which are currently provided by the local authority. These will include repairs and maintenance and perhaps rent collection, tenancy management, care-taking and security.

In the summer of 2003, the Chancellor of the Exchequer launched a new drive on PFI and highlighted both social housing and regeneration as two key areas for expansion. The Chancellor hinted that PFI could be used to build homes for social housing tenants and key workers.

6.10   Local Housing Companies

The government's emphasis on public/private sector partnerships and the lack of substantial new funding has prompted local authorities to look closely at stock transfers to Local Housing Companies. Local housing companies, like housing associations, are not-for-profit organizations constituted independently of the local authority. However, unlike housing associations, the local authority has a minority interest in them (and representation at board level) and they are structured to be formally accountable to the local authority and tenants, as well as other stakeholders.

Transferring the stock to local housing companies enables the use of private finance to meet repair and improvement costs and may attract government support where the transfer would generate a negative value for the local authority in question.

The Housing Act 1996 enables local housing companies to register with the Housing Corporation as social landlords, providing the equivalent status to registered housing associations. It is a radical way of attracting investment for local authority estates which have been cash-starved.

Local housing companies are companies limited by guarantee with class voting rights at membership level, which normally reflects the balance of power on the board, split between councillors, tenants and independents.

Any decision to transfer stock to a local housing company needs to be preceded by a positive tenants' ballot with the majority of tenants being in favour. The ballot is usually conducted by the Electoral Reform Society.

Local housing companies have to take on the 'risks' involved, i.e repairs, design, construction, operation, demand and financial.

Tenants of local housing companies become assured tenants.

Local housing companies have been supported by the new Labour government; in 1997 the then Housing Minister, Hilary Armstrong, stressed at the Local Government Association Conference that 'we will not force them down local authorities throats, but it is a necessary way to get regeneration and renewal of an area'.

6.11   Housing Investment Trusts

Housing Investment Trusts were set up to revive the private rented sector. Housing Investment Trusts are

- seen as the 'son' of Business Expansion Schemes, which attracted millions of pounds into residential property from private investors during the 1980s;

- designed to attract institutional investment in portfolios of residential property and provide a boost to the private rented sector;

- expected to provide good returns of 8% or 9%;

- exempt from capital gains tax and pay a preferential rate of corporation tax;

- deemed unattractive by City institutions because of poor tax incentives;

- restricted by the limits on the type of rented property that can be held in trust's portfolio – they are highly restrictive *and* cannot be tenanted.

The number of Housing Investment Trusts has been very small.

Summary

In this unit, we have looked at the balance that exists between private enterprise and public enterprise in housing. There are four important points to remember:

- there will always be those needing social housing (a social need) and there will always be those expecting to own their homes.

- legislation and other measures are generally aimed at the borderline, where the balance between public and private sectors can be affected.

- private enterprise is very much governed by market forces (especially by the prevailing desire to become an owner-occupier), although legislation also has its effect. You should be able to discuss the reasons why owner-occupation is desirable, what has facilitated its rise, and what its potential problems are.

- public enterprise is very much governed by legislation. However, that legislation must obviously take into account prevailing market conditions. Housing as a public need is difficult to quantify and predict, but to some extent public enterprise can be seen as the other side of the coin to private enterprise.

We have also looked at how building societies, and to some extent banks, are involved in housing, in their usual role of providing mortgage finance and also in:

- the extension of owner-occupation and, in particular, the 'one-stop shopping centre' concept;

- specialist housing projects;

- rented housing;

- urban renewal.

You should also remember that the Building Societies Act 1986 opened the door to a whole new commercial world for the building societies, and allowed them to compete with banks and other financial institutions.

7

THE NATIONAL HOUSING FRAMEWORK

Objectives

After studying this unit, you should be able to:

- outline the many organizations involved in providing housing in the UK;

- write detailed notes on local authorities, housing associations, the Housing Corporation and other regulatory bodies;

- describe 'Best Value' in housing.

7.1   Introduction

No single body has the responsibility for providing housing in the United Kingdom, either in the public sector or in the private sector. Instead there are a number of organizations, each filling a particular niche in the overall housing framework.

7.2   The Government's Role

Government Offices were set up by the Conservative government in 1994 in various parts of the country to cut through the bureaucracy of all matters going through one central point in London. More recently in 2000, the Labour government's Regional Co-ordination Unit was set up to work with the Government Offices to provide a mechanism for a significant step forward in the delivery of a range of government services and programmes, not just housing.

The aim is to cut through bureaucracy and add value to delivery through shared experience and best practice; bring together key stakeholders and local partners and provide a high quality service by combining skills in the Government Offices at the local level with the co-ordination role of the Regional Co-ordination Unit in influencing policy design and implementation in Whitehall.

Government Departments

There are various government sections involved; we shall examine some of them below.

Housing Directorate

This is divided into various aspects of housing, all of which are self-explanatory and indeed covered in this study text. These aspects are:

- local authority housing;
- registered social landlords and private finance;
- homelessness and housing management;
- housing renewal;
- private rented sector;
- housing policy and home ownership.

Housing is a key role in the present government's broad social agenda with its main purpose being to offer everyone the opportunity of a decent home. The provision of good-quality, efficiently managed social housing plays an important part in meeting that aim. Subsidies are provided by the Directorate for local-authority rented housing. Funds are channelled through the Housing Corporation (see later in this unit) for registered social landlords most of whom are housing associations (see later in this unit).

Regeneration Directorate

This Directorate maintains and develops the policy framework and administrative and financial structures for domestic and European regeneration programmes in England. It is also responsible for the New Deal for Communities Programme (see later in this unit).

Construction Directorate

The Construction Directorate is responsible for overseeing improvements, quality and value-for-money from construction, both for commercial and domestic customers, and to modernize construction methods and procedures.

Wildlife and Countryside Directorate

The Wildlife and Countryside Directorate is responsible for the conservation and enhancement of England's countryside; the economic and social development of rural areas; environmental aspects of forestry and agricultural policy; policy on trees; access to and informal recreation in the countryside; National Parks policy; and coastal policy.

Regional Development Agencies (RDAs)

When elected in 1997, the Labour government's stated intentions were to decentralize, hence the subsequent Scottish and Welsh devolutions. Similarly in England certain functions of the then Department of Environment, Transport and the Regions have been delegated to Regional Development Agencies. There are eight Regional Development Agencies with twelve-member boards appointed by the Secretary of State together with the London Development Agency.

These RDAs are powerful new bodies that direct investment and plan regional economics. They have absorbed the functions of English Partnerships and the Rural Development Commission. They are responsible for:

- certain funding;
- dealing with European funding;
- furthering economic development;
- promoting business efficiency, investment and competitiveness;
- promoting employment;
- enhancing the development and application of skills relevant to employment;
- contributing towards the achievement of sustainable development in the United Kingdom;
- raising loans of up to £200 million nationwide for regeneration.

English Partnerships

English Partnerships is the national regeneration agency, supporting high quality sustainable growth across the country. With its flexible and innovative Investment Fund, English Partnerships works through its six regions to create development packages with the private, public and voluntary sectors to stimulate investment and create jobs through the reclamation of derelict, contaminated or unused land and buildings and the promotion of subsequent development opportunities. It is a key delivery agency for the urban renaissance and the government's Sustainable Communities agenda which we referred to earlier in this book.

New Deal for Communities

We looked at this Report in Unit 2. You need to be aware how this fits in with the Office of Deputy Prime Minister.

In 1998 the government published a report entitled *Bringing Britain Together: a National Strategy for Neighbourhood Renewal*. This report identified that there were 4,000 council estates and 44 districts suffering from high concentrations of deprivation. The Report urged the fostering of partnerships between local people and providers of housing and other services. The government allocated £800 million to the programme known as *New Deal for Communities*.

Many homeless people are unemployed and one of the government's initiatives is this New Deal for Communities. The aim of the New Deal is for councils to tackle social exclusion through drawing together regeneration and housing schemes and to involve residents, police and health services in transforming communities plagued by crime, unemployment and drug problems.

The government's priorities are:

- getting people to work;
- getting places to work by dealing with issues like housing management and anti-social behaviour;
- building a future for young people;
- providing access to services such as banks and shops;
- making the government work better.

The first of the money is being spread between 17 deprived neighbourhoods across England in Liverpool, Manchester, Newcastle upon Tyne, Middlesbrough, Nottingham, Leicester, Birmingham, Sandwell, Kingston upon Hull and Brighton and Hove, and Hackney, Tower Hamlets and Southwark in London.

More areas will be able to bid for funding in future years.

Greater London Authority (GLA)

Following the referendum held in May 1998, the Greater London Authority (GLA) has been created with a directly elected Mayor for London. The GLA has responsibilities for economic regeneration, strategic planning, police, fire, transport, environmental protection and promoting leisure and culture.

7.3   Local Authorities

We saw in Unit 4 how local authority housing has developed since 1919.

Local authorities that currently possess general housing powers are:

- district councils (metropolitan and non-metropolitan);
- London borough councils;
- the Common Council of the City of London.

In England there are 32 London boroughs and over 300 district councils.

The Housing Act 1996 sets out the key responsibilities of local housing authorities; these are:

- the assessment of housing needs in the area and the development of plans to meet those needs;
- the provision of rented accommodation and the management of that housing stock, including the allocation of dwellings, rent collection, arrears recovery and the enforcement of tenancy conditions;

- assisting housing associations and private developers to provide housing within their area – this is known as the 'enabling' role;

- the provision of accommodation and other services for the homeless;

- exercising powers to tackle disrepair in private-sector housing and in relation to houses in multiple occupation;

- the provision of housing advisory services;

- the administration of housing benefits for both private and public sector tenants.

Local authorities have a statutory duty under section 167(2) of the Housing Act 1996 to give preference in allocating dwellings to:

a) people occupying insanitary or overcrowded housing or otherwise living in unsatisfactory housing conditions;

b) people occupying housing accommodation that is temporary or occupied on insecure terms;

c) families with dependant children;

d) households consisting of or including someone who is expecting a child;

e) households consisting of or including someone with a particular need for settled accommodation on medical or welfare grounds; and

f) households whose social or economic circumstances are such that they have difficulty in securing settled accommodation.

The Housing Act 1996 states that all local housing authorities must have an allocations scheme for determining priorities and as to the procedure to be followed in allocating housing accommodation. The scheme must be published and available free of charge to any member of the public requesting a copy.

The objectives of the allocations policy could include the following:

- arbitrate fairly between applicants without discrimination based on gender, sexual orientation, race, ethnic origin, religion or disability;

- give priority to people in greatest housing need;

- meet applicants' preferences and give some degree of choice;

- make effective use of housing stock;

- avoid creation of difficult-to-let areas;

- make efficient and economic use of staff resources;

- minimize the turn-round time of properties between lettings.

Allocation schemes for determining priorities in allocating housing accommodation are usually made on a points basis. Although there is a suggested 'model' scheme produced by the government, local housing authorities tend to adapt this scheme to meet the needs of their areas. Points are awarded in respect of various aspects of the applicant's accommodation and those that are the most highly pointed are allocated appropriate accommodation. Points can be awarded for

- lack of living room;
- lack of bathroom;
- lack of inside wc;
- lack of sufficient bedrooms (overcrowding);
- sharing facilities;
- medical conditions;
- insecurity of tenure.

These are the usual ones although local housing authorities may choose to have additional aspect included.

Local housing authorities must allocate housing accommodation only to those who are 'qualified' to be allocated housing accommodation by that authority. Local housing authorities decide what classes of person are or are not qualified. However, the Housing Act 1996 specifically excludes a person subject to immigration control within the meaning of the Asylum and Immigration Act 1996.

Local housing authorities have to maintain details of income and expenditure just like any other organization. All details are recorded in the Housing Revenue Account. You should be aware of the main features of the Housing Revenue Account as indicated below:

Housing Revenue Account

Income	Expenditure
rents and service charges	debt charges
HRA subsidy (Central Government)	supervision/management
credit from loan charges	repairs/maintenance
any other income	housing benefit
	bad debts on rent arrears

It is important to note here that the government is overhauling Housing Revenue Accounts.

There are various contraints on the Housing Revenue Accounts that tend to support local housing authorities going for stock transfers. The main ones are:

- the 'ring fencing' of the HRA to prevent transfers to or from it to the General Fund, limiting the freedom of action a local authority has over its HRA income and expenditure;

- assumptions made by central government over the requirements for supervision, management and repairs, and maintenance which may be insufficient to cover the real costs, particularly catch-up costs of repairs and maintenance;

The Financing of Co-ops

Housing co-ops are, in the majority of cases, funded for development in the same way as housing associations through:

(a) Housing Corporation Social Housing Grant (SHG), which provides the capital funding for any schemes that co-ops wish to develop.

(b) mini HAG also provided by the Housing Corporation which enables dilapidated properties to be brought back into use.

A co-op would have to meet both the Housing Corporation and local authority's conditions if it were to obtain funding. Briefly the criteria for funding are as follows:

(a) that it meets the borough's strategic priorities;

(b) that it will work with a developing partner, if necessary;

(c) that it will provide units at a competitive cost within the limits of the local authority's Development Programme;

(d) that it can identify schemes where tenant control is a preferred option of the housing corporation (and the local authority) in order to underpin the capital investment, eg urban regeneration and existing communities.

Constraints on Funding

There is a continuing reduction in overall capital funding of social housing by the government. The implications are that the Housing Corporation will be increasingly reluctant to provide a capital allocation to a small organization without an existing 'track record' of social housing provision. Resources for funding are more likely to be directed towards mainstream housing associations.

Under the Housing Corporation's present 'mixed funding' arrangements, if a capital allocation were provided by the Corporation, it is unlikely that it would meet the total cost of the housing project. Mixed funding is funding from the public sector purse supported by private sector investment. The balance may have to be funded by members of the co-op taking out a loan in the private finance market. The cost of such a loan could be high because the co-op would have no other collateral or assets against which it might be secured.

Setting Up a Co-op

Any co-op needs to be registered with the Registrar of Friendly Societies. This enables it to borrow money and to enter into contractual arrangements.

If a co-op requires capital funding from the public purse, it also has to register with the Housing Corporation. To do this it needs to satisfy the Corporation's criteria:

(a) that it has been identified as needed within the regional Corporation strategy.

(b) that it meets identified needs within the council's housing strategy.

- control by central government to limit public expenditure and to limit local authorities' borrowing to help control Public Sector Borrowing Requirements;

- the combination of these factors for many local authorities limit their ability to meet the expenditure needed to ensure stock is in good condition and that management is to a high quality, leading to a consideration of alternative means of raising funding, including the transfer of stock to more private-sector bodies which can raise private finance and have more control over their finances.

Council rents increased rapidly after 1990, following the passing of the Local Government and Housing Act 1989. In 1997, the incoming Labour government restricted increases and in 1999, guideline rents allowed an increase of 1% in real terms and by 2% for the next two years.

7.4   Housing Associations

Housing associations are independent, private organisations providing housing and care services for low income households on a not-for-profit basis. They are controlled by unpaid voluntary committee members. Larger associations employ staff to carry out the day-to-day work of managing the associations on their behalf.

Under the Housing Associations Act 1985, a housing association is defined as

a society, body of trustees or company:

a)   *which is established for the purpose of, or amongst whose objects or powers are included those of providing, constructing, improving or managing, or facilitating or encouraging the construction of, housing accommodation and which*

b)   *does not trade for profit ...*

Housing associations existed before local authority housing. The origins of modern-day housing associations lie in the medieval almshouses. Housing associations were established in the 19th century with the aid of charitable donations from wealthy benefactors such as Peabody and Guinness; they provided dwellings at modest rents. In the 20th century, governments started to pay similar subsidies to housing associations, as the did local authorities.

Most housing associations tend to be small in size, with only 10% of housing associations owning more than 1,000 dwellings; however, these 10% own 89% of the housing associations' stock.

The growth of housing associations increased rapidly after the passing of the Housing Act 1974 which, *inter alia*, introduced housing action areas. By 1981 there were in excess of 3,000 housing associations but this number has been reduced to around 2,500, mainly as a result of mergers. It is interesting to note, however, that new associations register each year (approximately 70 per annum) particularly:

New co-operatives.

New black and minority ethnic associations serving particular communities in specific locations.

New rural associations.

New local community associations.

Black and Ethnic Minority Associations

Approximately 100 new black and minority ethnic associations have been registered since 1985; these now include Black Roof, Asra (housing for elderly Asians – 'Asra' is the Hindi word for 'shelter') and Tung Sing (housing some of Manchester's Chinese community).

Rural Associations

These have been established because of the lack of affordable housing in rural areas, and this has given growth to small rural housing associations, often based on administrative counties, eg Gloucestershire Housing Society. These associations aim to develop affordable housing, either for rent or for low-cost sale in small villages.

Local Community Associations

These have been set up to take over various local authorities' housing stock. The earliest transfer involved Chiltern District Council in December 1988, who transferred 4,635 properties to Chiltern Hundreds Housing Association. There have since been about half a million dwellings transferred under this scheme, with many, many more in the pipeline.

Housing associations work closely with local authorities and very often house people from the councils' housing department's waiting list together with those accepted as statutorily homeless. At least 50% of housing association tenants are nominated by the local authorities or through the National Mobility Scheme for local authority tenants wishing to move to another part of the country (see Unit 2).

Registered housing associations must send a copy of their allocations policy to the Housing Corporation and to appropriate local authorities.

Under the Housing Associations Act 1985 (as amended), registered housing associations are given powers:

- to acquire commercial or business premises as an 'incidental' part of their programme; to repair, improve or convert such premises and even continue, for a limited period, any business acquired;

- to acquire houses which will then be sold at a discount to tenants who would not otherwise be able to exercise the right to buy.

The Housing Act 1988 extends the objectives of all housing associations to encompass:

- providing facilities and amenities other than dwellings for rent, to the benefit of the association's tenants;

- acquiring or improving for sale or shared ownership terms;

- construction for sale on shared ownership;

- managing houses or blocks of flats on leasehold, owned by individuals or organizations that are not housing associations;

- setting up agency services for owners or occupiers of houses, to carry out or facilitate the carrying out of maintenance and improvement;

- giving advice on the formation of housing associations or providing services and/or advice to voluntary housing associations.

Since the Housing Act 1988, housing associations have been performing the role of a local authority with regard to housing and as such are now the main providers of affordable housing. As well as performing the role of a local authority, housing associations have since 1988 operated on a far more commercial basis and, as such, are actively involved in the following:

- housing association management agreements to lease private dwellings to house homeless families temporarily;

- low cost housing schemes in rural areas;

- voluntary transfers of local authority housing stock;

- housing schemes for vulnerable people under the Care in the Community Programme;

- many of the functions of a local authority.

Main Categories

Housing associations fall into seven main categories:

- General needs housing associations – the most common one.

- The early **charitable housing trusts** date back to the 19th century. Some are still operating effectively today.

- **Philanthropic housing associations** are set up to meet special needs, usually for particular categories of people.

- **Industrial housing associations** are sometimes set up by private industrial concerns to provide housing for staff.

- **Self-build housing associations** were very much in evidence shortly after the Second World War. Members usually, but not always, built houses with their own labour. Dwellings were provided for renting or owner-occupation. The Housing Associations Act 1985 gives a definition of a self-build society as:

... a housing association whose object is to provide, for sale to or occupation by its members, dwellings built or improved principally with the use of its members' own labour.

● The feature of **housing co-operatives** is that their members are the owners of the dwellings built. Arrangements are made to compensate a member for any depreciation in the capital value of the property, should he wish to vacate the property at any time.

● Special **government-sponsored housing associations** are set up from time to time, to serve a specific purpose.

The most common type of association is the general needs one; these provide housing for families, couples, single people and the elderly.

Housing associations usually provide self-contained unfurnished flats and houses of various sizes. New houses are built by housing associations, others are improved or converted. Some housing associations specialize in dwellings for certain groups:

Housing for People with Disabilities

Specially designed accommodation is available for people with physical disabilities, including wheelchair users.

Housing for the Elderly

Often specially designed housing is available and may include a resident warden and/or communal facilities for the use of tenants, eg laundry facilities.

Housing for people with Special Needs

These housing associations provide accommodation for people who for a variety of reasons require special support, eg mental health problems, ex-offenders, young people, leaving care, people with AIDS/HIV etc.

Self-build Housing Associations

Self-build housing associations were very much in evidence shortly after the Second World War and continued to be a way of obtaining low-cost housing. Once completed the dwellings are usually bought by the members and the association is wound up. The associations are non-profit-making ones.

These associations can start in one of two ways

(a) A group of people in the same locality may wish to improve their housing conditions and form themselves into an association, appointing a managing agent for administrative functions and raise funding to buy land or property and carry out the development; or

(b) a professional self-build management consultant obtains a site and advertises for members to form an association.

The funding of such schemes is usually through banks and building societies. When the individual members buy the completed dwellings, they then make arrangements to repay their share of the loan; the remainder being repaid through members' individual mortgages.

As the Housing Associations Act 1985 states, it is possible for members to rent the dwellings and in such cases the rent is used to pay off a long-term mortgage taken out by the organization.

Such schemes can be assisted by the Housing Corporation which has a statutory function to promote and assist the development of such an organization. The Housing Corporation can provide the smaller proportion of the total development money needed for outright ownership schemes and/or by providing Social Housing Grant (SHG) for shared ownership schemes development in conjunction with a registered Housing Association.

The development money is provided from a 'revolving fund' administered by the Housing Corporation and is used when 100% funding is not possible from private lenders such as building societies and banks. Such monies are only for associations not individual self-builders.

Self-build associations seeking funding must consist mainly of first-time buyers in housing need. Owner-occupiers will, however, be considered but only if they are in the minority and in housing need, such as substandard or dilapidated housing, overcrowded conditions or hardship associated with disabled or elderly relatives, or are able to contribute trade skills essential to the scheme.

Shared-ownership self-build

Shared-ownership self-build offers the opportunity for those self-builders who cannot afford full mortgage repayments. Here the self-builders own a share of the dwelling and pay rent on the remainder and are able to buy further shares in the dwelling until they own it outright. The initial share in the dwelling is acquired through the use of their 'sweat equity' together with an additional share which is purchased. This 'sweat equity' is the excess of the value over of the dwelling over the cost expressed as a percentage of the value.

Working closely with a registered housing association in order to get Housing Association Grant, the self-build association needs to ensure that its members can get mortgages for the share they intend to buy. At the same time, the registered housing association will be buying the freehold or leasehold of the land and enter into a development agreement with the self-build association.

Self-build for rent

Here again self-build associations work closely with a registered association which arranges funding.

Housing Co-operatives

Perhaps the most important of these types of housing association are the co-operative societies. The Housing Associations Act 1985 defines a housing co-operative as:

... a fully mutual housing association which is a society registered under the Industrial and Provident Societies Act 1965.

and it also defines 'fully mutual' as meaning that:

... the rules of the association:

(a) *restrict membership to persons who are tenants or prospective tenants of the association; and*

(b) *preclude the granting or assignment of tenancies to persons other than members.*

In effect, this means that a housing co-operative is:

- an association of people managing and controlling the houses in which they live; where

- each person has an equal say in management decisions and can stand for election to the management committee; and

- each member pays a fair share of whatever it costs the co-operative to provide and maintain the houses.

Housing co-operatives play a small, yet important, part in the provision of social housing. They have traditionally been centred in large cities eg, London, Liverpool, Glasgow etc, but have now extended their activities to suburban and rural areas. Co-ops are sometimes regarded as 'fringe' organizations providing dwellings for people who would not be rehoused through traditional housing routes.

There are various types of housing co-operatives and the main ones are indicated below:

Par Value or Equal Value Co-ops

These are perhaps the most widely recognized schemes in the co-op movement. 'Par Value' means that all the residents have a variable stake in the co-op. In Par Value Co-ops the residents collectively own or lease and manage their property.

Short-life Co-ops

These specialize in leasing and rehabilitating properties which require some rehabilitation and have a limited duration up to 10 years, eg, properties that are subject to Compulsory Purchase Orders prior to redevelopment.

The above co-ops can be divided into fully mutual and non-mutual co-ops. In a fully mutual co-op, all tenants must be members of the co-op. This gives the co-op tax advantages and also the ability to decide its own form of tenancy and rent-setting arrangements.

Non-mutual co-ops embrace the objectives of the co-operative movement but do not insist that every tenant or prospective tenant has to be a member of the co-op.

Self-build Co-ops

These are usually temporary organizations that provide a framework to enable participants to clarify their responsibilities and obtain the financial loans for the scheme. Once the properties are built the co-op is usually dissolved. These have, however, been experimental schemes where members have continued to rent the dwellings once they have been built.

Tenant Management Co-ops

These take over some or all of the management functions according to an agency agreement signed with their landlord (local authority or housing association). They do not, however, come within the strict definition of co-ops because the residents have no ownership or leasehold rights over the property. The management functions include administering waiting lists, letting properties, transfer requests, rent collection and organization of repairs.

Advantages of Co-ops

(1) offers residents more control over management functions than other forms of renting

(2) members of short-life co-ops have greater opportunities for participation in the future of their tenancies than they would in private rented accommodation.

(3) co-ops offer members a flexible administrative and management resource tailored to the communities needs.

(4) working in conjunction with professionals, co-ops can produce schemes which meet local needs; they are able to ensure that members views are influential throughout the design stage of a housing scheme.

(5) co-ops can form the basis of economic regeneration in run-down areas by fostering an identity for the community.

(6) although they tend to be small-scale organizations, co-ops are able to work with local authorities to meet specific needs.

Disadvantages of Co-ops

(1) most co-ops require the membership of all their residents as a condition of tenancy and so can be difficult to set up. This can also be a problem for local authority nominations; access to housing will depend not only on housing need but on nominees being prepared to participate in the co-ops 'philosophy', which may be a problem where there are language or cultural differences.

(2) any complexities that arise from nomination issues can result in longer void periods and additional work for local authorities. It may also mean that, at times, nominations may have to be considered from groups that are not necessarily regarded by the council as having a high priority.

(3) although, in theory, all members of co-ops can participate in the control of the co-op, management decisions tend to be made by a small number of activists. There have been criticisms that this lack of defined management structure does not offer the impartiality and objectivity of more conventional organizations.

(4) co-ops are not subject to the competitive element of the housing market and it could therefore be argued that members of housing co-ops have less choice than they would, for example, with a housing association or a local authority.

(c) that it can meet the financial and management standards required by the Housing Corporation as a condition of funding.

When co-ops do not meet the registration criteria, but have been identified as needed within regional strategies, the Corporation will allow those co-ops to hold an entitlement to a specific SHG allocation so that the co-op can select an appropriate development partner.

Housing trusts

Although a housing trust is not quite the same as a housing association, it is also covered by the Housing Associations Act 1985. The Act defines a housing trust as a corporation or body of persons that:

-    is required by the terms of its constituent instrument to use the whole of its funds, including any surplus which may arise from its operations, for the purpose of providing housing accommodation; or

-    is required by the terms of its constituent instrument to devote the whole, or substantially the whole, of its funds to charitable purposes and in fact uses the whole, or substantially the whole, of its funds for the purpose of providing housing accommodation.

Put simply, the difference between a housing trust and a housing association is as follows:

●   a housing trust is set up to look after the interests of certain specified people.

●   a housing association is set up to look after the interests of anyone who needs social housing.

Housing societies

Housing societies are also slightly different from housing associations. A housing society is defined in the Housing Act 1964 as a society:

-    which is registered under the Industrial and Provident Societies Act 1893; and

-    which does not trade for profit; and

-    which is established for the purpose of constructing, improving or managing houses, or where these activities are its sole or principal objects.

For these purposes, houses are defined as:

-    houses to be kept available for letting;

-    houses for occupation by members of the society, where the rules of that society restrict membership to those persons who are either entitled or prospectively entitled to occupy houses which it manages or provides.

In addition to constructing, improving or managing houses, a society may have as supplementary purposes or objects:

- the provision of land or buildings for purposes connected with the requirements of the persons occupying the houses provided or managed by the society;

- encouraging the formation of other housing societies;

- giving advice on the formation and running of such societies.

Societies with other additional objectives fall outside the Act's definition of a society.

The difference between housing societies and housing associations is very slight. It arises out of technicalities relating to their formation: a housing society is originally set up in a slightly different way to a housing association. However, for the purposes of your syllabus you may regard a housing society as being the same as a housing association.

The provisions of the Housing Associations Act 1985 also apply to housing societies.

Housing Association Finance

Like local authorities, housing associations need capital funding.

Housing association involvement in providing affordable housing expanded rapidly in the early 1970s. Before 1974, subsidies were given to housing associations from the Housing Corporation. These subsidies were annual contributions towards revenue and assisted in meeting the running costs.

In 1974, the financing of housing associations changed and capital grants (or Housing Association Grant (HAG)) were made as a lump sum once and for all payment. This HAG was calculated on likely annual costs of management and maintenance less rental income which was based on 'fair rents' (calculated by the Rent Officer) after the scheme was built. This was a very generous grant. In addition Revenue Deficit Grants were payable for any period when a registered housing associations expenditure exceeded its income.

Any profit made was placed into a Grant Redemption Fund (GRF) from which the government could claw back monies from housing associations.

The Conservative government in 1979 started to cut grants to housing associations in line with its general approach to social renting and public sector borrowing. Housing associations directed their attention towards low-cost home ownership schemes such as shared ownership or improvement for sale (IFS).

As much as 90% of the cost of schemes was funded by the public sector in the form of HAG and there was little incentive for housing associations to control costs because increased costs were met by increased HAG. The fair rents bore no relationship to the cost of the scheme.

Consequently the Housing Act 1988 introduced a new regime for housing association finance.

This was as a direct result of housing associations performing the role of local authorities and being the main providers of affordable housing. The capital grant remained but was calculated before the scheme was built unlike previously. Housing associations were encouraged to borrow from private lending institutions such as banks and building societies. By borrowing from the private sector, the public sector money went further. Rents, however, went up because of higher interest rates charged by the private sector.

Housing association tenants, who were in their homes before 15 January 1989, continue to be the secure tenants they were at the time and are subject to fair rents set by the Rent Officer; fair rents are reviewed every two years.

Since 15 January 1989, all housing association lettings are assured tenancies and housing associations are responsible for setting their own rents; they are expected to be based on an affordable rent but, for low income tenants, housing benefit kicks in. We looked at housing benefit in Unit 2. We shall look in depth at tenancies in the next Unit.

Some tenants were given the Right to Buy back in 1980 and this has been extended now to virtually all housing association tenants with the exception of those in rural areas. Grants have been introduced to help housing association tenants buy their current or another private house.

The 'improve for sale' scheme (IFS)

We have just referred to 'improve for sale'. This scheme is intended to assist housing provision and was introduced in the Housing Act 1980. It is also available to local authorities.

As far as housing associations are concerned, the purpose of the scheme is to:

● improve substandard housing;

● extend home ownership into areas of predominantly rented housing; and

● promote low-cost home ownership, preferably for first-time buyers.

The idea behind the scheme is that the previously run-down houses are improved and are sold at market value. Discounts of up to 10% are offered to prospective purchasers who are tenants of local authorities, new towns or housing associations and who have been so for at least six months prior to purchase.

Shared Ownership Scheme for the Elderly

Very often once people reach retirement age their dwelling is too big (their children, if any, having moved away) and the property is too expensive for them to maintain.

Various options are open to such people including the Shared Ownership for the Elderly. These are schemes to assist elderly people of limited income who have some money available and wish to buy sheltered housing (usually specially adapted accommodation, often with a full-time warden living on the premises or in the vicinity).

The schemes are organized by Housing Associations which build a group of homes, usually one or two-bedroomed flats or bungalows, with a resident warden and certain communal facilities. These dwellings are offered for sale on a 99-year lease to people of 55 years of age or over.

The buyers normally have a choice of buying a 25%, 50% or 75% share (or slice of value), depending on their available capital. If purchasing a 25 or 50% share, rent in addition to the purchase price is paid. No rent is paid where 75% (maximum share) is purchased.

A government grant is paid to the Housing Association which allows the sale to be on a shared ownership basis and so reduces the cost for elderly people with limited capital. Should the buyer need a mortgage, most building societies will give mortgages subject, of course, to the conditions they normally lay down for lending money.

The Shared Ownership Schemes for the Elderly have a resident warden or an alarm system in case of emergency. The occupants are responsible for the maintenance and repair of their own home. The Housing Association is responsible for the repair and maintenance of the building itself, the common areas and grounds, and for the management of the scheme as a whole. Occupants pay a service charge for these services. These charges vary between different parts of the country. The Housing Association is able to provide information on the annual costs of running the dwelling.

If a person wishes to sell the property in due course it can be sold to any person over the age of 55 years and the Housing Association will wish to have first option to nominate somebody from their waiting list.

Once the property is sold the vendor receives a share of the new sale price, less the Housing Association's costs, thus benefiting from any increase in the market value of the dwelling. Any mortgage outstanding will, of course, have to be paid.

Housing Association Tenants Guarantee

The Tenants Guarantee was introduced in the Housing Act 1988 which sets out the rights and services that 'assured tenants' can expect from their housing association. Although the concept was introduced in legislation, the Tenants Guarantee is not covered by law but has the full backing of both the Housing Corporation and the government.

Housing Association Rents

Rents for housing association tenants are fixed in two ways:

(1) for secure tenants (those entered into before 15 January 1989) these are fixed by the Rent Officer;

(2) for assured tenants, the rents are set by the housing association itself. Because the rent is generally the only income received by the housing association for managing houses in its care, it must ensure that it can cover:

  (a) repayments on monies borrowed to provide the dwelling;

  (b) cost of day-to-day management and maintenance;

  (c) a reasonable sum each year to finance major repairs;

  (d) an allowance for voids and arrears.

The rents charged should be rents that people on low incomes can afford, and housing benefit can therefore assist those who need help towards the cost of rent.

Assured tenants' rents cannot be increased more than once a year; any proposed increase must be notified at least a month in advance.

Rents for assured tenants can be dealt with in one of two ways:

(a) linked to an independent price index detailed in the tenancy agreement; or

(b) the housing association deciding on rent increases by looking at its own costs each year. A right to appeal to a locally-based Rent Assessment Committee exists.

The second method (b) is the more common method of reviewing rents.

Housing association tenants are usually responsible for inside decorations together with any damage they cause; the housing association itself is responsible by law for the structure of the buildings and for the repairs to the outside of the dwelling together with its plumbing, the electrics and the heating system.

The tenancy agreement should include all of the following items required by the Tenants' Guarantee:

- a statement that the association is registered with the Housing Corporation;

- a note that the tenancy is subject to the Tenant's Guarantee;

- the rent (with any service charge shown separately) and the arrangements for altering it;

- details of who is responsible for which repairs and replacement of furniture and fittings;

- the conditions of tenancy (the tenant's obligations);

- right to do repairs and be paid for them, if the association fails to;

- right to be consulted;

- right to information;

- right to take in lodgers and sub-let;

- right to exchange;

- right to make improvements;

- right of husband or wife to take over the tenancy on the tenant's death (a right by law);

- details of the security of tenure provided and the grounds on which courts can be asked to end the tenancy.

Housing associations are required to keep accounts like any other organizations, and below is a 'simplified' Income and Expenditure Account.

Income and Expenditure Account

Rents	Loan repayments
Revenue deficit grant	Management costs
(for pre-1988 schemes)	Maintenance costs
Interest	Major repairs provision
(payable on investment)	

Registered Social Landlords

The term resident social landlord is a new name for landlords that are independent – most are housing associations but there are also trusts, tenants' cooperatives and local housing companies. (These were all detailed in the previous unit).

Registered social landlords are now the main providers of new social housing.

National Housing Federation

The National Housing Federation was originally know as the National Federation of Housing Associations. This was formed in 1935. The Housing Act 1936 recognized that it was the 'central association' for the voluntary housing movement.

It is a non-profit making company limited by guarantee. It represents the independent social housing sector.

Housing Corporation

The Housing Corporation is a public body, currently responsible for funding for all new social housing provision in England. It has the responsibility for regulating housing associations together with housing companies introduced under the Housing Act 1996.

The Corporation was set up by the Housing Act 1964; the rationale was to create an entirely new social housing sector based on housing associations to fill the gap between the shrinking private rented market and the dormant local authority sector at the time. The Corporation was allocated £300 million for the development of cost-renting and co-ownership schemes by housing associations registered with it.

It has its headquarters in London and eight regional offices, employing approximately 650 staff. Its Chairman and an up to 15-member Board are appointed by the Secretary of State for Transport, Local Government and the Regions.

The Act states that its duties are:

> ... to promote and assist the development of housing societies, to facilitate the proper exercise and performance of the functions of such societies, and to publicise, in the case of societies providing houses for their own members no less than in the case of those providing homes for letting, the aims of such societies.

The Housing Corporation's mission is 'raising the standard for homes and neighbourhoods'. Its key aims are:

● to regulate to promote a viable, properly governed and properly managed housing association sector;

● to invest for the creation and maintenance of safe and sustainable communities;

● to champion a resident focus in the housing association sector; and

● to be a modern, customer-centred, forward looking organisation encouraging change in the sector.

Over the next ten years there was much concern as to the accountability of housing associations who were making use of these monies. As a result, the Housing Act 1974 extended the powers and responsibilities of the Housing Corporation. The government also hoped that housing associations would play a far greater role in housing policy, especially with regard to the inner cities.

The Housing Act 1974 spells out in more detail and in plainer language the general functions of the Housing Corporation:

... the Corporation shall have the following general functions, namely:

(a) to promote and assist the development of registered housing associations and of unregistered self-build societies;

(b) to facilitate the proper exercise and performance of the functions, and to publicize the aims of principles, of registered housing associations and unregistered self-build societies;

(c) to establish and maintain a register of housing associations, to exercise supervision and control over registered housing associations and, to such extent as the Secretary of State may require, to act as his agent with respect to the consideration of applications for the payment of grants to registered housing associations; and

(d) to undertake, to such extent as the corporation considers necessary, the provision (by construction, acquisition, conversion, improvement or otherwise) of dwellings for letting or for sale and of hostels and the management of dwellings or hostels provided by the Corporation.

The Housing Corporation also has the responsibility for ensuring that effective liaison exists between housing associations and other organizations involved in housing, particularly local authorities. Its mission is to improve people's quality of life through social housing.

This framework continued until the introduction of the Housing Act 1988. This Act marked a second turning point for the Housing Corporation. A new financial regime for associations came into being. No longer would housing associations receive 100% public funding for schemes and be insulated from development risk; the level of HAG would now cover only a proportion of a scheme's cost, on average, with the remainder increasingly to be borrowed from the private sector.

The government made it plain that, from this point hence, housing associations would be major providers of new social housing in England, taking over from local authorities, who were given the task of maintaining and managing their existing homes and the vital task of developing and coordinating local housing strategy.

The Corporation can fund a number of commercial bodies to build social housing and to regulate new organizations set up to own and manage the transferred local authority housing stock.

The Housing Corporation's role is to support the social housing sector by working with housing associations and others to provide good homes for those in housing need.

To summarize, the general functions of the Housing Corporation are to regulate, fund and promote the proper performance of registered social landlords.

Future development

The government intends to extend the function of the Housing Corporation. It is also clear from the Housing Act 1988 that the housing association movement is taking on at least part of the housing stock which is currently in the hands of the local authorities.

Since April 1989, the Housing Corporation's links with government departments have been strengthened. Now, not only can it act as a moneylender and as a watchdog, but it is also able to promote alternatives to council housing and can oversee the transfer of council assets.

The government's budget for the housing association movement, payable through the Housing Corporation, is known as the **Approved Development Programme (ADP)**. This ADP is agreed each year following the Budget, which gives the level of expenditure for the following financial year and indicative figures for the next two. This money is used for:

- rented housing;

- houses for sale, including incentive schemes and Homebuy;

- projects of mixed funding, involving both public and private sector funding;

- mini-HAG (a smaller version of the Housing Association Grant);

- mortgages etc.

	£ billions
1991/92	1.73
1992/93	2.37
1993/94	1.80
1994/95	1.52
1995/96	1.18

1996/97	1.06
1997/98	0.65
1998/99	0.60
1999/2000	0.56
2000/2001	0.56

The Approved Development Programme is agreed annually. The funding is determined by:

● the priorities and targets set by Ministers which shape the overall balance of the programme between rented accommodation and home ownership and other forms of provision to be delivered.

● the need identified by local authorities in their three-year strategic housing plans and coordinated decisions on local authority Housing Investment Programmes (HIPs) and the distribution of the ADP.

● the competitive bids received from associations based on the maximum level of grant.

More recently the Housing Corporation has summarized its role in relation to resident social landlords as to ensure that they:

● manage their affairs economically, efficiently and effectively, making responsible use of public resources.

● use their public funding to fulfil the housing priorities for which it was intended.

● maintain good standards of management and service delivery for their tenants.

● preserve their reputation for sound management and financial strength to enable them to continue to attract private funding for investment in social housing.

A high percentage of the capital programme administered by the Housing Corporation is now devoted to projects which, in addition to their housing purpose, have the additional benefit of supporting regeneration objectives, including work in designated renewal areas.

There has been much criticism of the Housing Corporation in recent years; back in 1997, a Labour-commissioned report (when Labour were in opposition) – the Millan Report – recommended greater regionalization of funding through government offices, based more on need. If the report were to be implemented, housing associations would negotiate directly with the government regions for greater input onto housing and regeneration initiatives. Such action would drastically reduce the role of the Housing Corporation. The criticisms of the Housing Corporation are:

● repeatedly inefficient in managing the housing association programme;

● not very accountable for its work;

● few appeal rights for aggrieved parties;

● local authorities having strategic housing responsibility should have more local say in distribution of resources;

- should be supervised by the Audit Commission to ensure consistent monitoring along with other public sector bodies and agencies.

You must remember that there are good points about the Housing Corporation as well, such as:

- the Housing Corporation has played an effective role in administering billions of pounds of grant funding a year and supervising registered social landlords;

- its supervisory role has, indeed, been praised by the Joseph Rowntree Report in early 1993;

- any alternatives are not as effective and because they are more general the special nature of the housing association movement and other registered social landlords could be obscured;

- the housing association movement is unique and requires a unique government agency to support it.

Housing Plus

The concept of Housing Plus was first promoted by the Housing Corporation in 1995, the purpose being to:

- create and maintain sustainable social housing;

- obtain added value from housing management and investment;

- build partnerships with stakeholders in communities.

The term 'sustainability' in housing terms means 'social housing that enjoys a continuous healthy demand for letting throughout its projected lifetime, without substantial unplanned expenditure'.

Sustainable social housing helps to ensure that investment in other social infrastructure (schools, roads etc) is met not underused or wasted.

The task of managing social housing has changed rapidly in recent years. This has been caused by:

- the emergence of concentrations of difficult-to-let dwellings;

- rapid deterioration of living conditions on certain estates;

- increase in numbers of homeless;

- increase in numbers on housing benefits;

- growing concentration of those who are socially and economically disadvantaged.

Social landlords now work closely with other agencies to support the letting of properties. Without proper planning, management problems could undermine the effectiveness of public investment in social housing and, more importantly in the last couple of years, the long-term viability of investment by private lenders.

Links and partnerships must be made with agencies etc. These links could include:

- improving education, eg adult/literacy training

- better healthcare, including links with residential and nursing homes for the elderly;

- benefits advice service and the creation of credit unions (co-operative organizations which consist of a group of people joined together to provide savings and loans facilities to its members rather than use loan sharks!).

Community action plans are an integral part of the Housing Plus Initiative. A community action plan is a natural extension of a business plan and establishes a way in which the dimensions of sustainability can be incorporated into social landlords' management processes at a community level. They should be regularly reviewed. It is necessary for the social landlords to consult with residents, local voluntary groups, etc.

There are five key areas that need to be addressed in any community action plan. These are:

- **Social and demographic mix in the community;**

    Social landlords need to develop processes for monitoring the letting of properties and produce sustainable balances taking account of:

    - tenants' ages

    - household type; and

    - socioeconomic groups.

- **Tackling social exclusion**

    Social landlords need to ensure good transport systems are available for access to employment, retail and leisure facilities, introduce training schemes for those lacking skills, assist services such as banks and shops to the area.

- **Tackling poverty**

    Social landlords should encourage access to benefits services, provide energy advice, encourage credit unions, endeavour to keep rents low.

- **Tackling multiple deprivation**

    Social landlords should encourage neighbourhood watch schemes, to reduce high rates of crime (especially burglaries and street crime), and health action groups.

- **Managing tenancies**

    Social landlords need to reduce conflict between tenants, otherwise anti-social behaviour can rapidly undermine the desirability of living in a community. To assist this social landlords need to:

    - have sensitive allocations and transfer policies to reduce conflict

    - access to a mediation service

- use of powers such as Assured Shorthold Tenancies and possession orders to protect the community from disruptive behaviour.

Involving the community in events assists social landlords. This can be achieved by involving the community in planning and managing services, setting up residents groups, forums and community-based newsletters.

Funding for the Housing Plus Initiative can be by way of grants from the Housing Corporation (Innovation and Good Practice Grants and the Social Housing Grants). Other money can come from charitable services, lottery funding, millennium commission etc.

7.5   New Town Development Corporations

The Second World War had created a desperate need for housing, following the destruction of some 200,000 homes and damage to some 3.5 million others. New Town Development Corporations were set up under the New Towns Act 1946. Generally each Development Corporation was given a target population, a target for induced growth and a date by which those targets should be met.

The Corporations were mainly active in the field of providing new houses for renting and were responsible for the letting and management of their own rented housing. Occasionally they built houses for sale, but more often they made land available to private developers so that they could build and sell their own houses. Strictly speaking, the properties provided by the Development Corporations were owned by local authorities, so to that extent the Corporations could be described as a part of the local authority system.

New Town Development Corporations were set up specifically to provide accommodation for people entering new jobs in the area. It is important to note that this is separate from the normal provision of council housing. Corporation houses were administered separately and businesses relocating in the area were often assigned blocks of the new town accommodation.

After two years a tenant had the right to buy his Corporation property, in exactly the same way as a council tenant and under exactly the same 'right to buy' conditions.

As we have seen, under the Local Government and Housing Act 1989, all the new town housing stock was transferred, either to the appropriate local district council or to a landlord approved by the Secretary of State.

Housing Inspectorate

Following the outcome of the Comprehensive Spending Revision in 1998, the Chancellor of the Exchequer announced the release of £3.5 billion for capital receipts. At the same time he announced the formation of a housing inspectorate within the Audit Commission. This had, in actual fact, already been suggested in a White Paper – *Modern Local Government – In Touch with the People.*

The government is determined that the Inspectorate would help to improve the management of council housing, set new standards for performance and guaranteee high-quality of investment.

The Housing Inspectorate is playing a key role in tying the resources local authorities receive to their performance under Best Value. Regular inspections and ad hoc reviews of 'failing authorities' are undertaken, together with setting new standards of housing management.

The Housing Inspectorate is an attempt to head off criticism from other rivals, government departments etc, who consider that expenditure on housing has not been spent wisely.

A New Financial Framework for Local Authority Housing – Consultation Paper

In July 1998, John Prescott, the Deputy Prime Minister, set out his plans for making use of additional resources made available for housing and regeneration as a result of the Comprehensive Spending Review. At the same time, the Deputy Prime Minister stressed that the current system of local authority housing accounting did not encourage efficient investment and by introducing resource accounts would put local authority housing on a more business-like footing.

In December 1998, the government produced a Consultation Paper entitled *A New Financial Framework for Local Authority Housing*. The main points in the Consultation documents are to

● put local authorities' housing accounts onto a more business-like basis;

● encourage more efficient use of housing assets;

● increase the transparency of the housing revenue account to provide clear and helpful information for councils and tenants;

● assist authorities in planning their housing strategy;

● bring council housing onto a more directly comparable basis;

● achieve consistency with central government resource accounting and budgeting;

● achieve consistency with resource accounting in authorities' other revenue accounts.

Housing Quality Programmes

In 1996 a report, *Investing in Quality*, proposed that local authorities and registered social landlords should be required, after consultation with their tenants and other service users, to produce and implement a housing quality programme, to obtain Best Value through the achievement of agreed service targets of quality and cost. To many, housing quality programmes were preferred to compulsory competitive tendering.

The key proposals in the report were:

- that each local authority and registered social landlord would produce a housing quality programme which would identify how its housing services would be delivered, and demonstrate how best value would be achieved;

- production of a housing quality programme would be a statutory requirement for local authorities. Following consultation with tenants and service users, they had to identify the costs of each element of the service, and describe how the service is to be monitored and reviewed in conjunction with tenants and other service users;

- there should be a statutory duty on local authorities to report as to whether standards and targets were met;

- the feasibility of developing a British Service Sector Standard using the principles of ISO 9000 to promote high-quality housing services;

- performance indicators currently used by local housing authorities and registered social landlords should be brought more into line with each other;

- performance indicators should be extended to take in more unit-cost indicators as well as measuring outcomes to test the qualitative aspects of housing services;

- national minimum standards should be introduced for all key aspects of the housing service for local authorities and registered social landlords.

Arms' Length Management Organisations

Arms' Length Management Organisations provide an alternative route for local authorities that wish to maintain their own stock. It gives them more borrowing freedom.

Tenants of ALMOs remain as local authority ones and are treated in the same way as other local authority tenants for housing benefit purposes.

Currently (summer 2003) there are 25 ALMOs in operation and they are responsible for managing and improving around 360,000 properties or one in eight of all their stock to decent homes standard.

7.6   Other Regulatory Bodies

We have seen that no single body has overall responsibility for providing housing in the UK; so far we have looked at:

- local authorities;

- housing associations;

- the National Housing Federation;

- the Housing Corporation; and

- New Town Development Corporations.

To complete our coverage of the main organizations involved in housing in the UK, we shall now take a brief look at a number of other bodies.

Architects Registration Council of the UK

The Architects Registration Council is a professional body which keeps a register of persons whom they regard as suitable to be consulted on matters concerned with the profession of architect. Anyone requiring the advice and services of a qualified architect can apply to the council for a list of persons practising in their area, however do not forget that an architect usually qualifies by taking examinations with the Royal Institute of British Architects.

British Standards Institution

The British Standards Institution is the body that sets British Standards for all kinds of items, not just those connected with house construction. It was formed in 1901 to coordinate the development of national standards. It monitors items to ensure that they conform with the relevant standards. As far as house construction is concerned, the importance of this body lies in the fact that it vets and approves the standard of manufacture of goods used in, for example, plumbing or electrical work.

It works with manufacturing and service industries, businesses and the government to facilitate the production of British, European and International standards.

Many of the standards are now linked to the Building Regulations. These specify that certain materials should conform to BSI standards. Any materials approved by the BSI carry the 'kite mark' of the institution, ie its own product certification mark.

Building Research Establishment

The Building Research Establishment was set up in 1821 and undertakes research work on the design and performance of structures, building materials, fire protection and prevention, and construction techniques. It is also concerned with heating, lighting and sound insulation of buildings and with improving these elements.

It was actively involved in giving advice on the Channel Tunnel.

It has recently become a private company after more than 75 years in the public sector. It remains the UK's leading centre of expertise on building control and construction, and the prevention and control of fire; this expertise is available to all in the construction and associated industries, from multinational companies and government departments to individual designers, builders and home owners.

Chartered Institute of Building

The Chartered Institute of Building is the leading professional body worldwide for managers in construction. It has pioneered the way in establishing, promoting and maintaining standards of excellence in the construction industry and now sets the pace on a global scale for the education and professionalism of those who manage the construction of the built environment.

Chartered Institute of Housing

The Chartered Institute of Housing was formed in 1965 and is chiefly involved in research and education. There are 12 regional branches throughout the UK and one in Hong Kong.

As an examining body, the Institute awards professional qualifications for those employed in housing practice.

It has issued various publications on housing and also monitors legislative changes.

The Civic Trust

The Civic Trust is the leading national environmental charity dedicated to enhancing the quality of life in villages, towns and cities where people live, work, shop and relax. It works with a wide range of partners and with citizens in their communities to deliver practical programmes and projects. It undertakes research and campaigns for changes in government policy and public attitudes towards urban areas.

House Builders Federation (HBF)

The House Builders Federation is the principal trade federation for private sector housebuilders and the voice of the house building industry in England and Wales. It has over 300 members, ranging from the very large to the very small. These members account for approximately 80% of all new houses built in England and Wales in any one year and include companies of all sizes, ranging from multinational household names through regionally-based businesses to small local companies.

The Federation is a lobbying body, dealing primarily with political and planning issues and with market forecasting. The promotion of brand new homes as a product is handled by the New Homes Marketing Board. This was set up by the Federation in 1982, but is a totally independent body engaged in corporate marketing.

The HBF has a national staff based in London and a regional staff at ten centres throughout England and Wales. It is part of the Building Employers Confederation, which represents employers in the building industry.

Housing Associations Charitable Trust

The Housing Associations Charitable Trust is a well-established and independent charity, run by trustees appointed by the National Council of the National Housing Federation. Its main aim is to provide grants and loans to housing associations and other charitable organizations who provide accommodation for people in housing need, to use for purposes for which statutory funding is not available. The trustees take a flexible view on the sort of projects they aid, but prefer to pioneer new ventures which could ultimately pave the way for statutory finance to follow. A large proportion of its funds are derived from city-based charities.

Housing Centre Trust

The Housing Centre Trust was formed in 1934 to work for the improvement of housing conditions. It does this through its bimonthly journal *Housing Review*, by a continuous programme of seminars and by published information through its bookshop and library.

The trust is particularly active in disseminating information about slum clearance, urban renewal, better standards of house design and layout, and a planned environment for better living.

National Housebuilding Council (NHBC)

The National Housebuilding Council, formerly the National House Builders' Registration Council, which was set up over 65 years ago, is a voluntary, non-profit making, non-political body made up of nominees from all interests concerned with private housebuilding. It aims to raise standards of new housebuilding by requiring all registered builders to meet minimum technical requirements, and will only register those builders and developers who can build to NHBC standards and who are financially sound. It works closely with the government and its technical research body, the Building Research Establishment, as well as standard bodies such as the British Standards Institution.

Repair systems are devised by the company and a warranty given when work is completed; the properties then become saleable and can be mortgaged. As such it is the world's leading warranty and insurance provider for new homes.

Many builders submit their buildings to the NHBC for building control inspection, as the NHBC is an approved inspector ensuring that Building Regulations are observed. However, when registered housebuilders submit each home for inspection by the NHBC, and if everything is to the satisfaction of the NHBC, then the property is given the 'Buildmark'.

Normally, only those houses with the 'Buildmark' are mortgageable; 99% of new homes are inspected by the 400 inspectors employed. These inspections are on a spot check basis and are carried out on average every three weeks; however, because construction can progress a long way between visits, certain faults may not be spotted. It is for this reason that the 'Buildmark' provides the purchaser with ten years' peace of mind.

Before April 1988, new properties built by registered builders were covered by a ten-year insurance cover. However, since that date new properties are issued with a 'Buildmark'. which covers against a builder going bankrupt after exchange of contracts, remedying of defects for the first two years and protection against major damage arising out of structural defects.

If a claim is necessary, a purchaser is required to pay an investigation fee of £100; this is to prevent frivolous claims and is returnable if the claim is valid.

The NHBC also issues a six-year warranty on converted and renovated properties.

Under the Building Act 1984, NHBC Building Control Service Ltd (a wholly-owned subsidiary of NHBC) has been designated an Approved Inspector. This means that the

Company has authority to inspect sites in England and Wales, and grant approval under the Building Regulations as an alternative to local authority building control.

Today some 21,000 builders are NHBC registered. Most of the new houses built for sale in the UK benefit from NHBC's services. Since the mid-1960s over 5 million homes have benefited from the protection the Buildmark provides.

Royal Institution of Chartered Surveyors

The Royal Institution of Chartered Surveyors has professionals involved in a variety of areas from the construction of major public buildings to surveying the sea bed! They offer strategic advice in the economics, valuation, finance, investment and management of all the world's physical assets.

It has four main roles:

- to maintain the highest standards of education and training;

- to protect consumers through strict regulation of ethics and standards;

- to advise global organisations, such as governments and regional boards;

- to publish market information and research.

Housebuyers and sellers can contact the Institution to ask how to find a suitable surveyor to carry out a valuation or survey.

The Royal Town Planning Institute

The Royal Town Planning Institute was founded in 1914. It is a membership organisation and a registered charity. Most of its members are fully qualified professional planners. Nearly two thirds work as planning officers for local councils. Others work for central government, for property developers and other organisations with significant landholdings, as consultants or as teachers and researchers in universities. The Institute works to maintain and improve standards of town planning. Town planning is the key to ensuring the best possible environment in which to live and work in cities, towns and the countryside.

Tenants Participation Advisory Service (TPAS)

TPAS is a national non-profit making organization for residents of social housing and their landlords. It provides training, information and consultancy services on social housing issues to members and non-members alike.

The Town and Country Planning Association

The Town and Country Planning Association is the oldest charity concerned with planning and the built environment.

Started in 1899, it campaigned to improve the quality of people's lives through effective planning, public participation and sustainable development.

The Town and Country Planning Association believes that:

● everyone has the right to a decent home in a good environment;

● the needs and aspirations of local communities should be reflected in planning policies;

● planning policies should promote sustainable development as a means of conserving natural resources and reducing pollution;

● effective planning creates economic, social and environmental well-being.

7.7   The Private Sector

In the private sector, the most obvious organizations involved in housing, apart from the builders, are the building societies. However, they are not the only ones. Financial help from the private sector can come in a variety of ways, as shown by the list below.

● Most people seeking finance for the purchase of dwellings obtain mortgages from building societies.

● In recent years, banks have also become major lenders of funds both to existing customers and to new ones.

● Insurance companies also lend monies for house purchase purposes.

● Surprisingly, some people still go to moneylenders for assistance.

● A number of people (especially from the ethnic community) borrow the money from family or friends to purchase a dwelling. For example, 13% of the Asian community buy their homes with finance provided by the family.

For various reasons, it is not as advantageous now to rent dwellings as it was at the turn of the century. In spite of this, the government is still endeavouring to supply a source of accommodation in the private rented sector by introducing assured tenancies and assured shorthold tenancies.

7.8   Compulsory Competitive Tendering (CCT)

The following paragraphs cover compulsory competitive tendering (CCT). However, this no longer exists and is replaced by Best Value. Although you must know Best Value for your examinations, it is useful to refer to some background, hence the next two pages or so refer to CCT.

The Audit Commission monitors and compares local authorities' performance. Using this information and through the appointment of auditors, the Commission promotes efficient management and better value for money among local authorities.

The Commission carries out a number of studies annually into how local authorities might provide better value for money. Individual auditors follow this up by identifying the savings available in particular local authorities.

One way of achieving 'value for money' was by compulsory competitive tendering (CCT), whereby local authorities could not carry out certain works through their own employees unless the work had first been exposed to competition. The in-house workforce had to meet a specified financial objective annually. CCT covered a wide range of mainly manual services: building, highway construction, maintenance services (eg refuse collection and street cleansing) and leisure facilities.

Research undertaken for the then Department of the Environment, Transport and the Regions indicated that competition produced a range of benefits, including greater responsiveness to complaints from the public, more effective monitoring of performance and clearer service standards and objectives. It also achieved average cost savings of 6%.

Compulsory Competitive Tendering was introduced by the Local Government Act 1988 and at the time was mainly aimed at services such as building maintenance and refuse collection.

In November 1992, the Secretary of State for the Environment announced the extension of competition to professional construction-related services (engineering, architecture and property management) and core corporate services (finance, computer, legal and personnel services). About 90% of construction related services were subject to competition, and for corporate services the figure was between 15 and 80%, depending on the service.

The previous government's consultation paper *Competing for Quality in Housing* suggested a progressive introduction of CCT for local authority housing management. The intention was to improve the quality of service for tenants to increase 'efficiency and effectiveness on the parts of the service deliverers together with a degree of involvement of those for whom the service was provided, were seen as essential to this end'.

Local authorities, even the small ones, had been discouraged from tendering their housing management in a single contract because this was seen as being potentially anti-competitive. Tenant involvement was crucial for the success of CCT but the tenants had no vote on the tender decision of the local authority. Compulsory Competitive Tendering, the previous government asserted, should not in any way jeopardize local authorities' ability to exercise central policy functions in respect of their housing. Local authorities were responsible for drawing up and implementing the strategy for social housing.

The government realized that CCT could not be introduced immediately for a large number of reasons:

(i)   authorities may have been considering Housing Action Trusts or Large Scale Voluntary Transfer;

(ii)   time was needed to encourage a market in potential tenders to develop;

(iii)   consultation was a lengthy business;

(iv)   proper internal accounting systems needed to be established

Deadlines for putting the stock out to tender varied 'according to the size of the authority and the nature of its stock'. Authorities had to be aware of the European Community Services

Directive which came into force in July 1993, requiring contracts in excess of £149,000 to be open to European competition.

If a local authority itself won the contract it would need to exercise separate accounting. It could not bid to undertake the work of another local authority.

Compulsory competitive tendering with regard to housing came in gradually from 1 April 1996 in England. The services the government had decided that should come under Compulsory Competitive Tendering were as follows:

- collecting rents and services charges, including arrears;
- arranging lettings (but not deciding who got a Council house);
- organizing repairs and maintenance;
- making sure buildings were kept clean and tidy;
- dealing with problems and complaints, such as noise and nuisance.

Tenants were asked their views on the services they received from the Council. The Council then decided how CCT services should be provided.

A contract that describes the services was drawn up and organizations were invited to bid for it. The Council itself could also make a bid.

A different part of the Council then judged the bids and gave a contract to the organization that offered the best value for money and quality of service.

The successful contractor (the Council or private company which won the contract) then had to provide the agreed services at the agreed cost. The contract lasted for up to five years.

If the Council won the contract, the Council had to provide the agreed services at the cost it promised when it bid for them. If the Council lost the contract, the Council would still be the landlord and would continue to:

- decide who got Council homes;
- set rents;
- decide how much was spent on housing, including repairs;
- make sure contractors delivered services to a good enough standard.

The new contractor provided the actual services for the Council in the way set out in the contracts.

Indications showed that fewer than 4% of council housing contracts were awarded to outside organizations.

Best Value

Best value is a new framework for the management of local authorities. It is about the delivery by local authorities of high quality efficient services that are responsive to the needs and aspirations of local people – the service users. This means that local authorities must review all the services they provide by the best means available. This must be done in consultation with the people who use the services and the wider community.

Best Value is central to the government's agenda for modernising local government as detailed in a White Paper entitled *Strong Leadership – Quality Public Services* which was published in December 2001. Local authorities have been required, since April 2000, to make continuous improvements to all of their services including housing. Best Value involves the following steps:

- a continuous programme of fundamental performance reviews looking at every aspect of an authority's functions over a five-year period;

- a local performance plan setting out what the authority is doing and what it will do to improve services the following year;

- national performance indicators for local authority services;

- independent audit and inspection;

- intervention by the Secretary of State in cases of failure.

The new regime puts a great deal of pressure on local authorities to ensure that they are delivering the best-quality services to their residents.

In making decisions about the services, local authorities have to prove that in their review and audit process they have carried out four key tasks. The review process must:

- *Challenge* – are services necessary and if so, in what form are they needed?

- *Compare* – how do they perform alongside other local authorities, private and voluntary sector and other public bodies?

- *Consult* – find out what the public wants and expects by consulting with local taxpayers, service users, partners and the wider business community and involve them in the setting of performance targets;

- *Compete* – local authorities must show value for money and consider fair competition as a means of securing efficient and effective services.

Local authorities owe a duty of care of best value to local taxpayers; targets have to be set and compared against national standards. The national and local targets, together with performance indicators, are set by Audit Commission and auditors judge the integrity and comparability of performance information.

Let us look a little further at best value and the housing services provided either by a local authority or a housing association.

Housing is a very important part of their work and the government wants to see it improve year by year.

All housing services are covered by best value even if a local authority has transferred its stock to a different landlord, it will still have certain responsibilities for housing. If a local authority still owns its stock, its responsibilities as a landlord include:

- repairs and maintenance;

- setting and collecting the rent;

- managing the tenancy;

- consulting and involving tenants; and

- allocating and re-letting houses.

If a local authority no longer has a housing stock it still has the following responsibilities:

- investment in private sector housing in the area in poor condition, home adaptations for disabled people and advice to help improve the energy efficiency of properties;

- responsibilities for homeless people;

- assessing housing needs; and

- housing advice.

Auditors will report whether local authorities have achieved best value and contribute to plans for remedial action (if necessary). Provision is made for the Department of the Environment, Transport and the Regions to tackle failing councils and expose services to competition. Local authorities will have to publish performance targets and agree a programme of performance reviews for all its services. The targets must be published in the Annual Best Value Performance Plan. In addition, the public are consulted in setting targets for service cost and quality.

Benchmarking is used to offer a robust guide as to how a housing association or local authority measures up as a landlord.

Savings of 10% are expected in running services as a result of Best Value.

Registered Social Landlords take the same rigours of the government's Best Value regime as local authorities and the objectives are to:

- strengthen the influence of residents over the design and delivery of the services they receive;

- deliver high-quality and cost-effective services;

- achieve continuous improvement in the services delivered to residents and others.

The processes to do this are:

- comprehensive service reviews;

- preparation of service statements;

- production of performance plans and performance reports.

Summary

In this unit, we have looked at the organizations and regulatory bodies that make up the greater part of the housing framework in the United Kingdom. You should now be able to list the main organizations and write brief notes on them.

In particular, the role of the housing association and registered social landlords generally have been examined in some detail, and you should be able to:

- define a housing association;

- make brief notes on the different types of housing associations, including co-operatives;

- be able to discuss the role of housing associations;

- write about housing association finance;

- make notes on schemes of mixed funding;

- explain the 'improve for sale' (IFS) scheme; and

- write detailed notes on Best Value.

8

TENANCY

Objectives

After studying this unit, you should be able to:

● explain the different types of tenancy;

● explain tenant participation compacts;

● describe rent control.

8.1   Introduction

Surprisingly, all land in England is owned by the Crown. When William the Conqueror arrived in 1066 and defeated the English, he made grants of land to his followers. These grantees became holders or **tenants** of the land.

The tenants created by William the Conqueror were known as tenants in chief (or tennants-in-capite). They in turn granted land to others in return for carrying out some duty. These mesne tenants would grant land to others and so on. The condition on which the land was held was called the **tenure**. Some tenures lasted indefinitely, others for a limited period. The duration of a tenure became known as its **estate**.

Those tenures whose duration is indefinite have become known as **freehold**. Those that last for a period of time only have become known as **leasehold**.

Tenancy is thus one form of tenure. The person living in a dwelling, or tenant, does not own it; instead he pays a rent to the owner, or the landlord. That sounds straightforward enough. However, to complicate matters, legislation has defined several different types of tenancy which we shall look at shortly.

The three requirements for creating a tenancy are

● exclusive possession, ie the tenant does not have to share with others;

● a 'term' – either a fixed period or rent paid at regular intervals;

● obligation to pay rent.

However there are exceptions even if all three of the requirements were met, eg service occupiers who are provided with accommodation for the better performance of their jobs.

If the accommodation is a fringe benefit or offered as an inducement then it is likely that a service tenancy will have been created and may be either a protected tenancy under the Rent Act 1977 or an assured tenancy under the Housing Act 1988.

Apart from tenancies, there are other ways a person can use premises:

- owner-occupier;
- tresspasser;
- licensee.

Owner-occupier

We have covered owner-ocupation in the early units of this study text.

Trespasser

A trespasser is one who occupies premises without any permission at all to do so. Squatting is a form of trespass and generally arises because of housing shortages. People may be forced to trespass simply to find somewhere to live. Many local authorities and housing associations consent to properties being 'squatted' for some specific time or until they are ready to be redeveloped/rehabilitated as this to some extent protects the property from being vandalised if it were empty.

Licensee

The term 'licence' means permission and licensee someone who is neither an owner-occupier nor a tenant. The classic example of a licensee is a person in a property which is either owned or rented by a member of the family, usually a parent. The non-owner or non-tenant is a licensee. Similarly a cohabitant is a licensee of his partner, if it is the partner who owns or who is the tenant of the accommodation in which they live.

A licence enables someone to use a property with permission but it does not give someone security of tenure under the Rent Act 1977 or the Housing Act 1988 because that right is dependent upon the existence of a tenancy.

Tenancies

The terms that you need to know about for your examination are:

- regulated tenancies;
- secure tenancies;
- assured shorthold tenancies;
- assured tenancies;
- introductory tenancies.

8.2   Regulated Tenancies

Most residential lettings by non-resident private landlords which began before 15 January 1989 are regulated tenancies under the Rent Act 1977; the letting can either be furnished or unfurnished.

A letting is not normally a regulated tenancy if any of the following apply:

- where the tenancy began on or after 15 January 1989;

- where the landlord and tenant live in the same house or flat and have done so since the start of the letting (ie a resident landlord);

- where the landlord is: a local authority, a new town development corporation, a housing trust which is a registered charity, the Housing Corporation or a housing association registered with the Housing Corporation;

- where the letting is by a university, or college or polytechnic to one of its students;

- where the letting is to be for holiday or business purposes;

- where the landlord provides board (ie cleaning linen etc, which forms part of the rent paid);

- where the rateable value of the property let is above the Rent Act rateable value limits of £1,500 (London) or £750 (elsewhere);

- where no rent is payable or the rent is a low rent (a low rent is an annual rent of less than two-thirds of the rateable value of the property on 23 March 1965 if the property had a rateable value then or, if it did not, the date on which it was given one).

Rights of a Regulated Tenant

Regulated tenants have certain rights which relate to rent and to security of tenure:

- it is a criminal offence for anyone to turn a tenant out of his home without a court order or to make him leave by intimidation, violence, withholding services such as gas or electricity or any other sort of interference;

- a regulated tenant cannot be evicted unless a possession order has been obtained from the courts and the courts only grant in certain cases;

- if a regulated tenant dies, his or her spouse will normally take over the tenancy, the tenant can, however, be succeeded by a member of the family who has lived at the dwelling by taking an assured tenancy (see later in the unit);

- a regulated tenant, or his landlord, may apply to the local authority rent officer for a fair rent to be registered. Once registered, the amount of the fair rent becomes the maximum that the landlord can charge until it is reviewed;

- even if the rent is not registered by the landlord the rent can only increase in certain circumstances;

- the landlord of a regulated tenant is usually responsible for major repairs to the dwelling;

- the landlord of a regulated tenant may be able to obtain certain house renovation grants;

- regulated tenants qualify for the housing benefit scheme where appropriate.

There are two basic kinds of cases where the landlord can seek a possession order from the courts.

(a) **Discretionary Cases**

In these cases the court does not have to grant an order for possession but it *may* do so if it thinks it reasonable.

(b) **Mandatory Cases**

In these cases the court *must* grant an order if it is satisfied that the case qualifies.

Discretionary Cases

1. The rent is in arrears or some other term of the tenancy has been broken.

2. The tenant has caused nuisance or annoyance to neighbours or has been convicted of immoral or illegal use of the premises.

3. The tenant has damaged the property or allowed it to become damaged.

4. The tenant has damaged the furniture.

5. The landlord has arranged to sell or let the property because the tenant gave notice he was giving up the tenancy.

6. The tenant has assigned or sub-let the property.

7. The tenant was an employee of the landlord and the landlord now requires the property for a new employee.

8. The landlord needs the property for himself or certain members of his family.

9. The tenant has charged a sub-tenant more than the Rent Act permits.

Mandatory Cases

1. The landlord lets his home with the intention of returning to live there again eventually.

2. The landlord let accommodation to which he intends to retire.

3. The premises were let for a fixed term of eight months or less, having been a holiday let at some time during the previous 12 months.

4.   The let was a student let for 12 months or less.

5.   The accommodation was intended for a clergyman and has been let temporarily to an ordinary tenant.

6.   The accommodation was to be occupied by a farm worker and has been let temporarily to an ordinary tenant.

7.   The premises were agricultural holdings occupied by an ordinary tenant temporarily.

8.   The property was let as a protected shorthold tenancy and the shorthold term has ended.

9.   The landlord was a member of the regular armed forces at the time the letting was made and always intended to live in the house at some future date.

There are two other grounds for possession which are not 'cases' as such. First, the court can grant possession if it thinks that it is reasonable and suitable alternative accommodation is or will be available for the tenant. Alternative accommodation can be suitable if:

● it is determined in a certificate from the local council, if they are providing the alternative accommodation, or

● if it gives the tenant equal or equivalent security of tenure and meets certain conditions about size, rent and other features. The second ground for possession is that there is statutory overcrowding in the property, as defined in the Housing Act 1985.

At the time of the passing of the Housing Act 1980 there were 400,000 houses in the private sector with controlled rents; under the Act these were converted to regulated tenancies whereby fair rents would be set irrespective of the condition of the properties.

8.3   Secure Tenancies

Secure tenancies give statutory protection to occupants of public-sector housing. When first introduced by the Housing Act 1980, public-sector housing included that provided by registered housing associations and charitable trusts; since 15 January 1989 such landlords have been unable to grant secure tenancies.

In order to qualify as a secure tenancy, a tenancy has to satisfy what legislation calls the 'landlord condition' and the 'tenant condition'.

● Under the **landlord condition**, the landlord's interest in the property must belong to one of the following authorities or bodies:

 -    a local authority;

 -    a New Town Corporation;

 -    an urban development corporation;

 -    the Housing Corporation;

- a housing trust that is a charity; or

- a housing association or housing co-operative.

- Under the **tenant condition**, an individual tenant must occupy the dwelling-house as his only or principal home. Where there are joint tenants, all must be individuals, and at least one of them must occupy the dwelling house as his only or principal home.

Both these definitions are taken from the Housing Act 1985.

Under Schedule 1 of the Housing Act 1985, there are a number of exceptions to these general rules. Although you may wish to look them up for interest, there is no need to commit the details of the schedule to memory. The most important exceptions are that a tenancy is not a secure tenancy:

- where it is a long tenancy;

- where the tenant is an employee of the landlord, or of:

  - a local authority;

  - a New Town Development Corporation;

  - the governors of a grant-aided school;

  and his contract of employment requires him to occupy the dwelling house for the better performance of his duties;

- where the tenant is a member of a police force and the dwelling house is provided for him free of rent and rates;

- in some circumstances, where the tenant is an employee of a fire authority;

- where the dwelling house is on land that has been acquired for development and the dwelling house is used by the landlord, pending development of the land, as temporary housing accommodation;

- where it is designed to provide temporary accommodation of less than one year's duration, to enable a person to move into an area and to take up an offer of work there;

- where it is designed to give private-sector tenants temporary accommodation while work is carried out on their homes;

- where the dwelling house is part of an agricultural holding and is occupied by the person who controls the farming of the holding (he may be the tenant himself or he may be a servant or agent of the tenant);

- where at least part of the dwelling house consists of premises licensed for the sale of intoxicating liquor for consumption on the premises;

- in most circumstances, where the letting is made to a student;

● where the licence to occupy a dwelling was granted by an almshouse charity. An 'almshouse charity' is a corporation, or body of persons, that is a charity and is prevented by its rules or constituent instrument from granting a tenancy of the dwelling house.

Under the Housing Act 1986, introductory tenancies are excluded. We shall look at introductory tenancies shortly.

Rights of a Secure Tenant

Being a secure tenant means what it says: secure tenants enjoy security of tenure. The security is very similar to that enjoyed by regulated tenants. In particular, you should note that:

● A secure tenancy cannot be terminated except by obtaining an order of the court for possession of the dwelling. The Housing Act 1985 lists several grounds for possession. The most important ones are:

- where the rent lawfully due from the tenant has not been paid, or an obligation of the tenancy has been broken or not performed;

- where the tenant or a person residing in the dwelling house has been guilty of conduct which is a nuisance or annoyance to neighbours, or has been convicted of using the dwelling house (or of allowing it to be used) for immoral or illegal purposes. The Housing Act 1996 extends this possession ground by including 'an arrestable offence committed in, or in the location of, the dwelling house'.

- where the condition of the dwelling house has deteriorated as a result of the tenant's neglect, or that of another person residing there;

- where the tenant is the person, or one of the persons, to whom the tenancy was granted and the landlord has been induced to grant the tenancy by a false statement made knowingly or recklessly by the tenant or by a person acting at the tenant's instigation. This last part was added by the Housing Act 1996;

- where the dwelling house had been made available for occupation by the tenant while works were carried out on the dwelling house which he previously occupied as his only or principal home;

- where the dwelling house is overcrowded;

- where the landlord intends, within a reasonable time, of obtaining possession of the dwelling house:

   ● to demolish or reconstruct the building or part of the building comprising the dwelling house; or

   ● to carry out work on that building or on land let together with the dwelling house and therefore treated as part of it; and

   ● he cannot reasonably do so without obtaining possession;

- where the landlord is a charity and the tenant's continued occupation of the dwelling house would conflict with the objects of the charity;

- where the dwelling house has features that are substantially different from those of ordinary dwelling houses and that are designed to make it suitable for occupation by a physically disabled person.

A further new ground for possession was added by the Housing Act 1996:

- domestic violence when the dwelling house was occupied (whether alone or with others) by a married couple or a couple living together as husband and wife and

a) one or both of the partners is a tenant of the dwelling house

b) one partner has left because of violence or threats of violence by the other towards

(i) that partner or

(ii) a member of the family of that partner who was residing with that partner immediately before the partner left and

c) the court is satisfied that the partner who has left is unlikely to return

Should a secure tenant die, then a member of the tenant's family may be able to take over the tenancy. The relevant section of the Housing Act 1985 reads:

A person is qualified to succeed the tenant under a secure tenancy if he occupies the dwelling house as his only or principal home at the time of the tenant's death and either:

(a) he is the tenant's spouse; or

(b) he is another member of the tenant's family, and has resided with the tenant throughout the period of twelve months ending with the tenant's death.

Under the Housing Act 1988, lettings by housing associations are now assured tenancies and affordable rents are determined by the housing associations themselves unless:

- the contract was agreed before the Act came into force (15 January 1989); or

- the tenant was previously the protected or statutory tenant of the same landlord (this excludes tenants of protected shortholds); or

- there is 'suitable alternative accommodation'.

Therefore housing association tenants who have signed their tenancy agreement before 15 January 1989 keep their existing tenancy and the rights that go with it. This tenancy would have been a secure tenancy and the fair rent would be set by the rent officer. This also applies when the tenant moves to another home with the same housing association.

All housing association tenants who signed their tenancy agreement on or after the 15 January 1989 have assured tenancies. Assured tenants do not have the right to buy except those council or new town tenants whose homes are taken over by a housing association. These tenants have an assured tenancy with a preserved Right to Buy.

Otherwise, secure housing association tenancies continue to be governed by the Housing Act 1985. This provides for succession to a further secure tenancy as of right. Should a protected tenant die, a surviving spouse, or partner living as a spouse, is able to succeed to the protected tenancy under the 1988 legislation, provided that he had been living with the tenant. Where there is no surviving spouse or partner, a member of the tenant's original family living with the tenant at the time of death and for two years previously can succeed him, in the case of an assured tenancy.

In *Sanctuary Housing Association v Campbell* (1999), it was held by the Court of Appeal that a wife who was the sole tenant of a maisonette was entitled to surrender her tenancy although her husband was living in the property at all material times.

The tenant was granted a secure tenancy of the dwelling in April 1990 which she occupied with her children and the defendant (whom she married in July 1995). She left the dwelling the following year allegedly as a result of violence. The tenant was housed elsewhere and gave her keys back to the Housing Association who in this case gained possession of its dwelling.

In another interesting case, the *Royal Borough of Kingston-upon-Thames v Prince* (1999), the Court of Appeal ruled that a minor could succeed to a secure tenancy under the Housing Act 1985. In this case, the local authority had let a house on a secure tenancy. When the tenant died in 1996, living with him at the time had been his daughter and his 13-year-old granddaughter. The daughter had lived there for only six months at the time of the original tenant's death and therefore was not a person qualified to succeed the tenant. However, the Court of Appeal ruled that the granddaughter (who had lived with her grandfather for the past three years) could succeed, with the property held in trust for her by her mother until she reached the age of majority.

Anti-social behaviour

The Housing Act 1996 provides that in cases of anti-social behaviour local authorities can apply under the Act to the High Court or County Court for an Injunction prohibiting a person from:

a)   engaging in or threatening to engage in conduct causing or likely to cause a nuisance or annoyance to a person residing in, visiting or otherwise engaging in a lawful activity in residential premises to which this section applies or in the locality of such premises;

b)   using or threatening to use residential premises for immoral or illegal purposes; or

c)   entering residential premises or being found in the locality of such premises.

This legislation is strengthened by the Crime and Disorder Act 1998 which gives local authorities and the police joint responsibility to develop local partnerships to tackle and prevent crime in consultation with the local community. The key themes of the Crime and Disorder Act 1998 are:

● prevention from offending by children and young people;

- local partnerships protecting against anti-social behaviour, sex offenders and drug misusing offenders;

- promoting public confidence.

In *Woking Borough Council v Bistram* (1998), the tenant and family were found to have subjected their neighbours to continued torrents of foul abuse, other forms of annoyance and nuisance. Possession was ordered because their anti-social behaviour was almost definitely likely to continue or even worsen.

8.4 Assured Shorthold Tenancies

In 1914, only 10% of the dwellings in this country were owner-occupied; the other 90% were rented. These proportions have altered dramatically, especially since the 1960s: 70% of dwellings are now owner-occupied. The government intends to expand the private rented sector, which represents only 10% of dwellings, but landlords have been reluctant, until recently, to rent their vacant properties, preferring instead to sell them into the owner-occupier market. In an effort to change this attitude, the government initially introduced the concepts of assured and shorthold tenancies under the Housing Act 1980.

The Housing Act 1988 brought about incentives for private landlords to let free of Rent Act restraints as to a fair rent. The assured shorthold tenancy was born replacing the shorthold tenancies introduced in the 1980. 'Market' rents are payable on assured shorthold tenancies subject to one appeal to the Rent Assessment Committee. The Housing Act 1996 reduced the right of appeal against the agreed rent to once during the first six months of tenancy. There is now no maximum initial fixed period for an assured shorthold tenancy. (Prior to 28 February 1997, the first tenancy had to be for a fixed period of at least six months with no power for the landlord to terminate the tenancy before this time; now there is no minimum period specified.) An assured shorthold tenancy cannot be created if, immediately beforehand, the person to whom it is to be granted had been an assured tenant of the same landlord.

Under the Housing Act 1996, landlords must provide in writing within 28 days returns of the assured shorthold tenancy including:

a) the date on which the tenancy began;

b) the rent payable under the tenancy and the dates on which the rent is payable;

c) any term providing for a review for the rent payable under the tenancy; and

d) in the case of a fixed term tenancy, the length of the fixed term.

Similarly the Act provides that when giving tenants notice it must be in writing.

When the fixed term expires, the landlord has a right to possession.

If granted on or after 28 February 1987, any assured tenancy is automatically an assured shorthold tenancy unless:

a) the landlord serves notice to the contrary;

b)   the tenancy agreement states that it is not a shorthold;

c)   it is granted to a person who was previously the tenant under an assured tenancy by the same landlord.

Rights of an Assured Shorthold Tenant

The court will grant an order for possession if the assured shorthold tenancy has come to an end and the landlord, or in the case of joint landlords at least one of them, has given to the tenant not less than two months' notice stating that he requires possession of the dwelling. During the initial term of a first shorthold tenancy, the tenant may apply to the Rent Assessment Committee for it to set a market rent. The Rent Assessment Committee will set the rent only if it thinks there are enough similar properties let on assured tenancies (whether assured shorthold or not) and the rent being charged is significantly higher for that tenancy than the landlord should expect in view of those other rents.

The Rent Assessment Committee is a body of independent people who have been appointed by government Ministers. They usually comprise two or three people – usually a lawyer, a property valuer and a lay person. There are six Rent Assessment Panels in England and Wales, these are in London, Cambridge, Birmingham, Manchester, Chichester and Cardiff. These Panels are independent of both central and local government. There is no appeal against a committee's decision except on a point of law.

Tenants who renew an assured shorthold tenancy must pay whatever new or amended rent has been agreed. If, however, the tenant considers the new rent payable to be significantly higher than what the landlord might reasonably be able to charge, having regard to other dwellings in the locality, he may apply to the rent assessment committee to have the rent determined.

Where the new rent has been determined, it is effective from such date as the committee may direct, although this cannot be earlier than the date of the application. No notice of further increase can be served until one year after the rent assessment committee's determination.

As with regulated tenancies, there are two basic kinds of cases where the landlord can seek a possession order from the courts.

(a) Discretionary Cases

In these cases the court does not have to grant an order for possession but it *may* do so if it thinks it reasonable.

(b) Mandatory Cases

In these cases the court *must* grant an order if it is satisfied that the case qualifies.

In the case of assured shorthold tenancies these are

Discretionary cases
The court may order possession where the:

1. tenant in rent arrears when landlord started possession proceedings or tenant persistently late in paying rent;

2. tenant has broken one or more of the terms of the tenancy agreement;

3. condition of the property has got worse because of the behaviour of the tenant or any other person living there;

4. tenant or someone living in or visiting the property has caused or is likely to cause a nuisance or annoyance to someone living in or visiting the locality;

5. tenant or someone living there has been convicted of using the property or allows it to be used for immoral or illegal purposes, or an arrestable offence committed in the property or locality;

6. ill-treating furniture in dwelling;

7. landlord was persuaded to grant the tenancy on the basis of a false statement knowingly or recklessly made by the tenant or a person acting at the tenant's instigation

Mandatory cases

The court must order possession where the:

1. property is subject to a mortgage which was granted before the tenancy started and the lender (mortgagee) wants to sell it, normally to pay off mortgage arrears;

2. tenant owed at least two months rent if the tenancy is on a monthly basis or 8 weeks rent if on a weekly basis, both when the landlord gave notice seeking possession and at the date of the court hearing.

8.5   Assured Tenancies

Assured tenancies, which replaced protected tenancies as the vehicle of statutory protection for private-sector tenants, were also introduced by the Housing Act 1980. Their purpose, initially, was to allow new dwellings (and now substantially renovated dwellings, under the Housing and Planning Act 1986) to be let by approved landlords (approved by the Secretary of State) at freely negotiated rents, with full security of tenure being given to tenants for the duration of their initial tenancy. Assured tenancies are now governed by the Housing Act 1988. Landlords no longer have to be approved by the Secretary of State.

An assured tenancy is held by either individual or joint tenants, who live in accommodation which is let as a separate dwelling and who use it as their only or principal home. The rent is a market rent which is agreed between landlord and tenant when the tenancy commences.

Although rents are freely negotiated, security of tenure is protected as at the end of the tenancy an assured tenant is entitled to a further assured tenancy. A tenant has the right to remain in the property unless the landlord can prove to the court that he has grounds for possession. We shall look at these grounds shortly.

A spouse has the automatic right to succeed to a tenancy on the death of an assured tenant. There is no right to a second succession and other relatives have no right at all to succeed.

Where no provision to do so exists within the tenancy agreement, any landlord wishing to increase the rent must serve upon the tenant a notice in a form laid down by the legislation. If the tenant is unhappy with the new rent and cannot agree any variation of it with the landlord, he can refer this notice to the rent assessment committee, who will then set the rent. Except in the case of a statutory periodic tenancy, no rent increase can take place within one year of the tenancy's inception.

The following are the exclusions detailed in Schedule 1 of the 1988 Act:

- tenancies created or entered into via a contract that was agreed before the Act came into force (15 January 1989);

- tenancies where no rent is paid, or the rent is less than two-thirds of the rateable value of the property;

- business tenancies;

- tenancies of licensed premises;

- tenancies of properties that include more than two acres of agricultural land;

- tenancies of agricultural holdings occupied by the person who controls the farming of the holding;

- student lettings;

- holiday lettings;

- tenancies with resident landlords;

- Crown tenancies;

- public-sector tenancies, including Housing Action Trusts and co-operative housing associations.

Rights of an assured tenant

When an assured tenancy comes to an end, it can be removed on assured terms on whatever the tenancy says or the landlord can, if the tenant agrees, replace it with a shorthold tenancy.

As with regulated tenancies, there are two basic kinds of cases where the landlord can seek a possession order from the courts.

(a) Discretionary Cases

In these cases the court does not have to grant an order for possession but it *may* do so if it thinks it reasonable.

(b) Mandatory Cases

In these cases the court *must* grant an order if it is satisfied that the case qualifies.

In the case of assured tenancies where the tenancy is for a fixed term and the tenancy is not at an end, the grounds for possession are exactly the same as for assured shorthold tenancies that we have just looked at. However, when a fixed term tenancy comes to an end the grounds for possession can be any of those we looked at (under assured shorthold tenancies) *and the following*

Discretionary cases

1. suitable alternative accommodation is available for the tenant, or will be when the court order takes effect;

2. the tenancy was granted because the tenant was employed by the landlord, or a former landlord, but he is no longer employed by the landlord.

Mandatory cases

1. the property was previously the landlord's only or main home and requires it to live in as his main home;

2. the tenancy is for a fixed-term of not more than eight months and at some time during the 12 months before the tenancy started, the property was let as a holiday let;

3. the tenancy is for a fixed-term of not more that 12 months and at some time during the 12 months before the tenancy started, the dwelling had been let as a student let;

4. the property is held for use for a minister of religion and is now needed for that purpose;

5. the landlord intends to demolish or reconstruct the property and cannot do so with the tenant there. (NB: This case cannot be used where the landlord bought the property with an existing tenant, or where the work could be carried out without the tenant having to move.)

6. the former tenant, who must have had a contractual periodic tenancy or statutory periodic tenancy, has died in the 12 months before possession proceedings started and there is no one living there who has a right to succeed to the tenancy.

Where the court makes an order for possession to enable the landlord to carry out demolition or reconstruction works, or in the case of a tenant for whom suitable alternative accommodation is available, the landlord must pay reasonable removal expenses to the tenant under the Housing Act 1988.

Where the landlord obtains an order for possession by misrepresenting or concealing certain material facts, the Court may order him to pay compensation to the tenant under the Housing Act 1988.

Tenants cannot assign or sublet the tenancy without the landlord's permission. Reasonable access should be afforded to the landlord to inspect and, if necessary, to carry out repairs.

Where a sole assured tenant, who is not a successor, dies and the tenant's spouse has been resident in the property as their only or principal home immediately before the death, that spouse can succeed to the tenancy. A tenant will be a successor if he:

- succeeds under this section; or

- succeeds by virtue of the previous tenant's will or intestacy; or

- becomes the sole tenant of a previous joint tenancy, upon the death of the other joint tenant(s); or

- had been a successor to an earlier tenancy of the same or substantially the same dwelling house as is let under the new tenancy.

A person who lives with the tenant as wife or husband will be treated as a spouse for these purposes.

Succession to a statutory or protected tenancy can be obtained only by a person who was a relation to the deceased tenant:

- a spouse or;

- someone living with him or her as wife or husband or;

- a member of his or her family resident with him or her in the dwelling at the time of and for a period of two years before the death (Rent Act 1977).

In *Harrogate Borough Council v Simpson* (1984), it had been established that the phrase 'living with him or her as wife or husband' applied to heterosexual relationships only.

This was challenged in *Fitzpatrick v Sterling Housing Association* (1997). The Court of Appeal ruled (by two to one) that a man could not take over his partner's tenancy of the home he had shared with his gay lover for over 20 years. He had given up his job to be his partner's full-time carer after he suffered a stroke. The appellant had argued that he was entitled to succeed to the tenancy either as a member of his family or as a person who was living with him as his husband or wife.

This case went to the House of Lords in 2000 and by a majority of three to two, the House of Lords held that the appellant was entitled to succeed to the tenancy as a member of the deceased's family. Under the established case law, family membership was not restricted to purely legal relationships. Family membership was categorised by 'a degree of mutual inter-dependence, of the sharing of lives, of caring and love, of commitment and support'. In legal relationships these elements were presumed; in de facto family relationships, the person seeking to succeed has to establish them.

The judgement is of limited impact as it concerns the provisions of the Rent Act. The House of Lords unanimously rejected the alternative argument that the appellant was entitled to succeed as a person who was living with the deceased as his or her husband or wife. Furthermore, family membership is defined in relation to secure tenancies in Section 113 of the Housing Act 1985 in such a way that same sex partners are precluded. The appellant would not have had a statutory right of succession if the tenancy had been secure or assured.

8.6   Introductory Tenancies

These tenancies were introduced under the Housing Act 1996. Under the Act, local housing authorities or housing action trusts are given the power to operate an introductory tenancy regime. This means that 'trial periods' are introduced for tenants. The trial period is the period of one year beginning with:

a)   in the case of a tenancy that was entered into by a local housing authority or housing action trust

    (i)   the date on which the tenancy was entered into, or

    (ii)   if later, the date on which a tenant was first entitled to possession under the tenancy; or

b)   in the case of a tenancy that was adopted by a local housing authority or housing action trust, the date of adoption.

If the landlord wishes to bring the introductory tenancy to an end because of anti-social behaviour or rent arrears the landlord must serve notice on the tenant. The tenant has the right to an internal review of the landlord's decision but if he is unsuccessful an Order for Possession of the dwelling must be processed and the Court must grant possession provided the landlord has abided by the formal procedures necessary to obtain possession.

A person can succeed the tenant under an introductory tenancy if he occupies a dwelling house as his only or main home at the time of the tenant's death and either

a)   he is the tenant's spouse, or

b)   he is another member of the tenant's family and has resided with the tenant throughout the period of 12 months ending with the tenant's death.

An introductory tenancy is not capable of being assigned except in those cases of succession referred to in the previous paragraph.

Introductory tenants have the same right as secured tenants with regard to the Right to Repairs (see next section).

In *Manchester County Council v Cochrane* (1999) the Court of Appeal had to determine whether an introductory tenant could defend possession proceedings on the grounds that the internal review had not been conducted fairly. In this case, the local authority had served a notice because of allegations of nuisance and annoyance to neighbours; the tenant claimed the internal review had not been conducted fairly.

The court held that a decision on an internal review may be challenged only by Judicial Review in the High Court. The tenant could not raise the local authority's conduct as a defence against possession proceedings.

Introductory tenancies raise the important question of human rights.

In 2001, a case was brought against Bracknell Forest District Council by two of its tenants claiming that the introductory tenancy regime was incompatible with several of the articles under the European Convention on Human Rights. It has been held that introductory tenancies were not a breach of human rights because the Housing Act 1996 gives introductory tenants the right to request an independent review of the landlord's decision to seek an order for repossession. Hence there was no case for making a declaration of incompatibility under section 4 of the Human Rights Act 1998.

If a local authority or housing action trust decides to operate introductory tenancies, then there must be information published for the general public.

8.7   Other Rights and Benefits

Other rights and benefits available to tenants include the following.

The Right to Repair (Private Tenants)

A Right to Repair scheme was introduced with effect from 1 January 1986 which permits tenants to execute works for which the landlord is responsible, recouping the costs from the landlord.

Under the scheme the tenant sends a notice to the landlord explaining the proposed works, why they are needed and the materials to be used. The landlord has 21 days to respond, either granting or refusing the tenant's repair claim.

There are grounds on which the landlord *may* withhold consent and those on which he *must*.

The *discretionary* grounds for refusal are:

(a)   The landlord's costs would be more than £200.

(b)   The landlord intends to carry out the works within 28 days of the claim.

(c)   The costs are not reasonably necessary for the personal comfort or safety of the tenant and those living with him and the landlord intends to carry them out within one year as part of a planned programme of repair.

(d)   The works would infringe the terms of any guarantee of which the landlord has the benefit.

(e)   The tenant has unreasonably failed to provide the landlord with access to inspect the works.

The *mandatory* grounds for refusal are:

(a)   The landlord's costs would be less than £20.

(b)   The works do not constitute a qualifying repair.

(c)   The works, if carried out using the material specified, would not, in the landlord's opinion, satisfactorily remedy the lack of repair.

Assuming the landlord accepts the claim, he must serve a notice specifying:

(a)   The date by which a claim for compensation must be made following completion of the works (which must allow at least three months).

(b)   The amount of the landlord's costs (ie those he would be willing to pay if he were to carry out the works).

(c)   The percentage of the costs that the landlord would be prepared to pay (at least 75%).

When the landlord fails to serve a notice to carry out works within the time limit specified in the notice in reply, the tenant may serve a default notice if the estimate for the works is less than £200. The landlord must respond to this within seven days, either approving or refusing. Once this has happened the tenant may carry out the works. Once they have been completed the tenant must submit a claim for payment within 21 days. The landlord can refuse to pay if he is not satisfied with the works or if the authorized materials have not been used.

Right to Repair (Council Tenants)

As part of the Citizens Charter Scheme, a new Right to Repair scheme was introduced for Council tenants from 1 April 1994.

The new Right to Repair is a scheme for Council tenants and makes sure that certain small repairs which might affect health, safety or security of tenants are undertaken quickly and easily. Councils have to carry out these repairs within a specified time period.

If the Council does not carry out the repair in time, tenants can request another contractor to do so instead. If the contractor does not do the repair in time, the Council will pay compensation to the tenants. The Council tells tenants which repairs come under the scheme and how long it has to carry them out. Repair times vary depending on the type of repair. For example, if the toilet is not flushing, the Council usually has one working day to come and repair it. Other examples are that it has three working days to mend a loose bannister and seven working days to mend a broken extractor fan in a bathroom or kitchen.

Tenants can get certain small urgent repairs done (up to the value of £250) if they are likely to affect health, safety or security. The are called 'qualifying repairs'. Qualifying repairs include:

-    unsafe power or lighting points or electrical fittings;

-    blocked flue to open fire or boiler;

-    leaking roof;

-    toilets which do not flush;

-    blocked sink, bath or basin;

-    leaking from a water or heating pipe, tank or cistern;

-    loose or broken bannisters or handrails.

The Council has a full list of repairs that come under the scheme and is able to tell tenants if a repair needed is included in the scheme and similarly how long it has to get the repair done. The Council must tell tenants how it deals with repairs that are not covered by this scheme.

Tenants should inform the Council what repairs need to be done and the Council may need to send someone to check the problem first. If the repair comes under the Right to Repair scheme, the Council would tell a contractor to do it within the set time. The Council will also send a copy of the Repair Notice it sends to the contractor to the tenant. This notice will show:

- the name, address and telephone number of a contractor who will undertake the repair;

- the arrangements made for the contractor to carry out the repair (date/time);

- what the repair is;

- when the repair should be completed by.

If the contractor does not do the repair in time tenants receive £10 in compensation. For every extra day the tenant waits the tenant receives another £2. The most compensation for any one job is £50. The Council will pay compensation unless the tenant already owes it some money, for example for rent. If money is owed to the Council then the Council will take away the amount owed by the tenant from their compensation.

Right to Manage

As from 1 April 1994, council tenants' organizations have the right to take over management of their homes; it must be stressed here that it is to manage their properties not take over the actual ownership.

Council tenants have usually been managed by the local housing authority which has provided services such as:

Collecting rents and service charges;

Organizing repairs and maintenance, and making sure buildings are kept clean and tidy.

Tenants' Organizations can take over various services such as:

Repairs	General repairs; inside and outside decorations; glazing; outside window frames; removing graffiti; fences; outside light fittings and rubbish chutes.
Services	Cleaning public areas; gardening; heating.
Financial services	Collecting rents and service charges; setting service charges and paying repair bills.

Tenancy   Letting vacant homes; taking action to stop squatting and approving
management   sub-letting requests.

This Right to Management scheme is part of the previous government's Citizens Charter Scheme and applies only to Council tenants, including leaseholders.

A Tenants' Organization can have the Right to Manage if it represents the views of all its members and does what they ask it to do. The Tenants' Organization needs to inform the Council in writing clearly detailing which homes it seeks to manage.

Training is provided by professional advice agency from the government's approved list; training will show tenants' organizations how to draw up a management agreement with the Council which will list the services to be managed. Furthermore, the advice agency will also calculate the money a local authority will provide to manage the Tenants' Organizations homes.

Voting is then needed to ascertain whether the tenants accept the management agreement; assuming it is a yes vote, the Council will then decide an operative date for the Tenants Organization to take over the management of the homes.

Right to Compensation

As part of the Citizens Charter Scheme, a new Right to Compensation for Council tenants was introduced for home improvements from 1 April 1994 under the Leasehold Reform, Housing and Urban Development Act 1993.

A Council tenant whose tenancy is ending may be able to claim compensation from the Council for improvements made to the home.

Where a tenancy ends because of the death of the tenant, or other special circumstances, compensation can still be claimed. Compensation will not, however, be paid to those buying their homes through the Right to Buy or Rent to Mortgage scheme, because improvements are not included in the purchase price in these cases. (We shall look at the Right to Buy and Rent to Mortgage Schemes in the next unit.)

The Right to Compensation applies to improvements that were started on or after 1 April 1994. The Right to Compensation applies to the following improvements:

- bath or shower, wash-hand basin and toilet;

- kitchen sink and work surfaces for preparing food;

- storage cupboards in bathroom or kitchen;

- central heating, hot-water boilers and other types of heating;

- thermostatic radiator valves;

- pipe, water tank or cylinder insulation;

- loft and cavity wall insulation;

- draught proofing of external doors or windows;

- double glazing or other window replacement or secondary glazing;

- rewiring or the provision of power and lighting or other electrical fittings (including smoke detectors);

- security measures (excluding burglar alarms).

Internal decorations such as painting and wallpapering do not qualify for compensation.

A claim for compensation can be made up to 14 days after the tenancy has ended. The Council will need to know:

- the name and address of the tenant;

- what improvements have been made;

- how much each improvement has cost;

- the date the improvements began and finished.

The Council will then look at the cost of the improvements and if financial assistance (a grant) was given to help make the improvements, the Council would deduct the amount the grant was worth from the cost of the improvements.

The value of any improvement will go down as it gets older and as more use is gained from it. The Council may give less compensation if it thinks that costs of improvement was too high or the quality was higher than it would have been if the Council had undertaken the work itself.

The Council may also adjust the compensation – up or down – depending on the condition of the improvement when the compensation claim was made. The Council can also take off any money owed to it by the tenant from the compensation the tenant receives when the tenancy ends. Up to a total of £3000 for any one improvement can be paid but no compensation will be paid if the amount is less than £50. Compensation can be claimed for:

- the cost of the materials (but not appliances) and

- labour costs (but not the tenant's own labour)

Tenant Participation Compacts

From the early 1980s the previous government encouraged tenant participation. Proposals for a national framework for tenant participation were laid down in a consultation document produced by the then Department of the Environment, Transport and the Regions in January 1999 and included in the document was the concept of Tenant Participation Compacts.

Tenant Participation Compacts are an agreement between tenants and their landlord, the council, about different ways tenants can 'be involved' in the decision making and how services are provided.

They are part of the government's agenda to modernise local councils in order to improve local services for people. We saw in the last unit how under the duty of Best Value, (which came into force on 1 April 2000), local authorities have to show that its services provide the best value for residents.

There are two levels:

- borough-wide areas or issues;

- estate or neighbourhood level.

These compacts set out:

- how tenants can get involved collectively in local decisions on housing matters which affect them;

- what councils and tenants want to achieve locally through compacts, such as better ways of working together, improving local services or a better quality of life; and

- how the compact will be implemented and checked to make sure it is working properly.

As a result of Compacts, councils now regularly consult and involve their tenants in how their homes are managed and consequently tenants enjoy better services and a better quality of life as a result. Compacts give both councils and tenants the opportunity to look together at how tenants can have a proper say in their housing services.

The timetable for the introduction of Tenant Compacts was tight; local authorities had to negotiate a borough-wide Compact from 1 April 1999, to be implemented by April 2000, and locally negotiated Compacts had to be negotiated in tandem.

The principles for successful Compacts are:

- the council and tenants must work in a collective equal partnership;

- tenant participation must be valued and properly supported;

- tenants decide how they want to be involve and set out their priorities;

- tenant participation must be resourced in order for tenants to be involved at whatever level they choose.

Core standards ensure tenants participate and are involved in 'defining local problems and issues, deciding priorities and planning and implementing local solutions and initiatives'.

The core standards cover a number of areas. They include:

- services should be efficient and responsive and reflect local needs and priorities;

- tenants should be involved from an early stage in the decision-making process;

- the council shows its commitment to tenant participation public by publishing its tenant participation policies and strategies;

- tenants and the council agree a budget for tenant participation and the implementation of Tenant Participation Compacts;

- communication is tailored to tenants' needs;
- tenants' groups have to meet the council's formal and published recognition criteria;
- tenants and the council agree performance standards and monitoring arrangements;
- specified range of services covered by Tenant Participation Compacts. These are:
    1. the council's housing policy and strategy, identifying investment options, monitoring and review;
    2. capital works and renovation programmes;
    3. regeneration and improvement programmes;
    4. budgets, finance, rent setting;
    5. allocations and lettings policies;
    6. housing management services;
    7. tenancy agreements and decisions;
    8. leaseholder issues and charges;
    9. anti-social behaviour policies;
    10. setting targets and indicators, monitoring and reviewing service performance and agreeing remedial action if standards are not met;
    11. neighbourhood issues that affect tenants' homes and management of the housing service;
    12. environmental works;
    13. customer care.

Under the Local Government Act 1999 and standards set out in the *National Framework for Tenant Participation Compacts* (1999), there are national benchmarks for Tenant Participation Compacts. In addition there is a need to have systems to deal with complaints and disputes with regard to Tenant Participation. Tenant Participation Compacts must be regularly reviewed and monitored. Tenant Participation Compacts will form part of the assessment of the Council's performance.

Rent Control

Rent control is the restriction, or holding down, of rents. Landlords want to charge as high a rent as possible. However, they cannot be allowed to overcharge as they might try to do because, for example, of a shortage of accommodation. Legislation controlling otherwise unsupervised, and probably substantial, rent increases is called rent control.

Rent control and legislation

Since the beginning of the last century, a considerable body of legislation that relates to housing has developed. Some of it deals with rent control. Since your syllabus states specifically that a detailed knowledge of rent control legislation will not be required, the summary given below should provide you with all the information you need to know.

- Rent and Mortgage Interest (War Restrictions) Act 1915

  This Act fixed rents (mainly at levels existing in August 1914) and gave tenants some security against eviction.

- Housing Act 1930 (the Greenwood Act)

  The Greenwood Act encouraged local authorities to use their subsidies for rent rebates for the first time to assist poorer tenants in paying rents.

- Rent and Mortgage Interest (War Restrictions) Act 1939

  This Act brought rents under control and provided security for tenure (in a similar way to the 1915 legislation).

- Rent Act 1957

  The intention behind this Act was that the better privately-owned houses should be freed from rent control, creating an incentive for the poorer houses to be repaired and improved so that they too could escape rent control. The effects of the Act varied widely from place to place.

- Rent Act 1965

  The idea of 'fair rents' was introduced.

- Housing (Finance) Act 1972

  - Local authorities lost the power to charge 'reasonable' rents. Instead they were obliged to charge 'fair rents'. Consequently rent rebate schemes were made mandatory.

  - Rent allowances were made available to private tenants living in unfurnished accommodation and to housing association tenants.

  - Housing associations also became eligible for subsidies, but were obliged to apply the 'fair rents' concept.

- Rent Act 1974

  This Act gave security of tenure to tenants in furnished dwellings.

- Housing Rents and Subsidies Act 1975

  This Act repeals the controversial parts of the Housing (Finance) Act 1972, concerning reasonable and fair rents.

- Rent Act 1977

  This consolidating Rent Act is the one currently in force.

- Housing Act 1980

Assured and shorthold tenancies were introduced.

- Housing and Planning Act 1986

  This Act extended assured tenancies to include not only new buildings, but also those that had been substantially renovated.

- Housing Act 1988

  This Act saw the phasing out of rent controls and the further extension of assured and assured shorthold tenancies.

- Housing Act 1996

  This Act made further amendments to assured shorthold tenancies.

Fair rents

A fair rent is calculated by a Rent Officer or Rent Assessment Committee under the Rent Act 1977.

The Rent Officer acts independently of central or local government in fixing 'fair rents'.

The Rent Officer or the Rent Assessment Committee must consider all the circumstances, together with the state of repair of the house or flat, its character, locality and age, how much furniture is provided and what it is like. The Rent Officer or the Rent Assessment Committee must assume that the demand for similar houses or flats available for letting in that particular area does not greatly exceed supply; ie that the rent would not be forced up by shortage. Note, however, that the personal circumstances of the landlord and tenant are disregarded.

Summary

In this unit, we have looked at the very important topic of tenancy and considered the different types of tenancy: regulated, secure, assured shorthold and assured. Legislation plays a key role in this part of the syllabus. We have also looked at other rights and benefits; however, you should remember that a detailed knowledge of rent control legislation is not required.

9

THE RIGHT TO BUY

Objectives

After studying this unit, you should be able to:

- define the 'right to buy';
- state who has and who has not got the right to buy;
- explain how the right to buy works, quoting rules and figures;
- outline the concept of 'rent to mortgage'.

9.1   Introduction

The sale of council houses has existed since the first council houses were built in 1919 with local authorities selling houses to better off tenants. Some, but not all, local authorities offered discounts but the number of dwellings sold was very few. Discounts were introduced back in 1957 under the Housing Act of that year. However, you need to note here that council tenants could not demand the right to buy, as councils only had a discretionary right to sell. The former Greater London Council and Birmingham City Council, when they were both Conservative controlled found that there was a very keen interest from council tenants to purchase their properties. Consequently in their manifesto in 1979, the Conservative Party promised to introduce a statutory right for tenants. This statutory right was forced upon councils including those that did not wish to sell, notably the London Borough of Islington and the London Borough of Camden.

The right to buy scheme itself is targeted at well established public sector tenants. As we work through this unit we shall see that the scheme is open to virtually any secure tenant who can afford to buy with the exception of dwellings occupied in connection with their employment and housing specially provided for the elderly and in certain cases the disabled.

It has helped about 1.5m council tenants in England (1.85m in Great Britain) to realise their aspirations to own their own homes. In many cases, it has encouraged more affluent tenants to remain in the neighbourhoods they have lived in for many years, helping to create stable, mixed communities.

It has led to the removal of more desirable homes from the social rented sector, leaving local authorities with a smaller stock of poorer quality properties in which to house people who need help. It has also led to many thousands facing difficulties in meeting the costs of maintaining their homes.

The sale of council dwellings means a saving in the council's repair bills and management costs, although it can be argued that it becomes less efficient to manage the remaining council stock because of the 'pepper potting' effect, ie the scattering of those left in the council's ownership. The council does, of course, lose the rental income and any housing subsidy that may be payable.

Most sales of council dwellings are financed from building societies and banks and, therefore, the council receives the sale price at one go; this income is known as a capital receipt and as mentioned in Unit 1, 75% of capital receipts have to be allocated to the redemption of debt charges across the whole range of council services.

Many of the properties sold under the right to buy have been sold for far more than the original debt on the house, eg an average three bed council house built in the 1950s cost just £1,000! Needless to say the council properties which sold first were the houses on the most attractive and desirable estates in addition the houses had gardens, unlike flats. Flats proved difficult to sell even with the enormous discounts available. Those who have purchased their council houses have tended to be the better off tenants in secure and reasonably well paid jobs. In the 21st century, those remaining in council accommodation tend to be elderly tenants and very young tenants with families and who are on low income.

The Housing Act 1980 was the Act that introduced the phrase 'the right to buy'. It is a phrase widely used in housing today. Subsequent pieces of legislation, namely the Housing and Building Control Act 1984, the consolidated Housing Act 1985, the Housing and Planning Act 1986, the Housing Act 1988, the Local Government and Housing Act 1989 and the Leasehold Reform, Housing and Urban Development Act 1993, have amended parts of the 1980 legislation with regard to discounts and so forth, as part of the Conservative government's continued policy to sell off publicly-owned dwellings.

At the time of passing the Housing Act 1980, the government tried to extend the legislation to include housing associations being allowed to sell dwellings under the right to buy. However, many housing associations had been set up as charities and as such had both legal and moral issues to address if selling properties to tenants. Because of the opposition, at the time, only non-charitable associations could sell dwellings to tenants and even then only if it did not conflict with the association's trust.

So between the passing of the Housing Act 1980 and 1984 only just over 5,000 housing association dwellings were sold compared to 625,000 council dwellings during that period.

As we work through this unit, we shall see how schemes were devised to assist housing association tenants purchase dwellings.

Most people know that the right to buy means broadly that public-sector tenants are entitled to buy their own homes. But does every public sector tenant have the right to buy? How does a tenant go about exercising his right, assuming he has it? What legal pitfalls await tenants who choose to exercise their right to buy? The detail which underpins the right to buy concept forms the subject of this unit.

9.2   Definition of the Right to Buy

The Housing Act 1980 does not waste words. Part of the preamble states that it is:

> *... an Act to give security of tenure, and the right to buy their homes, to tenants of local authorities and other bodies ...*

The very first section of part one defines the position thus:

> *A secure tenant has the right:*
>
> *(a)   if the dwelling house is a house, to acquire the freehold of the dwelling house;*
>
> *(b)   if the dwelling house is a flat, to be granted a long lease of the dwelling house.*

This definition summarizes the right to buy very neatly. However, there are occasions when the right to buy does not arise.

9.3   Exceptions to the Right to Buy

The following types of dwellings and tenancies are excluded from the right to buy:

1.   Sheltered housing for the elderly, the physical disabled, the mentally ill or the mentally disabled. There are special rules that must be met in these cases.

2.   Homes that were first let before 1 January 1990 and which are particularly suitable for occupation by elderly people and had been let to be lived in by someone aged 60 or more.

3.   Houses and flats on land that has been bought for development and which are being used as temporary housing before the land is developed.

4.   The tenancies of employees who have to live in homes owned by their employers so that they could be near to their place of employment.

5.   The tenancies of employees whose home is inside the boundary of a school, a social service home, another type of operational building or a cemetery.

6.   The tenancies of members of a police force whose homes had been provided free from rent and rates.

7.   The tenancies of fire authority employees who have to live near to the fire station they work in and whose homes had been provided by the employer.

*8. Temporary lettings (of up to three years) of homes usually let to the employees mentioned in 4, 6 or 7 above.

9. Some homes that are let as part of a business or agricultural premises, eg public houses, farms, shops.

10. Homes that the landlord has leased from someone else and which have to be given up empty when the owner wants them.

11. Almshouses.

12. Houses that are let by a charitable registered social landlord, a charitable housing trust or association, by certain co-operative housing associations, or by housing associations or other registered social landlord that have not received grants from public funds.

*13. Tenancies given to students so they can follow certain full time courses at a university or college. This rule does not apply if a tenancy continues for more than six months after the tenants stop attending the course.

*14. The tenancies of people moving into the area from another district to take up a job and given a home temporarily while they look for a permanent home. This rule does not apply if the tenants are still living there after one year.

15. Tenancies given to homeless people under the Housing Act 1996.

16. The tenancies of people who used to be squatters but have now been given a licence to occupy a home.

17. Long fixed-term leases (of over 21 years).

18. Temporary lettings to people who were not secured tenants in their previous homes which are being improved or repaired for them to be returned to.

* for exclusions 8, 13 and 14 to count the tenant must be notified before the start of the tenancy.

9.4 Who Has the Right to Buy?

The Housing Act 1980 contains a good deal of complicated and interrelated information on exactly who has the right to buy. Most of the complications are beyond the scope of your syllabus. However, you should remember the following points:

● the tenancy must be secure;

● the tenant must rent from certain specified landlords;

● certain time conditions must be satisfied.

Specified Landlords

In order to qualify for the right to buy, tenants must rent their homes from one of the landlords listed below.

- landlords whose tenants qualify for the right to buy;

- a district council;

- a London borough council;

- a non-charitable housing association of other registered social landlord; or

- a Housing Action Trust.

There are certain other bodies from which a tenant may purchase but you, for your examinations, only need to be aware of the above.

Time Conditions

To qualify for the right to buy, a tenant must have spent at least two years with his present landlord or with another specified landlord. Alternatively, he must at present rent from a specified landlord but in the past have been a tenant of one of various public bodies for at least two years.

The qualifying period for discount can include time spent in different homes with different landlords and this does not have to be continuous. There are numerous bodies who cannot sell properties, eg British Waterways, British Airports Authority, Water Authorities etc, but the length of tenancies with these before becoming a local authority tenant count towards the two-year qualifying period and discount.

Under the Housing Act 1980, there is a further time condition where a tenant wishes to buy his home in co-operation with his family.

> *A secure tenant may ... require that not more than three members of his family who are not joint tenants but occupy the dwelling house as their only or principal home should share the right to buy with him; but he may validly do so in the case of any such member only if:*
>
> *(a) that member is his spouse or has been residing with him throughout the period of 12 months ending with the giving of the notice; or*
>
> *(b) the landlord consents.*

The Housing Act 1980 also provided that for a deposit of £100 (refundable), a tenant could exercise his right to buy but defer completion for up to two years.

9.5   Discounts

So far, we have looked at the definition of the right to buy, at who does and who does not possess the right to buy and at the exceptions where the right to buy does not arise. But does the right to buy offer any particular incentive to council tenants to buy their homes? Apart from the usual one of wanting to become an owner-occupier, is there any other reason why a tenant should choose to exercise his right to buy?

In fact, the right to buy offers a very tempting incentive to tenants in the form of discounts on the house price. The rules governing how much discount a tenant can receive are fairly complicated. These are the more important provisions.

- For houses, the discount is 32% after two years, increasing by 1% for each subsequent year up to a maximum of 60% for a qualifying period of 30 years or more.

- For flats and maisonettes, the discount is 44% after two years, increasing by 2% for each subsequent year up to a maximum of 70% for a qualifying period of 15 years or more.

- Maximum discounts under the right to buy were revised in 1999 (under a Statutory Order) to a maximum of £38,000 for London and the South East down to £22,000 in the North East.

- In March 2003, under a Statutory Order, the maximum right to buy discount available to tenants was lowered from £38,000 (£34,000 in one area) to £16,000 in 41 local authority areas. These areas were judged to be under the greatest housing market pressure as evidenced by high levels of homelessness (reflecting high demand for social housing) and high local house prices (reflecting the demand for social housing) and high local house prices (reflecting the demand for private housing and affordability). The government has emphasised that it does not wish to reduce the discounts available to tenants unless there is clear evidence of housing pressure.

- Where a property bought under the right to buy is resold within three years, the discount is repayable on a sliding scale, which reduces by one third each year. There are exceptions to the repayment of discounts when the property is sold under the Matrimonial Causes Act 1983, Inheritance (Provisions for Family and Dependents) Act 1975 or the Children Act 1989.

9.6   Exercising the Right to Buy

Should a secure tenant decide that he wants to exercise his right to buy, he notifies his landlord on a form RTB 1. The landlord then has four weeks or, in certain circumstances, eight weeks in which to reply to the RTB1. Either he must accept the tenant's application or he must state why he is not accepting it. This response is made on a form RTB 2.

Once the right to buy has been established, either because he has accepted it or because he has been obliged to accept it, the landlord has a further eight weeks (or occasionally 12 weeks) in which to tell the tenant the price of the dwelling and the terms on which it can be bought. This price will be the amount that the dwelling would command on the open market at the relevant time, less the discount to which the tenant is entitled. The notification by the landlord is called a Section 125 notice, because it is provided for in section 125 of the Housing Act 1985.

The Section 125 Notice sets out important issues to the prospective buyer. The notice:

- describes the property to be purchased;

- states the price – this is done by calculating what the home was worth at the date of the application then deducting the discount;

- details service charges or improvement costs to be paid for;

- describes any structural defects the landlord knows about;

- details terms and conditions;

- tells the prospective purchaser about the government initiatives of Rent to Mortgage.

Once these preliminaries have been completed, the tenant goes about the purchase in the usual way. He commissions a structural survey if he wants to and applies for a mortgage. This application may or may not be made through the landlord.

In due course, the transaction is completed. The tenant becomes an owner-occupier. Now he must stay in his new home for at least three years, or be obliged to pay back all or part of whatever discount he has received except as stated earlier.

9.7   Other Legislation

One important provision of the 1980 Act that we have not yet mentioned is section 23, which gave the Secretary of State the power to intervene; this is now section 164 of the Housing Act 1985.

Under this section, the Secretary of State may use his powers to order done anything that he believes a housing authority should have done, and to charge the authority with any costs arising out of its default, where it appears to him that tenants generally, a tenant or tenants of a particular landlord, or tenants of a particular type of landlord, may be having difficulty in exercising the right to buy. These powers may be exercised only after he has given the landlord or landlords notice, in writing, of his intention to do so and, while the notice is in force, such a notice shall be deemed to be given 72 hours after it has been sent.

As well as the originating Housing Act 1980 (since consolidated into the Housing Act 1985), five other Acts have affected the right to buy. These are:

- the Housing and Building Control Act 1984;

- the Housing and Planning Act 1986;

- the Housing Act 1988;

- the Local Government and Housing Act 1989;

- the Leasehold Reform, Housing and Urban Development Act 1993.

The Housing and Building Control Act 1984 made several important changes to the right to buy scheme.

- It reduced the right to buy qualification period from three years to two years.

- It increased the maximum discount allowable on houses to 60% after 30 years of qualifying tenancy.

- It introduced the idea of a public-sector tenancy, which enabled tenants to include in the qualification periods any time spent as tenants of landlords not previously included, such as British Airways, British Airports Authority, Water Authorities etc.

- In certain circumstances, the right to buy was extended to include dwellings where the landlord had only a leasehold interest.

- New guidelines were set as to whether tenants in disabled, sheltered and non-sheltered accommodation for the elderly could exercise the right to buy.

- It introduced the right of council tenants to purchase a shared ownership in their property.

The Housing and Planning Act 1986 included a number of significant provisions.

- It prevented the right to buy where the relevant dwelling was particularly suitable for persons of pensionable age and was let either to such a person or to a physically disabled person.

- It increased the discount rates for flats and maisonettes to the present 44%-70% range. It also provided for the present 2% annual increase in discount for each completed year of tenancy, up to a maximum of 70% for 15 years' qualifying tenancy. Note that this is only in respect of flats and maisonettes.

- It reduced the period during which there is a liability to pay the discount from five years to three years.

- It introduced the £35,000 limit on discounts. (In March 1989, this was increased to £50,000 under the Housing (Right to Buy) Maximum Discount Order 1989.)

- It increased the deposit necessary from £100 to £150 and extended the period during which a tenant could exercise his right to buy from two to three years. A tenant could exercise his right to buy but defer completion.

The Housing Act 1988 included the following:

- Where there are delays in expediting a purchase under the right to buy, Section 124 provides that any rent paid during the delay periods can be deducted from the price of the property being purchased. If a person believes that the local authority is delaying the right to buy application then he or she can serve a 'Notice of Delay' on the local authority. The local authority then has one month to rectify the delay or deny that a delay on its part is holding up the application. This reply from the local authority is known as a 'Counter Notice'.

- If after one month the local authority has not rectified the delay (or replied) then the purchaser should send a 'Notice of Operative Delay'. This has the effect that if there are further delays by the local authority then the purchase price is reduced by the amount of rent paid.

- Section 129 allows local authorities to make grants and payments to assist local authority tenants to obtain other accommodation in the private sector, ie not purchasing a local authority dwelling. These grants are known by several different names, such as home buyers grants, portable discounts, transferable discounts or cash incentives. Currently grants of up to £26,500 can be paid. These payments may be used as follows:

  - to acquire an interest in a dwelling house;
  - to carry out works in a dwelling house to provide additional accommodation;
  - to undertake both of these.

It is up to each local authority to decide whether to run these schemes; tenants have no mandatory right to a grant.

Local associations can target the schemes to free up accommodation in areas of the borough where there is a shortage of social housing or to release types of property for which there is a high demand, eg family sized accommodation.

In 2003, there was no money available from central government for these schemes (unlike the figures allocated ranging from £60m in 1996/97 to £109.1m in 1998/99). The local authorities need to fund from their own capital resources.

A similar scheme was introduced in April 1990 for charitable housing association tenants known as the Tenants Incentive Scheme. This is referred to later in this unit. This was replaced by the voluntary purchase grants scheme which provided grants of between £9,000 and £16,000.

The Local Government and Housing Act 1989 ends the exemption from the right to buy on all homes for the elderly, let for the first time after 1 January 1990, unless they are in sheltered schemes. Where an application for the right to buy is made on an elderly person's flat or bungalow let before 1 January 1990, the local authority may apply to the Secretary of State to have it excluded from the right to buy.

The Leasehold, Housing and Urban Development Act 1993 abolished the following rights related to the right to buy:

- right to a mortgage;
- right to defer completion;
- right to a granted shared ownership.

Shared ownership is dealt with later in this unit.

9.8   Current Situation

So far over 1.85 million households in Great Britain have purchased under the right to buy.

Sales peaked at over 100,000 a year in the early 1980s and again in 1988/89 following a rise in the housing market. In the late 1990s/early 2000, the figure was steadying out at around 50,000 dwellings a year.

An interesting law case to note is *Dyer v Dorset County Council* (1988). Mr Dyer was a secure tenant. He lived in a house built within the 100 acre grounds of a college, but situated some 450 yards away from the main college buildings and fronting on to a public road. He exercised his right to buy under the Housing Act 1980. The County Council contested this on the grounds that the house was within the curtilage of the college buildings, of which it formed a part. Since the Act does not define curtilage, and having regard to other cases and the dictionary definition of 'curtilage', the court decided at the time that Mr Dyer did possess the right to buy the property. However, this type of dwelling is excluded from the right to buy now.

Another interesting case arose in 1992 in which a tenant exercised his right to buy twice. The case concerned a tenant in Scotland who purchased his house for £8,500 (after discount) in 1980 from Bearsden and Milngavie District Council under the Right to Buy. The house was classified as defective under the Housing Defects Act 1984 and the local authority was obliged to buy the property back at £37,525 (the price set by the District Valuer). The owner then reverted to being a secure tenant in the property. Three years later no work having been done to the property by the local authority, the secure tenant decided to purchase at a price of £30,260 (33% discount!).

In 1991, again in Scotland, the House of Lords ruled that Edinburgh District Council had to complete the sale of a house under the Right to Buy even though the tenant had died. It had been decided earlier in *Sutton LBC v Swann* (1985) that if a tenant ceased to be such before completion of the purchase (eg by moving out after starting the procedure) the right to buy was no longer available.

In *Bristol City Council v Lovell* (1998), a secure tenant served a right to buy notice in April 1994 which was accepted by the council. In the meantime, the police raided the dwelling believing that the tenant was selling drugs from the address. Consequently the council served a possession notice on the grounds of illegal use of he dwelling. The tenant, however, considered that he could proceed with the right to buy. The tenant applied for an injunction against the authority enforcing his right to buy. The case went to the Court of Appeal which granted the application for the injunction. The House of Lords in 1998 held that the court could adjourn the right to buy injunction to await the result of the council's claim for possession for the illegal sale of drugs. This case has, in effect, set new law on when landlords can resist a right to buy claim by a tenant.

Further recent problems have been highlighted of financiers pressurizing elderly tenants to buy their homes. The tenants, who are eligible for discounts of up to 60% of the purchase price, agreed to pass on the house to the financier when they died.

The Housing Act 1985 makes provision for tenants who transfer to a new landlord under Large Scale Voluntary Transfers to retain the statutory right to buy their homes. This is known as the 'Preserved Right to Buy' or 'Right to Acquire'; this gives to tenants comparable statutory rights to buy their homes to those they had with the Council.

Most people who have purchased dwellings under the Right to Buy consider their purchase good value for money. However, some people are in difficulty, in particular those who bought their council flats and are unable to pay the service charges and in some cases cannot re-sell. Many of them did not realise the full extent of their obligations. Some local authority properties, particularly tower blocks and other system built estates, can be very expensive to maintain. Local authorities have been required to reduce high service charges in certain cases. This helped many people who found themselves in financial difficulties. However, for some people the cost and strain of home ownership was too much and they were desperate to become tenants again. Others wanted to move and buy elsewhere (for employment, health, family or other reasons) but could not find a buyer, or the prospective buyer could not find a lender willing to give a mortgage. The government, therefore, agreed back in 1999, to meet part of the costs incurred by local authorities of buying back such dwellings.

9.9   The Rent to Mortgage Scheme (RTM)

At its annual conference in October 1990, the Conservative Party announced its intention to introduce the Rent to Mortgage Scheme, the idea being that the rent should be regarded as a mortgage repayment. Secure tenants would thereby have the opportunity to purchase their homes with the mortgage repayments amounting to about the same costs as the rent they had formerly paid.

The government tried out the idea in Scotland initially, involving both Scottish Homes and the Scottish New Towns, and in Wales, involving the Development Board for Rural Wales.

In February 1991, the government commenced testing this scheme in Basildon and Milton Keynes. (These two towns were used because they were still at the time classed as 'New Towns' and hence governed by New Towns legislation and amendment to any Housing legislation was not necessary.)

The Leasehold Reform, Housing and Urban Development Act 1993 gives a right for secured tenants to buy their homes under the Rent to Mortgage Scheme.

Under the scheme secure Council tenants – traditional non-charitable housing association tenants and Housing Action Trust tenants – qualify, provided that they have two years tenancy. The criteria are very similar to those for the right to buy, namely:

Up to four people can purchase, providing that they have lived there for the previous 12 months.

Discounts are as for the right to buy (33% to 60% for houses and 44% to 70% for flats and maisonettes), subject to a maximum discount.

Discounts are repayable pro rata if the dwelling is sold within three years.

This scheme enables a tenant to buy his home by paying just part of the right-to-buy price to begin with. Tenants do not have to pay the rest of the price until later. The amount of later payments is linked to the value of the dwelling at the time payment is made. Some or all of the rest can be paid later. The final payment must normally be made when selling the dwelling on death.

There is a bigger discount on the initial payment than on later payments.

The legal charge has to be repaid in full if the owner dies.

The charge must be paid off on disposal unless the Matrimonial Causes Act 1973, the Inheritance (Provision for Family and Dependants) Act 1975 or the Children Act 1989 applies. In any of these cases the charge is waived.

The charge must be paid off within one year of the death of the purchaser unless it passes under a will to a spouse.

The property is valued at open market price (ignoring improvements).

Rental payments are used to arrive at an 'initial minimum payment' (based on a 25-year mortgage at local authority interest rates). The initial minimum payment is deducted from the Right to Buy price and the difference is made up by a legal charge on the property which is paid off when the property is sold, with the monies going to the Council.

It is not possible however to use the Rent to Mortgage Scheme if:

(i)   housing benefit has been paid at any time during the last 12 months;

(ii)   the initial payment is more than 80% of the purchase price.

Tenants of flats pay 80% of the amount that would have been paid in rent to take account of additional service charges.

The following are excluded from the Rent to Mortgage Scheme:
-    sheltered accommodation;
-    accommodation for the disabled;
-    temporary accommodation for council employees;
-    council accommodation used with a temporary licence to allow improvement work to be done to another property which is privately owned, ie a property 'lent' by a local authority to enable works to be carried out in the private sector.

The *advantages* of the Rent to Mortgage Scheme are that:
-    it allows people to purchase over a period of time if they cannot afford to do so at present.
-    outgoings are little greater than for renting the property.
-    it generates variety of tenure within a local authority housing estate, which may help protect an owner's investment.
-    it generally brings the advantages of home ownership.

The *disadvantages* of the Rent to Mortgage Scheme are that:

- it increases outgoings because some of the costs previously borne by the landlord have to be incurred by the tenant, eg repairs and insurance.

- it entails the general responsibilities of home ownership.

- where few Council properties have been sold on an estate there may be doubts about the investment performance of the property in question.

- there is apparently no flexibility to return to renting if the initiative does not work for particular individuals.

In reality the Rent to Mortgage scheme is rarely used; usually tenants who embark on this actually purchase their dwellings under the Right to Buy, particularly at present with the lowest interest rates seen for over 50 years.

In the first three years of the Rent to Mortgage Scheme only 23 dwellings were sold, although a further 100 applications were being processed. This was after £414,000 had been spent on publicity.

9.10   Shared Ownership

The Right to Buy is all very well but it does not help those who cannot afford to buy their homes even taking into account the available discounts. The government introduced the shared ownership schemes under the Housing and Building Control Act 1984. Shared ownership gives tenants the opportunity to part buy and part rent a property entirely. Such schemes normally involve housing associations and a limited number of local authorities. There are also some private-sector schemes. There are two main types of shared ownership schemes (i) conventional shared ownership and (ii) do-it-yourself shared ownership.

Conventional shared ownership

Under this scheme registered social landlords build or purchase and renovate existing dwellings for sale to purchasers on shared ownership terms; this is sometimes known as 'stair casing'.

If a house is being purchased on a shared ownership basis the purchaser is responsible for all repairs and redecoration both internally and externally. The housing association insures the structure of the dwelling although the purchaser makes a small service charge to cover this and to meet the costs of rent collection.

If a flat is being purchased on a shared ownership basis, the purchaser is responsible for all repairs and redecoration internally. The housing association undertakes to keep the dwelling in good structural repair, the structure insured and to keep any common parts, such as the staircase and corridors, decorated, cleaned and provided with adequate lighting. A service charge is made by the housing association in respect of this service. However, the purchasers must be informed of how the service charge is calculated and be consulted before any major repair or maintenance work is put in hand.

Traditional Shared Ownership

Many housing associations offer property on a shared ownership basis which is usually known as 'staircasing'. The tenant starts by buying a tranche or slice on a long lease and pays rent on a proportional basis on the tranche or slice not purchased. The purchaser at some future date increases his share of the equity (ie staircasing) by purchasing subsequent slices of the lease, resulting in an increase in mortgage repayments and a corresponding decrease in the rent – the idea being that the freehold may be acquired and the rent payable extinguished. The initial share may be as small as 25% or as much as 75%. The minimum share would depend on the type of shared ownership being offered. The rent is assessed as a 'fair rent' by the rent officer and takes into account the repayments made as an owner occupier and the share to be met of insurance, maintenance and repairs. It is possible to get help under the housing benefits scheme towards the rent.

Initially when purchasing property on a shared ownership basis, it is on the basis of a long lease. As a first owner, this will be a 99-year lease. If the dwelling is eventually purchased, ie 100%, then the owner obtains the freehold of such property or if a flat the lease will be amended to indicate this.

The scheme is intended to help those in housing need and who would otherwise be unable to purchase a property outright. Priority is given to existing council and registered social landlord tenants and to those on housing waiting lists.

Do-It-Yourself Shared Ownership (DIYSO)

Do-It-Yourself Shared Ownership (DIYSO) is offered to a limited number of local authorities. It is designed to enable people on low incomes to gain access to home ownership. DIYSO is similar to conventional shared ownership except it allows a purchaser to select a property on the open market and then buy it on shared ownership terms, paying rent to a registered social landlord on the share they do not own. Applicants choose a property on the open market. The amount of equity initially purchased is normally between 25% and 75% with an overall average of 50%. There are price limits set on the value of the property which might be bought under DIYSO. There is no statutory right to DIYSO.

The Housing Corporation used to fund this scheme, but although it still exists a new scheme called 'Homebuy' assists tenants to purchase dwellings. (See 9.13 later in this unit.)

Shared Ownership Procedure

Let us now look at the procedure for those wishing to participate in shared ownership. The first steps are identical to those under the right to buy system:

- the purchaser applies to buy the dwelling, asking the landlord for the right to buy claim form RTB 1.

- the landlord makes his first response within four, or sometimes eight, weeks on form RTB 2.

- he notifies the prospective purchaser of the purchase price.

- the prospective purchaser applies for a mortgage.

- the landlord, who must respond to the application within four weeks, gives a notification of the contribution required from the purchaser. This will take into account any discount and the price of the share.

- the mortgage must be arranged and the purchase completed.

As you can see, these steps are very similar to those taken under the Right to Buy Scheme, except that they involve the purchase of a share of a dwelling rather than the whole of it.

9.11   Right to Acquire

This scheme was introduced in the Housing Act 1996, and gives tenants of registered social landlords (eg housing associations) a statutory right to buy their home at a discount, generally between £9,000–£16,000 depending on the local authority area. It only applies to registered social landlords' properties built or purchased with public funds or transferred from a local authority after 1 April 1997, subject to certain exceptions. Eligible tenants must have spent a total of two years as a public sector tenant. The discount is funded by a grant from the Housing Corporation. Sales receipts are required to be recycled to provide replacement housing for rent.

There are, however, certain properties exempt from the Right to Acquire

- those in certain rural areas defined on maps by the Office of Deputy Prime Minister, with a population of less than 3,000;

- properties where the landlord is a co-operative housing association;

- tied accommodation occupied because the tenant is employed by the registered social landlord or other social landlords;

- a home that is one of a group of homes designed with special features for letting to people with physical disabilities;

- a home that is one of a group of homes let to tenants who are suffering or have suffered from a mental disorder where social services or other special facilities are provided;

- a home that is one of a group of homes let to tenants who have special needs and require intensive housing support;

- a home which is one of a group of homes particularly suitable for elderly people and is let to a person aged 60 or over;

- properties held on Crown tenancies;

- a property which is valued at or below the landlord's loan for that property.

New regulations came into effect in December 1999 which restricted the amount of discount paid in circumstances where the discount amounts to more than half of the value of the property. The intention was to stop the irregularity whereby some tenants were able to buy their home for a nominal value in areas with low property values.

9.12 Tenants of Charitable Housing Associations

Unlike most other public tenants, tenants of charitable housing associations were not given the right to buy under the Housing Act 1980. They had to wait until 1984 until a home ownership scheme for them was introduced under the Housing and Building Control Act 1984. Even then, fairly stringent rules on eligibility were applied.

- The property could not be eligible for normal right to buy terms.

- It had to be run by a housing association and must have been built or converted using a Housing Association Grant.

- The tenant must have been a tenant of a housing association for at least two years.

- His rent could not be in arrears.

- He must have been a tenant of the relevant property on 26 August 1984. If his tenancy started after that date, he must have been in his present tenancy for at least two years to be eligible for the scheme.

The discounts available under the scheme were the same as those available under the right to buy. However, the prices to which the percentage discounts were applied were different. For tenants of charitable housing associations, the percentage discount was applied to whichever was the lower of the following:

- the value of the dwelling;
- its purchase price;
- the building society's valuation of the dwelling;
- the price limit set set for the area in which the dwelling was situated.

The scheme was known as the Home Ownership Scheme for Tenants of Charitable Housing Associations (HOTCHA). This Scheme was replaced by the Tenants' Incentive Scheme which we referred to briefly earlier, and has been replaced through a new Voluntary Purchase Grant worth (introduced in 1996) a discount of between £9,000 and £16,000 depending on location. Housing associations are allowed to keep receipts for investment in new stock.

The Scheme makes it possible for tenants of registered housing associations to receive financial help to purchase a home of their own. By assisting tenants to move out from their rented property into a home of their own, it enables the vacant property to be used by a statutory homeless household. The housing association must demonstrate that the grant given has resulted in the immediate rehousing of a homeless household in another of its properties. It is not a statutory right and funds are limited. The scheme is targeted at those areas where the problem of homelessness is greatest.

To qualify for the scheme a tenant must:

- be a secure tenant or an assured tenant;
- have rented from a housing association, local authority or any other public sector landlord for a minimum of two years;
- not be in rent arrears;
- not own a residential property already.

The tenant can select a residential property on the open market anywhere in the UK provided that the property is:

- immediately habitable;
- acceptable for mortgage purposes;
- within set price limits for the scheme

Originally tenants could select anywhere in the world but following adverse publicity the scheme was amended.

The cash payment cannot be used to purchase:

- a commercial property (including premises with residential accommodation);
- a property at auction;
- mobile homes, caravans and houseboats;
- a property being sold by a government-funded agency, such as a housing association or local authority, where the property is being sold through a grant-aided scheme;
- a plot of land on which to build;
- a property requiring renovation that is not immediately habitable;
- a home you are building yourself which is not immediately habitable.

The cash cannot be used towards any government-funded shared ownership property.

9.13   Homebuy

The Homebuy scheme was introduced in April 1999 in England and replaced the Tenants' Incentive Scheme (TIS) and the Housing Corporation funded Do-It-Yourself Shared Ownership Scheme (DIYSO). The Homebuy scheme enables tenants of Registered Social Landlords (RSLs) and local authorities, as well as others in priority need on local authority waiting lists, to purchase a home on the open market with the help of an interest free equity loan from the RSLs equal to 25% of the purchase price, subject to certain limits. The remaining 75% is funded by the applicant through a conventional mortgage and savings. The loan to cover 25% of the purchase price of a home does not involve the purchaser in making monthly payments. It is paid back when the property is sold instead. The amount paid back is 25% of the value of the property at the time it is sold. In view of the fact that house prices tend to be increasing, the amount repayable will generally be greater than the value of the original loan.

One of the key objectives of Homebuy is to release existing social lettings which can then be re-let to people in housing need. Homebuy is, therefore, targeted on areas where there is a shortage of social housing. Applicants have no statutory right to Homebuy; acceptance depends on funds being available in a particular area and the suitability of the home being vacated for those in housing need.

9.14   The Future of the Right to Buy

At the time of writing this text (summer 2003) changes are proposed to the Housing Bill 2003 to tackle 'profiteering' from the right to buy. The following proposals are suggested:

- initial qualification period to be extended from two to five years;

- former tenants would have to pay back discount if they move up to five years after purchase (rather than three at present) and the amount to be repaid would be calculated as a percentage of the value of the property;

- landlords to be able to deny right to buy where demolition was likely. (This arose from the Ocean Estate in London where tenants purchased knowing that they would receive full market value (plus 10%) home loss payments and disturbance allowances when their properties were demolished);

- a five-year ban on letting right to buy properties to be introduced.

Summary

In this unit, we have looked at one of the most important estate management concepts of recent years – the right to buy. We have considered it in some detail, including what it is, to whom it applies and how it works. You should also be able to write about the relevant legislation, concentrating on the Housing Act 1980, but including the changes introduced by subsequent Acts.

Finally, we have considered the related topics of the 'Rent to Mortgage' scheme, shared ownership and charitable housing association tenancies.

10

URBAN RENEWAL

Objectives

After studying this unit, you should be able to:

● outline the problems relating to poor housing;

● explain the concept of the former General Improvement Areas and Housing Action Areas;

● describe the purpose of Housing Renewal Areas and Housing Action Trusts;

● outline the problems experienced in inner cities;

● explain how 'Priority Estate' Projects work;

● outline the proposals with regard to housing in *Towards an Urban Renaissance*;

● describe Local Strategic Partnerships.

10.1   Introduction

We have seen that housing conditions have gradually improved since about the time of the First World War and, in particular, that housing slowly came to be seen as a social service. However, problems related to housing conditions still remain.

10.2   Problems of Rehousing

It is all very well for a housing authority to clear a slum and plan for redevelopment. What happens to those people who until then had lived in the slums? Where do they go? Rehousing displaced families is a well-known problem and has been the subject of many reports and pieces of legislation in the past. When rehousing is planned, the three main factors that might cause a problem are:

● poverty;

● reluctance to move;

● the complications of belonging to an ethnic minority (or other well-defined group).

Poverty is a problem if the family or person concerned cannot afford the rent on whatever property they are moved into. This used to be more of a problem in the past. Nowadays, rent rebates in the form of housing benefit are available to those in need of financial aid.

Some families are extremely reluctant to move: they would rather stay in poor conditions, with their friends and relatives about them, than move to another area where they would feel out of place and alone. This problem is compounded if the new housing is to be provided on an estate some distance from their old home. Where the housing authority can rehouse people near to their former homes, then it will do so in an effort to make the move more acceptable to those concerned.

Housing for ethnic minorities, the elderly or the disabled has its own particular problems. These problems occur just as much in rehousing as they do when housing is being built or made available at other times. Special considerations have to be taken into account when moving a member of one of these specific groups to a new home.

10.3   Dealing with Unfit Houses

The criteria for judging whether a home is unfit for human habitation are given earlier in this text. Assuming that a dwelling is unfit, what can be done about it?

A local authority has various courses of action open to it when it comes to dealing with unfit houses in the private sector; it may:

- require an abatement of nuisance;
- issue a repair notice;
- issue a compulsory improvement notice;
- use a closing order;
- use a demolition order;
- use a compulsory purchase order;
- use the clearance procedure.

Abatement of Nuisance

Under the Public Health Acts, a local authority can require the abatement of a nuisance by a house owner, particularly in respect of defects in older houses.

Repair Notice

If a local authority decides that a house can be made fit at a reasonable cost, a repair notice can be served on the owner compelling him to carry out the work specified in the notice. Where the owner fails to comply, the local authority is itself empowered to carry out the work and recover the cost from the owner.

The owner of a house may, of course, feel that the serving of a repair notice is unjustified. If this is so, then he may appeal against the decision, usually on one of three grounds:

- that the house is not unfit;
- that the required repair works are unnecessary;
- that the works cannot be undertaken at a reasonable cost.

Compulsory Improvement Notice

If no action is taken by the landlord to undertake certain improvements for the benefit of tenants, the local authority can serve a compulsory improvement notice forcing the landlord to undertake the work and if he fails to do so, the local authority will carry out the necessary work and place a charge against the dwelling in order to ensure the costs of works is paid for.

Closing Order

Under the Housing Act 1985, a local authority can make a closing order in cases where it believes that a house cannot be made fit at a reasonable cost. The closing order is used when it is necessary to preserve adjoining buildings or when architectural or historic interest is involved.

Demolition Order

Similarly the Housing Act 1985 provides that a local authority can make a demolition order when it believes that a house cannot be made fit at a reasonable cost; such action is taken by a local authority as a last resort, when other actions have failed.

Compulsory Purchase Order

Local authorities can compulsorily purchase properties in the private sector to ensure that repairs or improvements are carried out. This is drastic action and is usually taken against a landlord who is unwilling to bring his property up to an acceptable standard.

Clearance Area Procedures

The Housing Act 1985 states:

> The local housing authority shall declare an area to be a clearance area if it is satisfied:
>
> (a) that the houses in the area are unfit for human habitation or are by reason of their bad arrangement, or the narrowness or bad arrangement of the streets, dangerous or injurious to the health of the inhabitants of the area; and
>
> (b) that the other buildings, if any, in the area are for a like reason dangerous or injurious to the health of the inhabitants of the area;

and that the most satisfactory method of dealing with the conditions in the area is the demolition of all the buildings in the area.

The situation where a housing authority decides that all the houses in an area should be demolished does not occur very often today. If it does, the Housing Act 1985 specifies the procedure that must be carried out. This includes making sure that suitable accommodation exists to rehouse those living in the clearance area.

10.4 Area Improvement

There are a number of area improvement schemes which we will now consider.

General Improvement Areas (GIAs)

In 1968, the government published a White Paper entitled *Old Houses into New Homes* which placed an emphasis on rehabilitation rather than redevelopment. As a result of that White Paper, the Housing Act 1969 made available various forms of grant designed to render house improvements a more attractive proposition. It also introduced the concept of General Improvement Areas. For the first time, grants were made available for the improvement of neighbourhood amenities, such as playgrounds for children or rest areas for the elderly, in these designated improvement areas, ie improving the environment. The provisions of the 1969 Act were consolidated into the Housing Act 1985.

Under the 1985 Act, if a local authority was satisfied:

- that living conditions in the area could most appropriately be made better through improving the amenities of the area or the dwellings in the area or both; and

- that such an improvement may be effected or assisted by the exercise of its powers under the provisions relating to General Improvement Areas;

then the local authority could declare the area to be a General Improvement Area.

After a General Improvement Area was declared, a local authority had to:

- publish in two or more newspapers circulating in the locality (of which one at least had to be a local newspaper) a notice of the council's resolution declaring the area to be a General Improvement Area;

- make known its intentions to everyone living in or owning a property in the area;

- send to the Secretary of State for the Environment a copy of the General Improvement Area resolution, a map of the proposed area and a copy of any relevant reports; and

- make maps available for public inspection at reasonable times.

The Housing Act 1985 went on to say that in a General Improvement Area a local authority may, for the purpose of effecting or assisting the improvement of amenities of the area, or of the dwellings in the area, or both:

- carry out works on land owned by it and assist (by grants, loans or otherwise) in the carrying out of works on land not owned by it;

- acquire any land by agreement; and

- let or otherwise dispose of land for the time being owned by it;

- acquire land compulsorily within the General Improvement Area or adjoining it.

Grants were available for environmental improvements to the curtilage of dwellings in a General Improvement Area. Curtilage works are those works on the outside of a property and 'surround' it, eg garden walls, gates etc. Originally back in 1969, these grants were £50 per dwelling. Following a government review in August 1988, the level of these grants was increased from £400 to £600 per dwelling, but the new limits were applicable only to those GIAs declared after 1 January 1988 and only in respect of expenditure incurred after 1 September 1988.

One of the problems that arose in General Improvement Areas (and Housing Action Areas) was that some houses in a road were improved but others remained unimproved. This undermined the concept of area improvement. Following pilot schemes in Birmingham, the government introduced 'enveloping' schemes in 1978 whereby local authorities could improve the extensive fabric of a block or street of private houses by repairing roofs, windows and walls.

This scheme was enhanced by economies of scale whereby one contractor replaced roofs, windows or walls with new materials matching throughout the block or streets. This scheme was replaced by Group Repair under the Local Government and Housing Act 1989 which operated in a similar manner. The uptake of Group Repairs is low as a direct result of grants being means tested (and as from September 2003 virtually ceasing)!

You should note that the lifetime of a General Improvement Area was indefinite (unlike Housing Action Areas (HAAs) and Housing Renewal Areas (HRAs), as we shall see shortly. The Local Government and Housing Act 1989 terminated GIAs from 31 March 1991.

Housing Action Areas (HAAs)

A government White Paper entitled *Better Homes: The Next Priorities* was published in 1973. It proposed yet another new concept in area improvement: the Housing Action Area (HAA). These HAAs were formally introduced in the Housing Act 1974, which was later consolidated into the Housing Act 1985.

The idea of an HAA was that these residential areas should be seen as entities where both houses and the environment could be improved.

If a local authority was satisfied that both the physical state of the housing accommodation in an area as a whole and social conditions in that area were unsatisfactory, then it could declare the area to be a Housing Action Area, provided that certain requirements were met.

These requirements were defined in the Housing Act 1985 as meaning:

... that the living conditions in the area ... can most effectively be dealt with within a period of five years so as to secure:

(a) the improvement of the housing accommodation in the area as a whole;

(b) the well-being of the persons for the time being resident in the area; and

(c) the proper and effective management and use of that accommodation;

by declaring the area to be a Housing Action Area.

A two-year extension could be approved by the Secretary of State if there were justifiable circumstances. Such circumstances would be if a large compulsory purchase order was being processed – this can be a lengthy process with public inquiries, etc. After a Housing Action Area was declared, the fact had to be registered as a local land charge and revealed on searches made at the local authority. The declaration procedure for a housing action area was the same as for a general improvement area.

You may well be wondering why a local authority would want to go to the trouble of setting up a Housing Action Area. What was the point of it all? The answer was that once an area had been declared as a Housing Action Area, a local authority could exercise certain powers. The Housing Act 1985 defined these powers as follows, stating that a local authority:

... may acquire by agreement, or be authorized by the Secretary of State to acquire compulsorily, land in the area on which there are premises consisting of or including housing accommodation.

The Act went on to say that, once having acquired land, a local authority could undertake all or any of the following activities:

(a) the provision of housing accommodation (by the construction, conversion or improvement of buildings, or otherwise);

(b) the carrying out of works for the improvement or repair of housing accommodation (including works to the exterior or on land within the curtilage of buildings containing housing accommodation);

(c) the management of housing accommodation;

(d) the provision of furniture, fittings or services in or in relation to housing accommodation.

In addition, the Act made the following provisions:

For the purpose of improving the amenities in a Housing Action Area, the local housing authority may:

(a) carry out environmental works on land belonging to it; and

(b) give assistance towards the carrying out of environmental works by others.

The government reviewed the level of grant available for dwellings situated within Housing Action Areas as it had done with General Improvement Areas. The environmental works grant was £50 per dwelling back in 1974 when HAAs were first declared. This was likewise increased from £400 to £600 per dwelling. The new limits applied only to HAAs declared after 1 January 1985 and only in respect of expenditure incurred after 1 September 1988. As with General Improvement Areas, local authorities were encouraged to use 'enveloping' schemes.

Like GIAs, Housing Action Areas have been replaced under the provisions of the Local Government and Housing Act 1989. Housing Action Areas terminated their status with effect from 31 March 1991.

The aim of General Improvement Areas was to save and improve older houses that were still basically sound, whereas the aim of Housing Action Areas was to deal with poor housing conditions in areas where there might be considerable social stress.

The facility for declaring these areas forms part of an overall housing improvement policy. Although housing improvement clearly includes provisions relating to individual dwellings, it is probably in area improvements that housing policy has made the greatest strides in recent years.

Housing Renewal Areas (HRAs)

Housing Renewal Areas replaced the Housing Action Area and General Improvement Area concepts. They became operative from 1 April 1990, under the Local Government and Housing Act 1989. Housing Renewal Areas are more concerned with urban renewal and a range of activities can be considered including improvements, new building and clearance of areas where appropriate.

Before proceeding down the Housing Renewal Area path, local authorities need to undertake a thorough appraisal of the various options open to them: demolition, redevelopment, rehabilitation, etc. This can be carried out under a process called Neighbourhood Renewal Assessment (NRA), when all the areas in the borough are considered to ensure that resources are made available to the area most in need.

In order to qualify as a Housing Renewal Area, there should be a minimum of 300 dwellings and a maximum of 3,000 dwellings; of these, not less than 75% must be privately owned or rented. The properties in the area should be predominantly in poor repair and a minimum of 75% must be unfit or qualify for grant aid. At least 30% of the households in the area should be receiving one or more state benefits.

A copy of the resolution, map and statement must be sent to the Secretary of State for the Environment, along with details of the numbers of dwellings together with houses in multiple occupation (HMOs). Declaration of HRAs is the same as for HAAs and GIAs: a report, public advertisements, and so on. By declaring an HRA, the Local Government and Housing Act 1989 provides for a comprehensive approach covering renovation and redevelopment of housing alongside action on social, economic and environmental problems. The lifespan of an HRA is 10 years, which will enable a local authority to have sufficient time to complete its programme of works.

Priority should be given to HRAs in a local authority's Housing Investment Programme (HIP); where, however, a local authority considers that insufficient funds are available, it can approach the Secretary of State for additional funding for the first year.

Environmental works grants are designed to enhance the appearance of the area and contributions can be made for this purpose. The calculation is based on the number of dwellings in the area multiplied by £1,000 for each dwelling.

HRAs rely on partnerships developing between local authorities, residents and private-sector interests.

As with HAAs, there is power to compulsorily purchase dwellings in HRAs.

The current regime encourages block improvements (or group repair). Thus, when there is a large number of dwellings adjacent to each other, they can be rehabilitated together. This, however, is not always possible.

Compared to HAAs and GIAs few housing renewal areas have been declared since 1990. This is because of lack of finance from the public and private sector. There is also a limited success with Housing Renewal Areas because of the restrictions on the type of areas that can be declared coupled with the drastic fall in local authority funding.

Poor Housing Outside HRAs

Local authorities are also able to use powers to improve poor housing conditions outside of HRAs. Limited grants are available under the Housing Grants, Construction and Regeneration Act 1996.

10.5 The Problems of Inner Cities

The problems of inner cities have seldom been out of the headlines in recent years, especially following the riots in the late 1970s and early 1980s. In retrospect, the causes of the inner cities' problems are not too difficult to see.

● Large-scale slum clearance, while often necessary, takes a long time and has several adverse effects:

- it disrupts communities;

- it can sweep away jobs that existed in small firms;

- it often fails to provide a satisfactory new environment.

- Too little use was made of existing housing stock; it would probably have been better to undertake more rehabilitation and repair and less new development.

- The houses and flats, particularly the local authority blocks built in the 1930s and 1950s, were physically inadequate and were drab, poorly serviced and ill-maintained. People do not want to live in many of the 1930s or 1950s estates and are keen to leave them.

- On occasion, both central and local government have adopted a rigid and bureaucratic approach to inner area redevelopment, failing to adapt and modify programmes to take account of the facts of the local situation and the wishes of the people affected.

- Opportunities for people to choose between different types of tenure and different types of home have decreased, particularly as the private rented sector contracted so dramatically.

The inner cities do not all suffer from the same housing problems. However, five main problems can be identified.

- The neighbourhoods are untidy and shabby, and contain run-down housing.

- The local authority estates are often bleak and inhospitable, especially the high-rise flats.

- Inner cities offer a limited selection of tenure.

- In comparison with other areas, inner cities contain a large number of people with special housing needs.

- For various reasons, the people living in inner-cities are not very mobile and they would find it difficult to move of their own volition.

The problems of the inner cities are deeply entrenched and will be difficult to solve. Because there are no easy solutions they will not go away overnight. However, one obvious way to improve the situation is to encourage financial institutions (including building societies) to spend more money on the inner cities. It has been argued that, in the past, building societies 'redlined' the inner cities by declining to lend money secured on inner-city properties. Whatever the truth of this view, building societies are now actively participating in the regeneration of the inner cities.

- Many of the leading building societies assisted local authorities in their Housing Action Area programmes and in some Housing Renewal Areas.

- Some building societies lend money for grant work, on top of that provided by local authorities.

- Some building societies and banks (such as Abbey National, Woolwich, Nationwide, Leeds and Halifax) have teamed up with construction companies (including Barratt and Wimpey), in order to participate actively in urban regeneration.

It was announced in the budget in March 1999 that £170 million would be made available for 1999/2000 to tackle crime and disorder on problem estates and would be used to install CCTV cameras in the most crime-ridden locations.

10.6   Priority Estate Projects

We have already noted that council estates can pose problems for the relevant local authority. The estates themselves are often poorly designed, constructed and located. There is frequently no money to spare when it comes to repairing or maintaining estate houses or flats. Often the people living in the estates tend to have low incomes (or be out of work), so that they depend heavily on state benefits. They may be one-parent families or families with large numbers of children. It is, perhaps, not surprising that a local authority can be faced with absconding tenants, rent arrears, vandalism, drug abuse and crime.

Priority estate projects represent a government initiative, set up back in 1979, which attempted to deal with the problems of council estates. Under the priority project, a team was set up comprising staff working for the estate, local authority workers and the residents themselves. The key elements of a priority estate project are:

- the setting up of a full-time, estate-based office;
- the appointment of a local coordinator responsible for all local management functions;
- the use of resident caretakers;
- the use of a local repairs team;
- the application of a local lettings policy within the local authority constraints;
- the residents themselves defining priorities for improvement programmes;
- resident involvement in estate management;
- responsibility for rent collection;
- setting a local budget to assist local decision-making.

10.7   Housing Action Trusts (HATs)

Housing Action Trusts were established under the Housing Act 1988. A Housing Action Trust, or HAT as it is commonly referred to, is a publicly-funded, limited life trust set up by the government to improve run-down council housing estates. It is run by a board of elected representatives of residents on the estate and members of the local authority.

The HATs' main aim was to achieve a sustainable and long lasting improvement in the living conditions in their areas.

The original concepts of HATs as contained in the Housing Act was to enable the Secretary of State to transfer problem estates out of local authority control into the hands of a quasi-government body – the housing action trust (HAT).

The objects of HATs are to:

- repair and improve the housing stock;

- carry out effective management and use of properties;

- encourage diversity of tenure;

- improve the general, social, environmental and living conditions of the area, including the provision of shops, advice centres and other community facilities.

To achieve these objectives, a HAT may:

- acquire (including the powers of compulsory purchase), manage and dispose of land and other property;

- carry out building works;

- ensure the provision of water, electricity, gas, sewerage and other services;

- carry on a business.

HATs assist those local authorities who do not have the resources to improve the estates. Governments have made available large amounts of money to ensure that HATs are a success. The Treasury could guarantee the payments of loans raised other than from the government.

Six HATs were set up under the Housing Act 1988 to regenerate some of the most deprived local authority estates in England. HATs were bitterly opposed initially but eventually the first HAT in North Hull was set up only after the council had gained concessions from the government including the agreement that after completion, the tenants could transfer back to the council. The North Hull HAT has now completed its work and ceased operation in March 1999. The remaining HATs are in Liverpool, Castle Vale (Birmingham) and the London Boroughs of Waltham Forest, Tower Hamlets and Brent (Stonebridge HAT).

To summarize, HATs take over council dwellings and refurbish or redevelop some of the country's worst estates, tackle their social, economic and environmental problems and promote local employment and diversity of ownership then sell them onto a housing association, tenants co-operative or private landlord or hand them back to the local authority.

The HAT provides a unique opportunity for residents to participate fully in determining the future of their homes and environment.

A feasibility study is produced by the local council with help from the Housing Corporation. Residents can then look at what needs to be done to improve the estate and discuss initial proposals for regeneration.

Residents are consulted upon the terms upon which the HAT will be introduced; these are set out clearly in writing before they vote. Public meetings are arranged; newsletters prepared and the public kept well-informed.

A vote by ballot is then organized. When a ballot is announced the decision on whether there should be a Housing Action Trust on the estate is up to the individual. If the majority votes for a HAT then a HAT will be introduced. If not a HAT will not be introduced.

Nearer to the ballot on a HAT a 'shadow' (or prospective) HAT chair will be appointed. That person will set up a 'shadow' HAT office on the estate with a number of staff to discuss any concerns that residents may have and to provide advice generally.

The ballot is a secret postal ballot run over a period of about three weeks independently, often by the Electoral Reform Society. Those eligible to vote will be:

- all tenants whose names are on a rent book;

- all long leaseholders who have purchased under the 'right to buy';

- tied tenants, eg caretakers, resident business tenants.

If the majority of residents vote 'no' then a HAT will not be set up; if the majority of residents vote 'yes' then the HAT proposal must go to Parliament for approval. Once Parliament has given approval it takes about six to twelve months to set up the Housing Action Trust – staff needs to be appointed and the properties need to be transferred from the Council.

Once the work of a Housing Action Trust is finished, residents may, if they choose, return to the Council. Residents also have the option to buy or part own their property, form an independent housing co-operative or choose a new landlord such as a housing association.

Rents are frozen until either refurbishment of the dwelling is complete or a tenant is moved to a new property. It is likely to take several years to complete work on estates.

The rent for the new home will increase only to the same levels that Council tenants pay for similar properties in the area and housing benefit is still possible.

Establishing HATS has been a constant struggle and there remains bitter opposition to various proposed HATs in run down areas such as Lambeth, Southwark, Leeds and Sunderland. Many tenants prefer to remain council tenants (or even housing association tenants as we shall see shortly). Many tenants adopt the attitude 'the devil you know is better than the devil you don't – with the council being the devil they know!

Because the six HATs formed proved so costly, the programme has since ceased.

10.8　Towards an Urban Renaissance

In 1998 an Urban Task Force under the chairmanship of the leading architect, Richard Rogers, now Lord Rogers of Riverside, was set up and given the major task of trying to assess the ability of our towns and cities to absorb a great deal of the new housing implied in the demographic forecasts we looked at earlier in the Study Text.

Members of the Trade Task Force were chosen for their expertise in elements needed for an urban renaissance, including social exclusion, sustainable development, urban design and urban regeneration. They were asked to find out what had caused urban decline in England and to recommend practical solutions to turn our cities, towns and urban neighbourhoods into places where people want to live, work and play.

The Report was published in the summer of 1999 and is called *Towards an Urban Renaissance*. It is perhaps worthwhile to look initially at the mission statement of the Task Force:

> *The Urban Task Force will identify causes of urban decline in England and recommend practical solutions to bring people back into our cities, towns and urban neighbourhoods. It will establish a new vision for urban regeneration founded on the principles of design excellence, social well-being and environmental responsibility within a viable economic and legislative framework.*

Causes of urban decline are given limited space although recommendations (all 105 of them!) for solving problems abound. The Report identifies the Industrial Revolution with its rapid urban growth and pollution as developing English attitudes towards the role and function of the city. The popularity of the suburbs took root. These and peripheral council estates were pushed along by slum-clearance programmes and the growth in car ownership. Urban decline in the centre of towns and cities accompanied this outward growth and economic change during the 20th century has left underused sites and buildings, especially outside the South East.

The Report stresses that towns and cities should be well-designed, more compact and connected, support a range of diverse uses within a sustainable urban environment which is well integrated with public transport and adaptable to change. The key themes of the Report are:

- recycling land and buildings;
- improving the urban environment;
- achieving excellence in leadership participation and management;
- delivering regeneration.

Many of the recommendations and proposals are design-related and some transport-related. The main recommendations and proposals from a housing perspective are:

- local government to drive the urban renaissance;
- creating designated Urban Priority Areas, enabling local authorities and their partners in regeneration, including local people, to apply for special packages of powers and incentives to assist neighbourhood renewal;
- housing to take a large share of a £500 million regeneration bonanza known as the Renaissance Fund over 10 years – the money could be accessed by local community groups and voluntary organizations to tackle derelict buildings;
- enabling Urban Regeneration Companies and Housing Regeneration Companies to coordinate or deliver area regeneration projects;
- obliging all local planning authorities to carry out regular urban capacity studies on a consistent basis, where necessary, working together across borough boundaries;

- establishing a national framework for identifying, managing and communicating the risks that arise throughout the assessment, treatment and after-care of contaminated and previously contaminated sites;

- launching a national campaign to 'clean up our land' with a target to bring all contaminated land back into beneficial use by 2030;

- giving local authorities a statutory duty to maintain an empty property strategy that sets clear targets for reducing levels of vacant stock;

- facilitating the conversion of more empty space over shops into flats by providing additional public assistance, including public equity stakes and business rate reductions;

- introducing new measures to encourage the restoration and the use of historic buildings left empty by their owners;

- housing associations to set up regeneration companies to deal specifically with the problem of unfit and vacant private housing stock;

- piloting different models of neighbourhood management;

- reviewing the mechanisms by which local authorities use planning gain to secure affordable housing to ensure developers have less scope to buy their way out of obligations to provide mixed tenure neighbourhoods and that councils are not obliged to require social housing in areas where there is already overprovision;

- enabling more mixed income housing projects to proceed, including the use of more challenging planning ideas and discounts for low- to middle-income households in areas of high property values;

- allocating social housing by a more open and flexible system than just basic need;

- introducing a package of measures, including some debt cancellation, to enable authorities with a large stock to transfer to arms-length management organizations;

- restricting public subsidy for social housing developments of more than 25 homes to schemes where homes for rent are integrated with shared and full-ownership housing;

- tax incentives to encourage the use of brownfield sites;

- attracting people to the abandoned dwellings in the Midlands and the North;

- standardize VAT on renovated and new build homes.

10.9 Change of Landlord – Secure Tenants (Tenants' Choice)

Following the right to buy, councils still wished to off-load the remainder of their housing stock. In 1988, a scheme called 'tenants' choice' was introduced under the Housing Act of that year whereby private landlords were given the right to bid for selected parts of the council's stock. This was subject to a successful ballot of the tenants. Councils were reluctant to transfer to such landlords for the fear of losing public sector housing at affordable rents.

The Housing Act 1988 endeavoured to diminish the landlord role of the local authorities. Before 1988, local authorities could voluntarily dispose of their housing stock; under the 1988 legislation, such action could actually be initiated by tenants themselves or by the prospective new landlord.

The initiative gave secure tenants of a local Council or a Housing Action Trust an opportunity to change landlords while staying in their present home.

Tenants' Choice was largely unsuccessful and it was abolished by the Housing Act 1996.

10.10 Large Scale Voluntary Transfers

Tenants' Choice must not be confused with voluntary transfer of housing stock. This is where local authorities transfer their dwellings to a housing association and the stock remains in the public domain under large scale voluntary transfer, housing associations are able to borrow on markets (to which local authorities had limited access) to improve the housing stock. Thus the concept of *voluntary* transfer was created.

The new housing associations created are not regarded by central government as part of the public sector which makes borrowing much easier. Although money still needs to be raised, the money borrowed by housing associations does not count as public expenditure and unregulated – unlike council borrowing.

Large scale voluntary transfer commenced in December 1988 when Chiltern District Council sold 4,635 homes to the newly created Chiltern Hundreds Housing Association.

The policy has been a success as far as governments are concerned but the central government cost of housing benefit has increased dramatically.

There is no doubt that the future of social housing lies in this domain. Under Large Scale Voluntary Transfer, local authorities can initiate the sale of all or part of their stock to another body with the approval of its tenants.

Following financial constraints on local authorities under the Local Government and Housing Act 1989, more and more authorities have decided to sell their stock. Money received are used to pay off any debts on the properties and any surpluses can be used for community facilities. New landlords are able to raise money easily to undertake the necessary repairs. Well in excess of half a million dwellings have been transferred from local authorities to housing associations and the number continues to rise at 150,000 – 200,000 dwellings per annum. More than half of all remaining council landlords are on track to get rid of their housing stock to housing associations under the Large Scale Voluntary Transfer programme.

Voluntary transfer schemes give tenants the right to be consulted, although no formal procedure is laid down for voting. Particular effort must be made for those tenants whose mother tongue is not English. A ballot is held to vote for or against a new landlord. The transfer proceeds only if the majority of tenants eligible to vote cast their votes in favour.

The benefits for tenants in transferring to housing associations are as follows:

- rents pegged with limits on future rises;

- guarantees that major repairs and modernization would be carried out;

- status rise from council to housing association tenant.

Usually the local authority housing staff are transferred to the housing association and the staff then belong to an organization with housing as a core business rather than councils with much wider concerns, often conflicting with the housing department's own wishes or tenants' needs.

Some of the earlier transfers were led by councillors who believed that selling off the family silver would allow the purchase of much more popular items for the public such as leisure centres, while at the same time no longer having to pay the silver's custodian and cleaner.

More recently transfers have been seen as the only way tenants could have repairs and modernization, while maintaining affordable rents. The extra funding would also mean that more social housing could be developed for homeless families and other applicants in the future.

In 2002 the goal posts changed slightly and the government now takes into account a number of points when considering transfers of housing stock. The government looks for evidence that:

- transfers will promote enhanced levels of tenant and community involvement and empowerment;

- the needs of all tenants are addressed – particularly those in Black Minority Ethnic (BME) communities;

- they incorporate plans for neighbourhood renewal and regeneration where appropriate; and

- they involve the creation of effective and efficient social businesses run by skilled, accountable boards and strong senior management leadership.

In addition the government expects to see evidence that the local housing authority has understood and properly planned for its ongoing strategic enabling role. This will include planning:

- how it will continue to work in partnership with existing registered social landlords;

- the support it will offer to the transfer registered social landlords in relation, for example, to regeneration activities;

- how it will discharge its responsibility for homelessness;

- its plans for addressing the problems of private sector housing conditions.

Local Strategic Partnerships

The Social Exclusion's Unit introduced in 2001 a national strategy for neighbourhood renewal *"New Commitment to Neighbourhood Renewal: A National Strategy Plan"*. This new strategy identified a number of problems affecting the co-ordination of public services. It emphasised that disciplines such as housing, health and social services were poor at communicating with each other. It stressed the need for 'joined-up' working.

The plan was for joining up services at neighbourhood level and neighbourhood management was needed. Hence Local Strategic Partnerships were formed for the 88 local authority areas identified as the most deprived areas. These Partnerships are cross sectoral, cross agency, umbrella partnerships focussed and committed to improving the quality of life and governance in a particular locality. These are, as the name suggests, a partnership of residents and agencies working at local level bringing together housing, health (including the National Health Service), business groupings and the police and probation service, Learning and Skills Councils and the new Connexions Service and Employment Service with the aim of all working together to solve a community's problems.

The core tasks of a Local Strategic Partnership are to:

● prepare and implement a community strategy for the area;

● bring together local plans, partnerships and initiatives to provide a forum through which mainstream public service providers work together effectively to meet local needs and priorities;

● work with local authorities that are developing a local public service agreement to help in the process and then meet suitable targets;

● develop and deliver a local neighbourhood renewal strategy to tackle problems relating to health, unemployment, crime, poor housing and failing education.

The Strategy set out the government's vision for narrowing the gap between deprived neighbourhoods and the rest of the country so that within 10 to 20 years, no one should be seriously disadvantaged by where they live.

Compared to the rest of the country, deprived areas have:

● twice as many people dependent on means tested benefits;

● 30% higher mortality rates;

● three times more child poverty;

● 70% of all English ethnic minority residents.

Targets have been set across the sectors for reducing crime, improving school results, narrowing health inequalities and eliminating substandard housing.

The aims of the new Strategy are to:

● deliver economic prosperity;

- safe communities

- develop high quality education;

- have decent housing;

- provide better health to the poorest parts of the country.

At regional level, neighbourhood renewal teams have been set up in the nine government offices to provide a direct channel of communication from neighbourhood/community groups to the neighbourhood renewal unit and act as:

- facilitators to support the development of Local Strategic Partnerships;

- mediators to resolve difficulties which may arise over the participation of government agencies in Local Strategic Partnerships, and in the negotiation of partnership and plan rationalisation proposals;

- accreditors to assess whether Neighbourhood Renewal Fund grant conditions are being met and that Local Strategic Partnerships are effective and involve genuine community participation.

This is a new approach and differs from previous attempts to tackle deprivation by:

- attacking the core problems of deprived areas like weak economies and poor schools;

- harnessing the power of all sectors to work in partnership;

- focussing existing services and resources explicitly on deprived areas;

- giving local residents and community groups a central role in turning their neighbourhoods around.

To assist with Local Strategic Partnership, a Neighbourhood Renewal Fund has been set up which will provide £900m over three years in the 88 local authority areas. In order to be eligible for the money, councils had to produce a local neighbourhood renewal strategy agreed by the Local Strategic Partnership by April 2002.

A Community Empowerment Fund has been set up to support community and voluntary sector activity in the involvement within the Local Strategic Partnership. Such funding is used to assist community representatives attend Board meetings.

Summary

Although housing conditions have improved over the last 80 years or so, the problems have not been completely solved. Slums still exist and, more commonly, so do problem council estates.

In this unit, we have looked at some of the specific problems arising out of poor housing conditions and the various ways open to a local authority to deal with them. In particular, you should know in some detail about Housing Action Areas and General Improvement Areas, as well as newer initiatives such as Housing Action Trusts and Housing Renewal Areas. You should also be aware of the role of Local Strategic Partnerships

The problems of inner cities are topical and quite regularly turn up in the examination. You should be able to describe what the problems are, how they came into existence and how the government (and building societies) are trying to solve them.

Finally, we have considered Large Scale Voluntary Transfers.

11

GRANT AID

Objectives

After studying this unit, you should be able to:

- outline the background to grant aid;

- write detailed notes on the Labour government's reform of private sector housing renewal;

- describe the Neighbourhood Renewal Fund.

11.1   Introduction

Standards of housing have improved considerably in the last hundred years, as we have already seen. Perhaps just as importantly, expectations have risen. For example, it is now accepted that houses owned by private landlords should not be let unless they conform to accepted standards.

Because private owners cannot always afford all the modern amenities recommended or even prescribed by government, various forms of central government grant (Exchequer grants) have been available to private house-owners depending on the circumstances. Grants have helped to ease the costs of home improvement, conversion and modernization. We shall also look at funding available for regeneration of areas.

11.2   Background

Exchequer grants did not just appear overnight. They evolved over quite a long period of time and there were two reasons, in particular, for this:

- The need for a grant system had to be recognized and the form of a grant discussed and organized before any further steps could be taken.

- Exchequer grants were introduced through legislation, and the passing of new legislation can be a time-consuming process.

Several pieces of legislation served to establish Exchequer grants as an accepted and normal form of financial assistance in housing. They were:

- the Housing Act 1949;

- the House Purchase and Housing Act 1959;

- the Housing Act 1969;

- the Housing Act 1974;

- the Housing Act 1980;

- the Housing and Planning Act 1986

- the Local Government and Housing Act 1989; and

- the Housing, Grants, Construction and Regeneration Act 1996.

However, in July 2003, it was a complete 'all-change' with regard to grants. With the exception of Disabled Facilities Grants, which we shall look at shortly, all other grants stopped! This was under the Regulatory Reform (Housing Assistance – England and Wales) Order 2002. Local authorities can if they so desire pay some grants but these grants will be limited because of lack of funds.

We shall, therefore, look at a lot of the history of grants here, how they developed and indeed how they abruptly ended.

Housing Act 1949

The Housing Act 1949 represented the first serious attempt to provide grants to assist home-owners. The Act gave local authorities the power to make **discretionary grants** to owners, amounting to 50% of the cost of works approved by the local authority, subject to certain limits. Both the Exchequer and the local authority concerned were required to contribute towards the cost of the work. Owner-occupation was much lower at the time and not many owners took advantage of these grants.

House Purchase and Housing Act 1959

The House Purchase and Housing Act 1959 introduced a new grant called the **standard grant**. Provided that certain conditions were met, a house-owner could apply for the grant as a right. The local authority had no option but to award it; this grant was **mandatory**.

The purpose of standard grants was to give financial assistance to ensure the supply of the five standard amenities. These were:

- a fixed bath or shower;

- a wash-hand basin;

- a wc;

- a hot and cold water supply;

- a ventilated food cupboard.

Not surprisingly, the introduction of the standard grant proved a very popular measure. As a result, a great number of home improvements were made throughout the UK.

The Act also provided that discretionary grants should continue to meet the requirements of owners who wished to improve their property to a level higher than the standard.

Housing Act 1969

After various reports and other pieces of legislation, the Housing Act 1969 gave considerable prominence to home improvement grants. Instead of the discretionary and mandatory standard grants that had been available previously, the Act provided for improvement grants, standard grants and special grants. The format, however, was very similar to that of the previous system.

- An **improvement grant** was payable to owners for conversion and improvements that went beyond the provision of standard amenities. Grant payment would not be made unless the dwelling conformed to the standard prescribed.

- A **standard grant** was payable in respect of dwellings which lacked 'standard amenities', therefore grants were made available for:

    - a sink;

    - a wc;

    - a fixed bath or shower;

    - a wash-hand basin;

    - a hot and cold water supply at the sink;

    - a hot and cold water supply to a fixed bath or shower;

    - a hot and cold water supply to a wash-hand basin.

    As you can see, this list of standard amenities is very similar to the one which appeared in the 1959 legislation.

- A **special grant** could be provided when houses in multiple occupation needed finance for standard amenities. In effect, it was a standard grant for houses in multiple occupation.

Grants amounting to 50% of the cost of the eligible work were payable (65% in the case of dwellings in General Improvement Areas).

Under certain conditions, it was possible to obtain both a standard grant and an improvement grant. However, the improvement grant was reduced by the amount of any standard grant paid.

Like the Housing Act 1959, the 1969 Act stimulated rapid growth in house improvements across the UK. As well as providing for the improvement of individual dwellings, other parts of the 1969 legislation provided for the improvement of areas known as General Improvement Areas. (We referred to these in Unit 10.)

Housing Act 1974

The Housing Act 1974 reorganized the grants available to home-owners yet again. Five main grants were now available, although two of them were applicable only in General Improvement Areas or Housing Action Areas.

- An **improvement grant** was payable in respect of works required for the conversion of houses and other buildings, for the improvement of a dwelling or, in the case of a registered disabled person, works required for his welfare, accommodation or employment (where the existing dwelling was inadequate or unsuitable for those purposes).

- An **intermediate grant** was payable in respect of works required for the improvement of a dwelling by the provision of standard amenities which it lacked or which, in the case of a registered disabled person, were inaccessible.

- A **special grant** was payable in respect of works required to improve a house in multiple occupation by providing standard amenities or providing a means of escape from fire.

- A **repairs grant** was payable in respect of works of repair or replacement relating to a dwelling in a Housing Action Area or a General Improvement Area. These grants could, for example, include a repair or replacement of the roof of a dwelling.

- An **environmental grant** was available for curtilage works, such as fixing new gates or erecting garden walls, within a Housing Action Area or General Improvement Area. (A curtilage is an area or enclosure attached to a dwelling.)

These grants were discretionary except for the intermediate grant. Provided that the applicant met certain conditions, a local authority could not refuse to give an intermediate grant, ie it was mandatory.

Housing Act 1980

Repair grants had been payable only in respect of properties within Housing Action Areas and General Improvement Areas. The Housing Act 1980 removed this restriction, making them available in respect of properties built before 1919 with a rateable value of not more than £400 in London or £225 elsewhere. These rateable value limits were not applicable in Housing Action Areas or General Improvement Areas. The grants were payable provided the necessary work was substantial work of structural character.

The Act removed the requirement, contained in the 1974 Act, to repay grants in the case of sale.

Housing and Planning Act 1986

The Housing and Planning Act 1986 amended the Housing Act 1985, and introduced a new type of discretionary home improvement grant: the **common parts grant**. This enabled local authorities to offer financial assistance, subject to certain conditions, towards works of improvement or repair to the common parts of a building containing one or more flats.

Local Government and Housing Act 1989

The Local Government and Housing Act 1989 completely revamped previous grant systems.

Under the Act grants were available towards the cost of repairs, improvements, conversion of buildings and/or providing facilities and adaptations for a disabled person. In addition, minor works assistance was available to some owner-occupiers and tenants, who needed to carry out small-scale works to their homes.

Under the Local Government and Housing Act 1989, there were four major types of renovation grant available. These grants were:

- renovation grant;
- common parts grant;
- house in multiple occupation (HMO) grant;
- disabled facilities grant.

In addition to the above grants, assistance was given to carry out small-scale works including insulation work – this was known as minor works assistance.

Under this legislation, means-testing for grant aid was introduced. At the same time grants became mandatory in respect of unfit dwellings. This forced local authorities to provide grants for such dwellings and because of the large number of properties involved, waiting lists for grants were introduced. Consequently many local authorities decided not to bother to inspect dwellings within their area as they realised that they would have to provide funding for improvements in respect of unfit dwellings!

Housing Grants, Construction and Regeneration Act 1996

The four main grants that were available in the Housing Grants, Construction and Regeneration Act 1996 are outlined below:

- **renovation grant**: for the improvement and/or repair of houses (including maisonettes and flats), and for the conversion of houses and other buildings into flats for letting.

- **common parts grant**: for the improvement and/or repair of the common parts of buildings containing one or more flats.

- **HMO grant**: for the improvement and/or repair of houses in multiple occupation (HMOs), and for the conversion of buildings into HMOs.

- **disabled facilities grant**: for adapting or providing facilities for the home of a disabled person, to make it more suitable for him to live in. A disabled facilities grant is also available for adaptations to, or for providing facilities in, the common parts of buildings containing one or more flats for disabled people.

Under this legislation all grants became discretionary with the exception of certain work under disabled facilities grants.

Our Future Homes: Opportunity, Choice, Responsibility

This was a White Paper published in June 1995, by the then Conservative government. In the Paper it set out, among other things, a review undertaken earlier of the private sector renewal programmes and outlined proposals for changing legislation.

The White Paper emphasised that home owners were primarily responsible for repairing and maintaining their properties. However, financial assistance from public funds towards the cost of repair and maintenance should only be provided where owners did not have sufficient resources to undertake repairs themselves. The White Paper stressed that sometimes private housing was in a very poor condition and public intervention to enforce fitness standards could be justified. Similarly, assistance could be provided where regeneration of a whole area was taking place.

The White Paper stated that only a small minority of privately owned homes were unfit and owned by people who could not afford essential repairs. Any attempt to contribute to these costs could be carried out only over a period of time. In these circumstances the right that existed at the time to a mandatory renovation grant created unrealistic expectations. The demand for a mandatory grant greatly exceeded the resources available from local authorities for the purpose at a time of general expenditure constraint and reduced staffing resources. This meant that local authorities had been able to direct their budgets only to such grants and not tackle more comprehensive area renewal strategies such as Housing Renewal Areas.

It was for these reasons that all grants became discretionary (with the exception of certain work under disabled facilities grants) under the Housing Grants, Construction and Regeneration Act 1996.

Quality and Choice: A decent home for all – the way forward for housing

This White Paper was published by the Labour government in December 2000, and included in the paper were proposals for reforming legislation governing private sector renewal. The government acknowledge that poor quality housing impacts on the health of occupants and on the quality of life in the area. Whilst committed to improving housing quality in all tenures, the government consider that it is only right that the responsibility for maintaining privately owned homes (which for many people is their most valuable asset), should rest firmly and foremost with the owner, whilst acknowledging there were those in poor quality housing that could not afford to repair the dwellings, would need assistance. (This view was not dissimilar to the previous government's White Paper referred to above).

The White Paper points out that, under the previous grant systems there have been many unnecessary restrictions placed on local authorities resulting in many authorities taking a narrow and rigid approach to housing renewal.

One of the restrictions, under the previous grant regime prevented authorities from helping to develop equity release schemes in which capital in the home, rather than income, can be used to repay a loan. Equity release loans can often have a number of advantages over conventional loans. By avoiding the need for the borrower to make repayments from income, they provide access to capital without reducing people's living standards.

Under the changes approved under the Regulatory Reform (Housing Assistance – England and Wales) Order 2003, local authorities can from July 2003, provide assistance in the following ways:

- a grant;

- a loan;

- a loan guarantee or indemnity;

- by providing materials or labour;

- by incurring expenditure in other ways (such as paying a contractor to carry out work);

- or any combination of these.

Authorities are able either to provide assistance themselves or through another agency, such as a registered social landlord, charity or home improvement agency. We shall look at home improvement agencies shortly.

To ensure that the assistance they give is targeted effectively, authorities have the power to carry out mean-testing and to charge for any labour or materials they provide, should they wish to do so. They are able to set the conditions under which any financial assistance should be repaid and the period over which those conditions should apply. Where they chose to give a loan or to attach conditions to a grant or loan, authorities have the power to waive any requirement to repay it or to reduce the amount they require to be repaid.

Disabled Facilities Grant

A disabled facilities grant is designed to make the home of a disabled person more suitable for him to live in, and to help the person manage more independently in the home. An application can be made by a disabled owner-occupier or tenant.

The council will check that the proposed works are necessary and appropriate to meet the needs of the disabled occupant, and that the works are reasonable and practicable given the age and condition of the property.

Providing that the proposed works are necessary and appropriate, and the works are reasonable and practicable, then the grant becomes mandatory and an amount payable up to a maximum of £25,000. Where necessary an additional discretionary grant element of up to £15,000 could be payable as 'top-up' funding. In the case of an extended family the top-up element is means-tested having regard to all relevant persons. Examples of works qualifying for mandatory grant would be:

- making it easier to get into and out of the home;

- making access easier to the living room, bedroom, kitchen and bathroom;

- providing suitable bathroom and kitchen facilities that can be used independently;

- adapting heating or lighting controls to make them easier to use;

- making the dwelling safe for the disabled occupant;

- improving the heating system in the home;

- making provisions around the home which will help a disabled person to care for someone living there who is dependent on the applicant for care.

A discretionary grant is also available for a wide range of other works to make a home suitable for a disabled occupant's accommodation, welfare or employment. Works could include providing a safe play area for a disabled child or providing or adapting an existing room to enable a disabled person to work from home.

All applications are subject to a means-test to determine the amount to be contributed by the applicant towards the cost of the works. Generally, the means-test focuses on the disabled person and their spouse, but where that disabled person is a child, the parent(s) or guardian(s) are means-tested.

Depending on the local authority, applicants who own their property and who are unable to afford their contribution from the means-test, can possibly be assisted through the equity release scheme.

Warm Front Scheme (formerly Home Energy Efficiency Scheme (HEES))

You should note that it is possible to obtain grants to cover the cost of making a home warmer through the Warm Front Scheme. This is not administered by local authorities but by the Energy Action Grants Agency (EAGA). It was set up by the Social Security Act 1990 which endeavoured to improve the thermal insulation of dwellings and reduce or prevent the wastage of energy in dwellings.

The scheme was originally launched in 1991 It was then known as the Home Energy Efficiency Scheme (HEES). This was renamed in the winter of 2001/02 to the Warm Front Scheme.

Under the scheme households in receipt of a qualifying income related or disability benefit or older people can receive help in making their homes warmer. There are two types of grant:

(i) **Warm Front Plus Grant**

This is applicable for over 60s who are in receipt of an income-related benefit. Grants of up to £2,500 are given to cover the cost of insulation measures, such as loft, cavity wall and draught-proofing and where appropriate installing a central heating system in the main living areas.

(ii) **Warm Front Grant**

This is applicable for over 60s who are in receipt of a qualifying disability benefit or those where there is a child under 16 living at the dwelling and the householder receives a qualifying benefit.

No contribution is necessary unless the costs exceed those figures quoted above.

The grant is not repaid if the dwelling is sold.

We looked at fuel poverty earlier in this text. A household is said to be in fuel poverty when it needs to spend 10% or more of its income on energy to maintain an adequate standard of warmth (although it may not spend that money). One in eight households struggles to keep warm in winter.

For every 1°C the temperature drops, it has been estimated there will be an associated increase of 8,000 deaths. In the world's coldest city – Yakutsk in Russia – there is no excess winter mortality!

86% of low income households do not have adequate loft insulation, 67% do not have any draught proofing and 36% do not have adequate hot water tank insulation.

Most households with someone aged 60 or over are entitled to the £200 winter fuel payment, irrespective of whether they are living in England or abroad. Ironically, although this is paid automatically to women 60 or over, men aged between 60 and 65 have to claim, unless they are on income-related benefits. This is because payment is linked into those on pension and benefits. No attempt is made by the government to rectify this situation and each year many men between the ages of 60 and 65 miss out on this payment and suffer and even die. If temperatures average zero or lower over seven days, those aged 60 and over, who are on income support, receive a further payment of £8.50.

Current situation

Apart from disabled facilities grants which remain the same, it is very much down to local authorities to consider what assistance they can provide to owner occupiers to repair/improve their properties. As any other assistance is discretionary, it is all dependant on the budgetary constraints prevailing at the time. Furthermore, the types of grants payable and for what purpose are a matter for individual local authorities. The author has endeavoured to summarise this in a few paragraphs based on his experience of authorities in the South East. Let us look, therefore, at what is available.

Other grants

(i) **Repair Grants**

Repair grants, up to £5,000, may be approved for vulnerable applicants in receipt of income-related benefit for works to remedy defects which affect health and/or safety.

Typical works which may attract grant aid include the following:

- main structural work (including roof and windows);
- rising and/or penetrating dampness;
- disrepair to drains;
- disrepair to basic amenities necessitating their renewal;
- defects to the water supply;
- defects to electrical wiring;
- internal works such as plastering/rendering, condensation treatments and heating measures.

(b) Handyperson Grants

To qualify for assistance the client must meet one of the following criteria:

i.   be aged 60 or over;

ii. be disabled or infirm;

iii. be in receipt of an income-related benefit with child(ren) under 16.

The following conditions/limitations apply:

- total duration of work not to exceed six hours in any one year;
- clients must agree to a Council Officer carrying out brief survey to identify what work is necessary;
- all materials (other than fixings and smoke/carbon monoxide detectors) to be supplied by the client;
- grant will be limited to £250;
- clients must have the power or duty to carry out the works.

Typical works which may attract grant aid include the following:

- replacing light bulbs;
- setting thermostats/timers;
- fitting smoke/carbon monoxide alarms;
- unblocking sinks/basins/baths/wc;
- putting up curtains/tracks;
- fixing down hazardous carpets, trailing electrical leads etc;
- moving furniture (requiring one person);
- replacing wc seats, small areas of tiling, sealant around bath/sink;

- fitting grab rails, plugs, fuses;

- minor measures against condensation (eg mould removal, fitting air bricks, etc);

- energy efficiency advice and minor measures (eg fitting foil behind radiators, etc);

- initial help following hospital discharge (eg resetting heating controls, etc);

- minor repairs to paths (to eliminate trip hazards), gate and fences.

(c) **Landlord's renovation grants**

To qualify for assistance the landlord must:

- be the freeholder of the property or have a lease with at least five years unexpired at the time of the application, and

- except in cases where the works are to improve fire prevention and/or means of escape from fire,

  either enter into a nominations agreement with the Council to accept a tenant nominated by the Council*

  or enter into an agreement with the Council to lease the property to the Council*

  *for a period of five years starting from the completion of the works.

The following conditions/limitations apply:

- no grant will exceed £15,000;

- for eligible works/services costing up to £30,000 the applicant must contribute half of the total cost (ie grant to be match-funded by landlord);

- the applicant must fully fund the cost of any works above the match-funded threshold of £30,000.

Work which may attract grant aid:

- measures to improve fire prevention and/or means of escape from fire in houses in multiple occupation having three storeys or more where the works are required by the council;

- rehabilitation works to facilitate the re-occupation of a property.

(d) **Energy Grants**

Energy Grants may be approved in cases where applicants do not qualify for assistance under the government's 'Warm Front' Scheme.

Typical works which may attract grant aid include the following:

- loft insulation;

- cavity wall insulation;

- insulation to water storage tanks/cylinders and pipework;

- where necessary, clearance and disposal of roof contents to allow insulation placement.

The following condition/limitation applies:

- grant shall not exceed £750.

Home Improvement Agencies

Home Improvement Agencies were introduced in 1987, to assist vulnerable people living in poor or inappropriate private sector housing in providing practical help with repairs, improvements and adaptations. The agencies are small (currently 230 government funded agencies in England), not-for-profit organisations that assist the elderly, disabled and those on a low income to repair, improve or adapt their homes. They are supported by local authorities, housing associations (especially Anchor Housing Trust) and charities. The capital funding to assist required work can come from a variety of sources; local authority private renewal grants, charitable donations, a client's own sources of income or equity release.

The aim of Home Improvement Agencies is to improve people's living conditions, thereby enhancing their health and quality of life and enabling them to remain in their homes in greater comfort and security. They have been very successful and many older people would otherwise have been unable to remain in their homes resulting in the need for residential accommodation.

These agencies are sometimes known as 'Care and Repair' or 'Stay Put' agencies. The activities of a Home Improvement Agency include:

- visiting clients in their homes and advising on problems concerning the property;

- checking entitlement to welfare benefits;

- providing advice on financial options available to the client;

- assisting with the completion of forms, such as grant applications;

- drawing up a schedule of works;

- liaising with and monitoring the performance of contractors;

- liaising with social workers, occupational therapists, surveyors, environmental health and grants officers.

Some agencies provide additional services such as:

- handyperson services (usually minor plumbing, electrical repairs etc);

- gardening and/or decorating services (sometimes carried out by the handyperson);

- direct provision of aids and adaptations for vulnerable people living in the private sector.

11.4   Global Grants

So far in this unit we have looked at grants that have been (and some that still are) available towards the improvement, repair and conversion of individual dwellings. On a much larger scale, grants are available which are designed to stimulate urban regeneration. There have been other 'global' grants in the last 15 years or so; all of these have been, or are being, replaced.

(i)   City Grants

The City Grant was introduced in July 1988. It replaced urban development grants (UDGs) and urban regeneration grants (URGs). It also incorporated private-sector development land grants (DLGs), where the project fell within a priority area for city grant.

The city grant scheme was designed to support projects that were:

● undertaken by the private sector;

● capital investments;

● above £200,000 in total project value;

● within a priority area;

● unable to proceed because costs, including reasonable profits element, exceed certain values;

● and which would provide jobs, private housing and other benefits.

In most cases, the private-sector developer would be a company, although individuals, charities, pension funds or others could apply; local authorities could be involved. However, the risk-bearing rested firmly with the private sector, because there were no local authority guarantees that might bail the developer out should the project fail.

City grants could be paid in respect of industrial sites such as factories, workshops and warehouses; commercial sites such as shops and offices, sports and leisure centres; and for housing, which was for sale or for private letting at a market rent. City grants could also be available for projects falling within areas covered by Urban Development Corporations (UDCs).

Under the city grant system, the amount payable served to bridge the gap between the cost of a development and its sale or rental value.

(ii)   City Challenge

City Challenge was launched by Michael Heseltine in May 1991 to tackle urban squalor and revive some of Britain's most run-down inner cities. It offered local authorities from Urban programme Areas – working with private-sector, voluntary and community partners – an opportunity to compete for inner city and housing resources to tackle a wide range of economic and social problems, with funds made available to winners over a five-year period. The aim was to provide major impetus to area improvement, leading to self-sustaining economic regeneration.

City Challenge rewarded authorities that demonstrated imaginative approaches to inner city regeneration, with particular emphasis being placed on proposals aimed at creating an environment likely to attract people to live, work and invest in run-down urban areas.

(iii) Single Regeneration Budget (SRB)

The government introduced the Single Regeneration Budget in November 1993, building upon the City Challenge model and merging 20 separate programmes totalling some £1.4 billion in 1994/95.

The Single Regeneration Budget was a comprehensive national scheme which looked at regeneration issues in both the urban and rural context and not just housing; it enabled the problems of bad housing to be tackled alongside unemployment, education, training and crime. Its purpose was to boost business, create jobs and fight crime. The public and the private sector could bid for cash that would fund regeneration and last from one to seven years. The funding of the Single Regeneration Budget was flexible in being linked to the scale and nature of the problem. It was also based on a longer time frame than City Challenge (five years).

It provided resources to support regeneration initiatives in England carried out by local regeneration partnerships. It was an important instrument to tackle social exclusion. Its priority was to enhance the quality of life of local people in areas of need by reducing the gap between deprived and other areas and between different groups.

(iv) Challenge Fund

Within the SRB came the Challenge Fund worth some £450 million annually, which selected from competing bids for the most imaginative and best value local projects.

Regeneration is not just an urban problem; rural districts can face serious problems of unemployment, poverty, lack of skills and despair. The Challenge Fund, introduced at the same time as the Single Regeneration Budget, introduced a more comprehensive and holistic approach to regeneration. The Challenge Fund offered a chance of tackling problems in rural areas and in towns that were not previously eligible for City Grant or Urban Programme assistance. The Challenge Fund allocated limited resources through a competitive process.

The Urban Programme (referred to later in this text) had spread resources very thinly for individual projects. The Challenge Fund and its forerunner, City Challenge, favoured a spiral approach, focusing on a discrete geographical area with a critical maximum size – a population of 25,000 in the case of the Challenge Fund.

The Challenge Fund varied from the City Challenge, with the latter being restricted to just the larger metropolitan areas and the former being given to all.

It is unfortunate that the Challenge Fund was introduced at a time of severe financial pressure on public sector funding in general and regeneration programmes in particular, which had negative implications for the success of the system and its longer-term effectiveness in achieving sustainable regeneration.

(v) Capital Challenge Pilot Scheme

In May 1996, John Gummer, the then Secretary of State for the Environment, announced a pilot scheme for the Challenge Funding of local authorities' mainstream capital expenditure. Following consultation in the early part of 1996, the government decided to proceed with a practical test of how challenge funding of capital spending might work, the benefits it could bring and the possible opportunity costs of the approach.

The pilot scheme tested whether the 'challenge' approach could

- foster local choice and local decision-making and provide a clear incentive to developing local partnerships for the provision of mainstream services;

- give positive encouragement to those local authorities that took a strategic approach to planning capital investment; and

- lift some of the close controls that Whitehall exercised over investment decisions.

The Fund was administered and distributed on a regional basis.

(vi) Estates Renewal Challenge Fund

The Estates Renewal Challenge Fund was launched in November 1995 with the aim of funding to help towards the costs of transforming some of the remaining large, run-down local authority estates. This assisted the transfer of the stock to registered social landlords through a public and private sector partnership.

It was a competitive fund designed to facilitate the transfer of poor-quality local authority estates to new registered social landlords. These are the estates that would not be transferred without some public support.

11.5 Other Approaches to Urban Regeneration

The government has approached the problem of urban regeneration in a number of other ways in the past.

(i) Urban Development Corporations (UDCs)

Urban Development Corporations (UDCs) were set up by the government with the objective of regenerating designated areas. A UDC sought to bring land and buildings into effective use, to encourage the development of industry and commerce, and to ensure that housing and social facilities were available to encourage people to live and work within its area.

The SRB funds the remaining nine UDCs in England.

The Local Government, Planning and Land Act 1980 created the London Docklands Development Corporation among other things. This body has no shareholders, and is not run with a view to making profits. In 1981, the first acre of dockland was sold for £33,000. Now such land sells at an average of over £1 million per acre, while as much as £5 million per acre may be paid for exceptionally good locations!

The attractions of London's Docklands are:

- their proximity to central London;

- the fact that many dwellings abut quiet stretches of water;

- good transport for those needing to travel into central London;

- status.

(ii) Estate Action

Estate Action, which used to be called Urban Housing Renewal Unit, was set up by the Department of the Environment in 1985. It existed to try to improve the living conditions on the neglected and rundown Council estates.

The government confirmed in 1994 that it was its intention that Estate Action focus resources on major schemes intended to develop and implement strategies for the comprehensive regeneration of larger more rundown estates, but it is intended that resources should also continue to be available for schemes designed to promote carefully targeted small-scale improvements to forestall or reverse decline.

Estate Action promoted good practice, stimulated innovation and provided resources for estate improvement schemes that were cost effective and yielded value for money. It also supported schemes that met the following objectives of:

- physical improvements to housing;

- improving housing management (at the local authority and at the estate level);

- involving tenants in the regeneration and long-term management of their estate;

- diversifying tenure;

- attracting private-sector resources and;

- establishing estate-based training and enterprise initiatives.

(iii) Enterprise Zones

One example of targeting specific areas for regeneration effort can be seen in the Enterprise Zones, familiar from television and other advertisements. These were set up in the 1980s. They were the result of a government approach to help industry and stimulate development inside specially designated areas. An area designated an Enterprise Zone may receive financial assistance and a simpler framework of administrative controls. There are a number of benefits:

- Enterprise Zones were exempt from rates;
- 100% allowances, for corporation and income tax purposes, were available for capital expenditure on industrial and commercial development;
- a greatly simplified planning regime existed in an enterprise zone; developments that conform to the published scheme for each zone would not require individual planning permission.

There are a number of Enterprise Zones in England including:

Corby	Salford/Trafford
Dudley	Scunthorpe
Glanford	Speke (Liverpool)
Hartlepool	Telford
Isle of Dogs	Tyneside
Middlesbrough	Wakefield
North East Lancashire	Wellingborough
North West Kent	Workington
Rotherham	

(iv)   The Urban Programme

The Local Government Grants (Social Needs) Act 1969 authorized the Secretary of State for the Environment to reimburse local authorities which incurred expenditure by reason of the existence in urban areas of special need. The Housing and Planning Act 1986 permits the Secretary of State to give financial assistance by grant of a loan, or otherwise, to persons whose activities contributed to urban regeneration and who incurred expenditure which qualified for assistance. These grants were known collectively as the Urban Programme.

Local authorities were also given additional powers under the Inner Urban Areas Act 1978. Authorities designated under this Act were empowered to declare Industrial or Commercial Improvement Areas, where loans and grants could be given for improving amenities and improving or converting buildings. These schemes have now been phased out through the Single Regeneration Budget.

11.6   Current Initiatives

(i)   Urban Regeneration Companies

We saw earlier in the text how Lord Rogers' Urban Task Force had recommended creating urban regeneration companies (URCs) to lead and co-ordinate redevelopment and new investment in declining urban areas.

URCs are new independent companies established by the relevant local authority and Regional Development Agency, as well as English Partnerships, the private sector and other key partners. URCs work towards a co-ordinated approach to the problems and opportunities in their target areas. While their principle focus is engaging the private sector in an agreed physical and economic regeneration strategy, this needs to be within the wider context of a comprehensive approach to tackling the problems, and identifying the opportunities, of an area.

It is proposed by the government to set up 12 new URCs by 2004.

(ii)   Neighbourhood Renewal Fund

Following the Comprehensive Spending Review 2000, the government set targets for improved outcomes by public services in deprived neighbourhoods. The targets mean that government departments, local authorities and other service providers are being judged for the first time on their performance in the areas where they are doing worst – not on the national average.

A New Commitment to Neighbourhood Renewal – National Strategy Action Plan sets out the government's policies to tackle deprivation wherever it occurs in England. A key element of the strategy is the improvement of mainstream services to produce better outcomes in the most deprived areas. This means increased employment and improved economic performance, reduced crime, better educational attainment, improved health and better housing.

The Neighbourhood Renewal Fund aims to enable the 88 most deprived authorities, in collaboration with their Local Strategic Partnership, to improve services, narrowing the gap between deprived areas and the rest of England.

Funding of £900m has been made available to 2003/04.

(iii)   European Funding

It is sometimes possible to attract European Funding, and the two main funds available are:

● European Regional Development Fund (ERDF) for use in deprived areas;

● European Social Fund (ESF) for training and employment measures.

Summary

In this unit we have looked at grants for house improvement, conversion and modernization and other approaches to urban regeneration.

12

VALUE AND SALEABILITY

Objectives

After studying this unit, you should be able to:

- describe the different ways in which a property can be valued;

- outline the factors affecting the saleability of property;

- explain the legal situation on the 'duty of care' of surveyors and valuers.

12.1   Introduction

The term 'estate management' is open to several different interpretations, depending upon its context. According to Clive Thornton, estate management is:

> ... the direction and supervision of an interest in landed property with the aim of securing the optimum return. This return may not be financial but may be in terms of social need, status, prestige, political power or some goal of group of goals.

For our purposes, in other words, estate management is all about managing resources, which may be financial, human or physical, in order to bring about the best return. In the private sector, that return will be largely financial. In the public sector, where housing is intended to serve a need, it will be mainly social.

In this unit, we shall be looking at the private sector and, in particular, at the criteria which affect the value and saleability of private dwellings.

There are four occasions when the value of a house is assessed and there are four different types of valuation, which are carried out for different reasons, though not necessarily by different people. They are:

- a structural survey valuation;

- a building society or bank valuation; and

- a valuation for insurance purposes;

- investment valuation (for rented housing).

Structural Survey Valuation

Suppose that Mr A puts his house up for sale. Mr B quite likes the look of it and is interested in putting in an offer to buy it. The first thing Mr B should do is to arrange for a survey of the house to make sure that it really is all it purports to be. Such a survey is called a structural survey.

A structural survey should be carried out by a qualified surveyor and Mr B can either organize this himself, or he can arrange one through his building society or bank. In any event, he will have to pay for it, regardless of whether or not he eventually buys the house.

How much he has to pay for the survey depends partly on the value of the property, but also on exactly what depth of survey he requires. That is something he must discuss with the surveyor. Generally speaking, if Mr B is at all nervous about the house he wants to buy, or if it is an older property, he should ask the surveyor to conduct a detailed survey, often called a 'full survey'. This would include, for example, testing the drains and examining the central heating, whereas a cheaper survey might not. A full survey could cost anything up to £2,500, whereas a less detailed one might cost only £500.

There are certain points which any survey should cover. These are usually set out in a standard form by the surveyor or his firm. In any case, all surveys ought to state exactly what they cover and to what extent. They should also state the conditions of engagement, which are designed to protect the surveyor against future liability.

A good example of the layout of a report is the *Housebuyers Report*, which is published by the Royal Institution of Chartered Surveyors (RICS) for use by their members. It is not a full structural survey; neither is it superficial. It is designed to give prospective house purchasers who do not wish to incur the cost of a full survey, reasonable confidence in the condition of the house in which they are interested. Reproduced below is part of a Royal Institution of Chartered Surveyors leaflet, which gives some idea of its scope.

The standard RICS Housebuyers report and valuation provides intending purchasers with a concise report on the state of repair and condition of the house which they are proposing to buy, in a format prepared and published by the Royal Institution of Chartered Surveyors.

The scheme is intended to include houses and bungalows of up to 200 m^2 (2000 sq. ft.) of floor area not more than three storeys in height, but it is not intended for pre-1900 properties.

The inspection covers all those parts of the property that are readily visible or accessible, including the roof space if there is a readily accessible roof hatch. It does not, however, include an underfloor inspection where there is no direct access, or close inspection of the external faces of roofs where the roof height is more than three metres (ten feet) above ground level. In many properties even a surface inspection of the flooring may be precluded due to the presence of fitted carpeting and furniture and, in the case of some properties, of fitted hardboard over the floorboards.

Where possible, drain covers are lifted and electric wiring visually inspected, but a definitive report on the condition of services such as these cannot be provided without a test by a competent plumber or a competent electrician.

The difference between this standard form of report and valuation and a structural survey is that the latter is based on a very detailed examination with a detailed report. It is time-consuming and may involve the occupier in some inconvenience.

The RICS standard form of report, however, which is particularly attractive when time is short or economy is important, involves a less detailed inspection and a more concise report concentrating on the major defects only, being sufficient to enable a chartered surveyor to give a general opinion on the quality and condition of the fabric. It aims to assist a prospective buyer in deciding upon the soundness or otherwise of the proposed purchase. A structural survey will provide a very detailed report on the condition of the property with advice on the repairs and modifications required, but would not normally include a valuation. It will normally assume vacant possession unless otherwise instructed.

Source: Royal Institution of Chartered Surveyors.

Building Society or Bank Valuation

Suppose that Mr B is happy with the result of his structural survey or housebuyer's report. He decides that he wants to buy the house and applies to a building society or bank for a mortgage. Now it is the turn of the building society or the bank to look at the house and make a decision: is it worth accepting a mortgage of the property, or not? In other words, the lender must now carry out its own valuation, in order to assess whether the condition and value of the house is adequate security for the mortgage loan requested by Mr B.

A building society or bank valuation is made purely for the benefit of the financial institution, and it should be noted that:

● it does not imply that the house is worth whatever price is being asked for it; and

● it is not a structural survey. It does not imply that the house is necessarily structurally sound and free from defects, although a lender would obviously not wish to make a mortgage loan on any house that was on the verge of collapse.

Insurance Valuation

Any owner-occupier with a mortgage must insure his house against the possibility that it will need to be rebuilt, which would be the case if, for example, there were a serious fire. The cost of rebuilding need not bear any resemblance to the sale price, survey valuation or building society or bank valuation. The insurance value of a house, which reflects the cost of rebuilding, is generally lower than all the other valuations; it does not take into account the value of the land on which the house is built, nor any considerations relating to the location of the house, nor the contents of the house.

Valuation Summary

By now, you may be wondering just how many times a house is valued, and why. The following summary should clear the position.

- The building cost, or the amount it cost to build, represents the original 'value' of a house.

- Usually, the price a house fetches when it is sold for the first time is higher than its building cost, reflecting the profit taken by the builder. There are one or two exceptions to this general rule, such as where local authorities have made land available to builders at very cheap rates which we referred to earlier in this book.

- The sale price asked by subsequent owners will take into account the location, contents and maintenance of the house, as well as the effect of inflation.

- The value of a house for insurance purposes will bear no relation to any sale prices, because it reflects only the cost of rebuilding.

- The valuation a surveyor makes for a potential buyer will take into account the location of the house, and will probably be quite close to the sale price.

- The valuation made by a surveyor for a building society will be entirely for the purpose of deciding whether any mortgage loan will be justified and secure. For this reason it is likely to be cautious, and may well be lower than the asking price for the house. It will generally exclude items such as carpets or light fittings which are left behind by the seller.

Until October 1980, the valuation and report made by a building society's valuer were seen only by that building society. For his own security, the prospective purchaser was obliged to arrange his own structural survey. This reported on the condition of the house but did not always, at that time, include a valuation.

It was the former Abbey National Building Society (now Abbey National plc) that first released survey reports to prospective purchasers.

Nowadays, prospective purchasers are entitled to see all reports produced by building societies' or banks' valuers. Since these are not necessarily detailed enough to satisfy a nervous purchaser that the house is structurally sound, a compromise is often reached whereby a surveyor carrying out a survey for a building society or bank will carry out a structural survey on behalf of the prospective purchaser at the same time. This produces obvious savings in time and cost. It also means that the surveyor is able to comment more sensibly on house valuations, rather than looking merely at the structural aspects of a house or considering it simply as possible security for a mortgage.

12.3 Legal Aspects

Now that the reports prepared by building society and bank valuers are made available to prospective purchasers, a number of questions arise. Are prospective purchasers entitled to rely on such reports as indicating that the house is worth buying? What happens should the house subsequently prove to have serious defects? Does the building society or bank bear any responsibility towards the purchaser?

There is a technical way of phrasing these questions in law: does the building society or bank owe a **duty of care** to the purchaser?

In the case of *Hedley Byrne and Co Ltd v Heller* (1963), one bank relied upon the opinion of another as to the financial stability of a third party. The opinion given was incorrect, but it included a disclaimer which read 'for private use and without responsibility on the part of this bank or its officials'.

Since this case does not involve housing, you do not need to know its details. However, you should remember two important conclusions which were reached by the House of Lords.

● Since the disclaimer existed, no duty of care arose in this case. Therefore the action failed and no damages were payable.

● The House of Lords considered that where no disclaimer had been issued, there would have been a duty of care in these circumstances.

> ... *If, in a sphere in which a person is so placed that others could reasonably rely on his judgement or his skill as on his ability to make careful inquiry, a person takes it on himself to give information or advice to, or allows his information or advice to be passed on to another person who, as he knows or should know, will place reliance on it, then a duty of care will arise.*

We need to look now specifically at the duty of care, by a surveyor, to the purchaser of a dwelling. One of the most important cases you should know about is *Yianni v Edwin Evans* (1981). It was in this case that it was established that valuers who prepared valuation reports for building societies or banks were under a duty of care to mortgage applicants.

● *Case:* **Yianni v Edwin Evans (1981)**
E, a firm of valuers and surveyors, carried out a valuation for a building society and on the strength of E's report the building society granted a mortgage loan for £12,000. Subsequently, cracks which would have cost £18,000 to repair were discovered in the foundations of the house. Although the building society had recommended that Y should carry out his own independent survey, which he had not, and although the society had issued its standard notice that the making of an advance would not imply any warranty or that the purchase price was reasonable, Y sued E.

● **Held:** The society's willingness to make an advance of £12,000 implied that the house was worth at least that amount. The judge was satisfied that the society knew that E's report would be passed on to Y and that Y would place reliance on it, regardless of the standard notice. He therefore held that a duty of care did arise, and Y's case succeeded.

The importance of *Yianni v Edwin Evans* (1981) cannot be overstated. It means that, in general, building society or bank valuers owe a duty of care to mortgage applicants. If somebody buys a house on the strength of the fact that a building society or bank has relied upon its valuer's report to make a mortgage advance and subsequently finds serious defects in it, then he may sue the valuer. Although there is no guarantee that he will succeed, the law permits him to bring such an action, and he stands a chance of receiving damages.

One exception to the general rule has however occurred. This was the case of *Stevenson v Nationwide Building Society* (1984).

- **Case:** *Stevenson v Nationwide Building Society* (1984)

  S, an estate agent, purchased a property. He did not see the building society's valuation, which did not disclose the fact that the property spanned a river and was of an unusual design. Subsequently, part of the property's concrete floor collapsed and S sued the society's valuer.

- **Held:** The judge was in no doubt that the valuer had been negligent. However, the case failed for two reasons.

  - The mortgage application form contained the words: 'I/we understand that the report and valuation on the property by the society's valuer is confidential and is intended solely for the consideration of the society in determining what advance (if any) may be made on the security, and that no responsibility is implied or accepted by the society or its valuer for either the value or condition of the property by reason of such inspection and report.' The judge was of the opinion that the confidentiality of the report was neither here nor there. The words which followed clearly indicated that the survey was not intended to be a full structural survey and had limited purpose.

  - The judge might still have upheld S's case, but for the fact that he was an estate agent. He had also admitted that he knew all about the practice of building societies and their disclaimers. The judge therefore ruled that S should not have relied on the valuer's report. He had only himself to blame when the purchase turned out to be a poor investment.

The *Stevenson* case is an exception to the more general rule established in the *Yianni* case, but you should be aware that it exists.

The case of *Smith v Eric S Bush* (1987) suggests that an unskilled person can rely upon a building society or bank valuation, despite explicit warnings not to do so, unless the defects missed are such that they would have been picked up only on a proper structural survey.

- **Case:** *Smith v Eric S Bush* (1987)

  In 1980, Mrs S, a state-enrolled nurse, bought an old terraced property for £17,500. She received a mortgage from the former Abbey National Building Society, relying on the society's valuation which was carried out by B. For a fee of £21, she was shown B's report, which stated that there was nothing significantly wrong with the dwelling. In June 1982, a chimney which had been unsupported at the time of the survey collapsed, causing considerable damage. Mrs S sued B.

- **Held:** the surveyor was under a duty of care not only to the building society, but also to someone whom he knew would probably rely on his report since she possessed no special skill in valuing. Mrs S was awarded damages against B.

A similar case occurred in 1987, namely *Harris v Wyre Forest District Council*.

- **Case:** *Harris v Wyre Forest District Council* (1987)

  In 1987, Mr and Mrs Harris, then engaged, applied to the local authority for a mortgage loan to purchase a small Victorian house. They completed and signed the local authority's standard application, but did not read the disclaimer which appeared just above where they placed their signatures and which read as follows:

  To be read carefully and signed by all applicants ... we understand that ... the valuation is confidential and is intended solely for the information of Wyre Forest District Council in determining what advance, if any, may be made on the security and that no responsibility whatsoever is implied or accepted by the council for the value or condition of the property by reason of such inspection and report. (You are advised for your own protection to instruct your own surveyor/architect to inspect the property.)

  I/we understand that the valuation report is the property of the council and that I/we cannot require its production.

  The valuation report valued the property at its asking price. It made no mention of problems with the foundations. Three years later, Mr and Mrs H tried to sell the property and were advised that it required considerable underpinning, as well as other works, and was unsaleable.

- **Held:** The Court of Appeal ruled that Mr and Mrs H had accepted the terms of the mortgage application. Therefore, neither the Council nor their valuer owed any duty of care towards the couple and had assumed no responsibility for the condition of the house. Leave to appeal to the House of Lords was granted.

  In April 1989, the Lords overturned the decision of the lower court. Lord Templeman stated that 'valuers were professional men paid for their services and they knew that 90% of housebuyers relied on mortgage valuations. Many people could not afford a second valuation. They placed their trust in building societies, local councils and the professional valuers they appointed ... It is not fair or reasonable for building societies and valuers to agree together to impose on purchasers the risk of loss arising as a result of incompetence or carelessness on the part of the valuers.'

12.4   The Price of Land

The factors that affect the price of land are a combination of social and practical matters. Probably the four most important are:

- desirability of the land;
- density of population;
- suitability for development;
- planning restrictions.

Desirability

The most important single factor affecting the price of land is whether people want to live in that particular area. This in turn is the result of a number of factors.

- Is the area close to business and commercial centres? Those in work will want to be close to their jobs; others will want to be close to shopping and recreational centres.
- Is the area pleasantly situated? For example, a new building site next to a council estate will prove less popular than one close to a private residential area.
- Is the area accessible? Is it well-served by roads and public transport?

The desirability of an area is not always in direct proportion to the density of its population. Parts of London are densely populated but the demand for land there is not particularly high, whereas a high premium is placed on living in the countryside near to London, which is relatively less populous.

Density of Population

Generally speaking, the density of population in an area remains a significant factor in the price of land within that area. We have all seen the high price of land reflected in the high price of houses, when developers do manage to provide more homes in a densely populated area.

- Land will be more valuable in densely populated areas simply because it is scarce. Conversely, land in sparsely populated areas will be cheaper because more of it is available.
- Land in densely populated areas will be more valuable because it is in demand; presumably that is why the area has a high population in the first place. Conversely, land in sparsely populated areas will be cheaper because there is less demand for it.

This, of course, is the basic law of economics – supply and demand.

Suitability for Development

There is little point in buying land if there is no prospect of developing it (except, perhaps, as a speculative investment). This may seem an obvious point, but the factors that make land unsuitable for development are not necessarily so obvious.

The point to bear in mind is that if the land is, for one reason or another, of poor quality, then it will cost more to develop it. However, the price of the finished product will be unchanged: it will be whatever prospective housebuyers are prepared to pay. The developer has to bear the extra costs incurred in building on the substandard land.

There are a number of reasons why land might be classified as poor and not suitable for development:

● at one time there may have been mining in the area, making parts of the land unsafe;

● the land may have subsidence problems (not necessarily caused by mining);

● there may be peat under the subsoil, a substance not particularly suitable for building on;

● the land may have been used as a rubbish tip in the past and if so, there is an ever-present danger of vermin and underground fires;

● the land may be toxic – if, for example, it is the site of old gasworks.

In all these (and many other) cases, the land in question can usually be developed. However, the costs of development are likely to render the project uneconomic.

Planning Restrictions

The fourth major factor affecting the price of land is whether there are any planning restrictions on how the land can be developed. For example, a local authority might decide that a particular area should not be turned into a residential development. If that is the case, then clearly residential developers will not want to buy the land, there will be less demand for it and its price will drop.

There are other specific planning restrictions which could make a developer wary of buying land in a particular area. For example, suppose that there were some old, derelict properties on the land which needed demolishing.

● Can the same number of houses be put back up? The minimum requirements regarding the area covered by houses and the amenities contained in them are not the same as they were some years ago.

● Can the land be developed economically in such a way that parking is provided? Town planners now want parking facilities available for new houses and this was certainly not the case when many older houses were originally built.

12.5　Saleability

There are many things that can affect the saleability of a property. Some homes are obviously very desirable, whereas there are others that virtually no one would want to buy. The vast majority of private dwellings fall somewhere between these two extremes and in a number of cases it may be hard to tell whether or not a particular property will sell quickly or easily. There is no magic formula and all that anybody can do is to make a judgement based on past experience, bearing in mind the various factors that may be relevant.

- **Location**

  A house that is conveniently located should be easier to sell than a similar house in the middle of nowhere. Of particular relevance are:
  - transport facilities, such as bus, road and railway;
  - shops;
  - schools;
  - doctors, dentists, hospitals;
  - post office branches, which will be needed particularly by older people who have to collect their pensions, especially if they do not wish their pensions to be paid into a bank account;
  - recreational facilities.

  The proximity of different locations to areas of employment is also important. Houses in the 'commuter belt', which describes the area surrounding a major employment centre such as London, tend to fetch higher prices than do others which are further away.

- **Condition**

  The condition of a property will also affect its saleability. Where substantial expenses are likely to be incurred in repairing a property, it may prove difficult to sell. On the other hand, there are people who specialize in buying run-down property, upgrading it and then selling it at a profit. Where a property merely needs redecorating or perhaps a new coat of paint on the window frames, the effect on its saleability should be negligible.

- **Type of tenure**

  Freehold properties are normally more popular than leaseholds.

- **Type of property**

  Although some types of dwelling undoubtedly sell more readily than others, this is one of the hardest factors to quantify. For one thing, tastes differ across the country. Only by applying one's knowledge of the particular locality being considered will it be possible to tell whether a large semi-detached house will sell more easily than, say, a small detached house.

- **Specific facilities**

  It will be advantageous for a dwelling to have:

  - a large kitchen – indeed the larger the kitchen the more saleable the dwelling, generally speaking;

  - a garage or, failing that, a parking space;

  - a garden;

  - some form of heating – gas central heating is probably the most popular, although any heating is better than none.

- **Number of bedrooms**

  At first you might think that the more bedrooms a house possessed, the more readily it would sell. For demographic reasons, this is not the case. A single person, for example, is unlikely to want to buy a four-bedroomed house. Moreover, smaller houses are likely to prove more saleable in the future because the average size of households is decreasing and there will be an increase in the number of single people. Despite this general principle, whether a three-bedroomed house is more or less likely to sell than a similar two-bedroomed house will depend more on local circumstances than on anything else.

- **Appearance of the property**

  The condition of one house may not differ significantly from that of another. However, it may prove less saleable simply because either the inside or the outside looks less attractive. Frequently, vendors prefer to spend a small amount in remedying this situation before they put their houses on the market.

- **Local planning permission**

  Occasionally, plans for local development affect the saleability of a house. Some, such as for the erection of a factory nearby, or a new estate, or the construction of a new main road, will have an adverse effect. Others may actually boost saleability: the building of a new supermarket may make shopping easier, the construction of a new office-block might lift employment prospects in the area. Improvements to the road network might also increase saleability, as happened in the south-east with the building of the M25.

We looked earlier in the text as to how the proximity or otherwise of certain factors affected the price of dwellings.

12.6　Security

Regardless of their classification and of how repayment is to be arranged by the mortgagor, who is the person receiving the loan, all mortgages must be secure. There are two main criteria:

● A mortgage is secure if it complies with all the requirements of the Building Societies' Acts.

● The mortgage is secure if the property is readily saleable and is likely to remain so throughout the term of the loan, without any depreciation loss to the mortgagee.

Summary

This unit has described the different ways in which a property can be valued and outlined some of the factors behind them. We have seen that nowadays a valuer may be sued for negligence, even if his report had been intended for the building society or bank which employed him and not for a mortgage applicant.

Finally, we have looked at the general question of saleability and the need to obtain security for any advances made.

13

OTHER ASPECTS OF HOUSING

Objectives

After studying this unit, you should be able to:

- explain the need for various professional staff in the field of housing;
- describe the need for building contracts;
- outline the reasons for requiring Building Control.

13.1 Introduction

In this final unit, we shall look at various topics related to housing:

- the personnel involved in housing;
- building contracts;
- building control.

It should be remembered that, although these areas are comparatively small, they are nonetheless important.

13.2 Housebuilding Personnel

In this section we shall look at the professional personnel involved in building development projects. These personnel may be employed in specialist practices by a local authority, a housing association or by a private development company.

Architects

An architect is regulated and controlled by the Architects Registration Council of the UK, although the main institution that sets the examinations governing the ranks of professionally qualified architects is the Royal Institute of British Architects (RIBA).

An architect's primary role is to:

- design the building, or whatever extension or alteration is required;
- prepare working drawings;
- draw up contract documents and arrange the contract;
- supervise the work in progress;
- certify interim payments to the contractor;
- examine the contractor's final accounts.

The extent of preliminary work put in by the architect rather depends on what the client has in mind. If the client knows precisely what he wants and just does not know how to design it, then the architect's work is relatively straightforward. Where the client really has no idea of what he wants, then the architect may be involved in giving some preliminary advice before the design stage can begin.

Most people tend to think that an architect is someone who designs and that he draws diagrams of his designs so that others can carry out the necessary building work. This is certainly a central aspect of the architect's role in construction. However, as the list of his duties shows, his supervisory role continues throughout the whole of a building project, not just during the design stage.

The Penguin Dictionary of Building defines an architect as:

> *...one who designs and supervises the construction of buildings. His main duties are preparing designs, plans and specifications; inspecting sites; obtaining tenders for work, and the legal negotiations needed before building can start. His functions now extend into town planning and the study of the social and work activities that need buildings. The Architects (Registration) Acts 1931 to 1969 protect the title 'architect' in the United Kingdom so that only those who are registered with the Architects Registration Council may practise as architects. To qualify for registration a person must pass an architectural examination of university degree level as well as one in professional practice.*

The relationship between an architect and his client is governed by the law of contract. However, an architect may not have a written contract, which naturally leaves him vulnerable when it comes to payment of his fees. The answer, of course, is to draw up a written agreement whenever possible, although problems can still arise, as the following cases show.

- An architect may only recover fees for work actually done.

  Case: *Farthing v Tomkins* (1893)

  The plaintiff prepared plans for the building of a hotel, as requested by the defendant. The scheme was subsequently abandoned.

  Held: the plaintiff was unable to recover the scale fee relating to the total project cost, but was able to claim fair charges for work actually done.

- A negligent architect may be sued.

Case: *Greaves & Co (Contractors) Ltd v Baynham Meikle & Partners* (1975)

The plaintiffs, a firm of building contractors, were employed to build a warehouse for the storage of oil drums. Part of the contract provided that the plaintiffs employ the necessary architects and engineers. The plaintiffs were aware of the use for which the warehouse was to be built.

The defendants, a firm of consultant structural engineers, were employed to design the structure of the warehouse. The building was built to a new system of construction governed by British Standards. The defendants failed to study a circular, issued by the British Standards Institution, warning designers of the effect of vibrations caused by imposed loadings in such a structure, even though they were aware of its existence. Afterwards, construction faults were discovered in the floor and remedial works costing £100,000 were necessary.

Held: the design was inadequate for its intended use, and the defendants were in breach of duty and in breach of an implied term of the agreement that the design would be fit for its purpose.

- Over-certifying accounts constitutes negligence.

Case: *Sutcliffe v Thackrah* (1974)

The plaintiff wished to have a house built and employed the defendants, a firm of architects, to prepare the necessary plans. A standard RIBA form was used. This stated that the architect would issue interim certificates at specified intervals, stating amounts due to the builders in respect of work undertaken. Payment would be made within 14 days.

There were delays in the construction and the plaintiff terminated the services of the builder, who later became insolvent. An action was brought against the defendants for damages in certifying interim payments for work not carried out, or not carried out properly.

Held: the architects were negligent in issuing interim certificates for work not carried out, or not carried out properly, and were therefore liable for damages.

Building Surveyors

The role of a building surveyor falls somewhere in between that of an architect and a quantity surveyor. *The Penguin Dictionary of Building* defines a building surveyor as:

> *... a specialist in building construction and repairs and alterations to buildings. He supervises building, decorating, and sanitary work, and advises in disputes on party walls, easements, light and other legal matters. He is usually a quantity surveyor by*

training, being an Associate of the Royal Institution of Chartered Surveyors, or the Incorporated Association of Architects and Surveyors.

(**Note**: in law, an **easement** is a right which one person may have over another person's land, such as the right to walk over the land or to run a pipe through it.)

A building surveyor may also have qualified through the Chartered Institute of Building or through the Institute of Building or Structural Engineers.

Quantity Surveyors

A quantity surveyor, as defined by *The Penguin Dictionary of Building*, is:

> *... a person with somewhat similar professional qualifications to a building surveyor who looks after the technical accountancy of building contracts. He measures the work shown on the drawings and writes the quantities down, after he has compiled the bill of quantities, for use in tendering. He measures the work done by the contractor on completion (also every month for the certificate) and advises the client on the correct sum to be paid to the contractor at any time ... In the USA, the quantity surveyor is not always needed for civil engineering work, but British building quantities are very much more complicated and usually require one.*
>
> *In the nineteenth century, groups of competing contractors would collaborate during tendering to employ one man to draw up a bill of quantities so that the cost of this labour was shared between them. This was the origin of the profession. This also explains why those countries which do not use competitive tendering do not have quantity surveyors.*

Put simply, a quantity surveyor is a professional who deals with the quantities and costs involved in a project. He will:

- advise on the total work required;
- advise on the available size and standard of structure for a given price;
- prepare budgets;
- ensure that the proposed building can be erected within the approved expenditure limit;
- advise on tendering procedures and contracts, and prepare the necessary documents;
- provide advice ensuring that authorized costs are not exceeded;
- ensure that the contractor is paid a proper price for the work.

Structural Engineers

The main function of a structural engineer is to make calculations of the stress imposed on a given area by a given load. Usually he carries out this task by coordinating the work of a group of draughtsmen and designers.

The career structure of a structural engineer normally includes the following stages:

- draughtsman;

- steel detailer;

- structural steel designer; and

- structural engineer;

with the qualification usually being through the Institute of Civil Engineers.

The work of a structural engineer sounds distinctly less glamorous than that of the other professionals, but it is no less vital. For example, the wind can exert considerable pressure upon the roofs of dwellings and, without the help of a structural engineer, a roof might be built with insufficient strength to withstand that sort of load. The consequences of this could clearly be serious.

Contracts Manager

The Penguin Dictionary of Building defines a contracts manager as:

> *... a senior architect, surveyor, civil engineer or tradesman employed by a building or civil engineering contractor, who has worked for many years in building construction and takes full responsibility for the completion of the contracts under his authority. He deals with the architect, engineer or other client of each site, as well as with his own company directors.*

In short, the contracts manager runs the construction side of a project, dealing with the agents and foremen responsible for individual sites. He is a manager who also possesses technical expertise and he is responsible for the smooth and efficient progress of the work. Without him, the other personnel would lack direction and coordination, and the project would probably grind to a halt.

13.3   Contracts

Let us look in this section at the contract, who is involved, and the insurance side of housebuilding.

The Public Sector and the Private Sector

Housebuilding in this country is generally of one of two types. Social housing, ie local authority or registered social landlords, is normally for rent, and speculative developments within the private sector are normally for sale to the public at large.

- It is usual for social housing to be built under a construction contract by a builder, who will have no financial involvement in the development other than to be paid for the work he carries out.

- The private sector developer will usually build the dwellings himself. Employing the necessary labour either directly or on an individual subcontract basis, the builder is risking his investment in land acquisition and building against eventually being able to sell the finished dwellings at a profit.

While there are variations on these themes, the generality holds good for the vast majority of residential construction projects.

What Experts Are Involved?

Both public and private development requires input from three different types of consultant:

- Architects will design the houses and the layout of the estate.

- Engineers will work out the structural details of the house, and produce designs for roads and sewers serving the estate.

- Cost consultants or quantity surveyors will advise on the likely costs to be incurred in carrying out the works.

Each of these consultants may be employed in specialist practices, or by a local authority, or by a development company directly (in-house). Each of the professions is bound by a code of ethics to ensure a businesslike approach to its work, requiring very high standards of technical ability before admission to the separate societies or associations.

How a Plan is Drawn Up

Typically a developer, whether in the public or the private sector, contacts an architect with a proposal or an idea for how to develop a site and gives him details of the type of dwelling he thinks would be appropriate. This brief would include a suggested mix of dwellings (for example: 30% four-bedroomed detached houses, 30% three-bedroomed detached houses and 40% three-bedroomed bungalows) and perhaps an indication of the floor areas of the dwellings, plus the density at which they should be built (for example: eight dwellings per acre, or 17 dwellings per hectare).

The architect will then prepare outline schemes for the development, seeking his client's approval before embarking on the lengthy process of producing detailed working drawings. A preliminary investigation by the engineer and cost consultant at this stage will produce advice on ground conditions and on the approximate costs of the project. These details will be amplified as more information about the proposals becomes known.

Eventually, the scheme proposals will be fully drawn up and quotations sought, either for the whole contract from a general building contractor or for parts of the works from individual specialist contractors.

When the quotations have been assessed and it has been decided to appoint someone to carry out all or part of the works, a contract is drawn up between the employer and the contractor to protect their respective interests in the building. The employer wants to know how much he is going to be charged for the job. The contractor wants to be assured that he will be paid, at an agreed rate, for the work he has carried out.

The most common forms of building contracts are those prepared by the Joint Contracts Tribunal (JCT), a body that includes representatives from the parties most involved in building works. There are several versions of these standard contracts, to cater for most types of building works for both local authority and private employers and for minor works such as small subcontracts.

Having been awarded a contract, the builder will start work on the site and build according to details issued to him, to a time-schedule agreed between himself and the employer, and for a price that is contained within the contract.

If the developer undertakes to employ his own labour force, then no formal contract for the building as a whole will exist. He might decide to contract out individual sections of the works to separate specialist companies or individuals, in which case he might once again use a JCT form of contract.

Finding Suitable Contractors

The ability of companies to compete in pricing their work depends to a large extent upon their suitability to carry out the work. There would be no point in approaching a national contractor, used to building airports or multi-storey office blocks, for a quotation to build a pair of semi-detached houses; neither would there be any point in offering a contract to build the channel tunnel to the local maintenance or jobbing builder. The selection of suitable builders to appear on a tender list is part of the developer's or architect's role. Properly carried out, it will ensure that the contract is within the economic and technical capabilities of the successful tenderer, and that the price is the best that can be achieved.

Many builders are not interested in taking on maintenance or repair works, other than those incurred in their new building activities. They will therefore not be in a position to quote competitively. Normal routine repairs and maintenance are therefore best carried out by companies or individuals specializing in such tasks. However, the people concerned must be competent; a simple maintenance task which has been mishandled or bodged can prove expensive to correct. In the case of specialist contractors, it is always sensible to check with the relevant trade association if there are any doubts as to their capabilities. Most specialist contractors will guarantee their work, and the best will offer a guarantee backed up by an insurance policy. This provides additional security, should the company cease to trade during the life of the guarantee.

Developer Contributions

Local planning authorities have a responsibility to allocate sufficient land for housing in their development plans. Local planning authorities may require, as a condition of granting planning permission, that a proportion of affordable housing is provided as part of a proposed housing development. This is laid down in a Government Circular 6/98 entitled 'Planning and Affordable Housing' which came into effect on 8 April 1998. In exceptional circumstances local planning authorities and applicants may agree to an alternative arrangement for delivering an agreed element of affordable housing on a different site.

So when considering development proposals for private housing schemes comprising 25 or more dwellings or a site of one hectare or more is used, a local authority will seek to achieve agreements with developers to secure affordable housing, ie where the rent or price is permanently reduced, directly or indirectly, by means of a subsidy from the public, private or voluntary sector and which is provided or managed by a registered social landlord. The local authority will seek to secure the maximum reasonable proportion of housing to meet the needs of buyers or renters on low and middle incomes who are unable to gain access to general market housing, on all residential sites where this is practicable. This will be a priority in reaching agreement with developers in order to make adequate provision for housing needs identified in the local authorities Housing Investment Programmes.

The Town and Country Planning Act 1990 (section 106) introduced the concept of planning obligations. The legislation gives the council the option of requiring the developer, as part of the package, to make a contribution (financial or in kind) towards the infrastructure of an area – for instance, roads or community facilities which the planners regard as a necessary concomitant of the development. Planning obligations are a key means by which local authorities can secure contributions from developers for the provision of affordable housing. The system operates by granting planning approval, subject to the developer making a proportion of the homes in new developments affordable.

Section 106 agreements, as they are known, play a very important part. Since the legislation, 75% of all new sites in London include affordable housing. It is estimated that 15,000 affordable homes are built each year via section 106 agreements.

In London, Ken Livingstone as Mayor has provisionally set a target of 50% (35% social housing and 15% key worker/shared ownership homes) for affordable housing in all new developments.

There has been much criticism of section 106 agreements in that they are made 'behind closed doors'. It has been suggested that the current system of negotiation through section 106 agreements be replaced with one based on tariffs covering infrastructure projects and affordable housing. As a result such agreements would be more transparent to outsiders than the present approach and would be clear at the outset to developers and councils alike. They would, therefore, play a major part in bringing about more affordable housing. In local development plans, local authorities would set out a schedule of tariffs as an initial negotiating position.

The Building Contract

A building contract is a legal agreement between an employer and a contractor, to carry out certain work. On occasion, the employer will be the eventual occupier of a dwelling. More usually, the employer will be a housing development business or a local authority.

A small building contract, such as to erect a porch or to carry out a minor repair of some sort, can be made verbally. However, it is more common for the contractor to provide a written estimate of the costs for the proposed work. If the employer accepts the estimate, the contract is then entered into.

For large contracts, the necessary documentation will usually include:

● a set of drawings;

● a bill of quantities, consisting of a detailed list of items needed to fulfil the contract; and

● a document setting out the detailed conditions of the contract; these would include the purpose of the contract, a timetable and penalties for not completing on time.

Any building contract, whether verbal or formally documented, is subject to the law of contract. Its complications are beyond the scope of this study text, but you should have an idea of:

● the contractor's basic obligations under a building contract;

● the logic behind an agreement;

● the basic remedies for breach of contract; and

● the two most important types of contract.

We shall now consider these areas.

The contractor's obligations

In order to avoid later disputes with the employer, a contractor should know his rights and obligations at the outset of a contract. In addition, the employer should know exactly what is in the contract, so that he knows what to expect from the contractor. One way of trying to ensure that both contractors and employers are familiar with the contents of a contract is to use a contract that is in a standard form.

A contract in standard form will include the contractor's primary obligations. These are as follows:

● He should complete the building work in accordance with details specified by the contract.

● He should use materials of the standard specified by the contract and employ the level of workmanship specified by the contract.

● He should give all notices required by law, such as informing the local authority when works requiring inspection are completed.

● He should remedy all defects that appear within the time stated in the contract. Where no period is specified, it is assumed to be six months.

- He should carry adequate insurance against injury to people working on the site and against fire.

Agreements

Where a builder undertakes to carry out some relatively minor building works, such as an extension to a house, then the work may be subject to written agreement rather than to a formal, detailed contract. An agreement is subject to the same legal provisions as a contract, provided that it meets five conditions:

- An offer has been made which has been accepted. Although this sounds straightforward, 'offer' and 'acceptance' are legal terms which are subject to several complicated rules.
- Both the parties to the contract should be legally able to enter the contract. Some persons have only restricted capability to enter into contracts, and are not bound by agreements made outside those limits.
- The agreement must have 'form', such as being written out or supported by written evidence. Alternatively, it should be supported by 'consideration', such as some return, not necessarily financial, which one party to the contract gives to the other in exchange for the promise made to him.
- The agreement should come about through the genuine consent of the relevant parties. There should be no mistake, misrepresentation, duress or undue influence operating as it is created.
- The subject matter of the agreement must be legal. The courts will not enforce it if its purpose is deemed to be illegal or contrary to public policy.

Breach of contract

The standard remedy for breach of contract is the award of damages, as compensation for the loss caused by the breach. Alternatively, the injured party may in some cases claim payment for the value of what he has done, or seek a court order requiring the defendant either to perform the contract (specific performance), or to observe negative restrictions which he has accepted under the contract (an injunction). Where appropriate, he may apply for a declaration that the contract has been rescinded, or obtain restitution of property which he has transferred. The right to a remedy for breach of contract is subject to time limits and, if delayed, the right of action for breach may become statute-barred.

Types of contract

There are two main types of building contract:

- A lump-sum or fixed-price contract, as its name suggests, means that an overall price for the building works is fixed and agreed. Usually such a contract will include a fluctuations clause. Without this, the contractor could find himself caught out if the costs of building materials and labour increase.

- In other contracts, prices are not agreed in advance. The contractor carries out the building work, and then charges a price to cover his costs once all the work has been completed. Obviously, the employer should steer clear of this type of contract unless he has a good reason to believe that the contractor is fair and honest.

Guarantee schemes

Various guarantee schemes exist as a measure of protection for the employer; examples of these are:

- 'Buildmark' – probably the most well known of all guarantee schemes. This is offered by the National Housebuilding Council and covers:

    1. protection up to £10,000 or 10% of the purchase price whichever is greater against a builder going bankrupt where, after exchange of contracts, a purchaser loses his/her deposit or actually suffers loss because of faulty building;

    2. first two years – the builder is required, at his expense, to remedy defects which arise as a result of his not conforming to NHBC standards for materials/ workmanship. However, some items are excluded, such as normal wear and tear, normal condensation or shrinkage;

    3. from the beginning of the third year to the end of the tenth – protection is provided against major damage arising out of structural defects, resulting from a failure to comply with the NHBC's technical requirements. Damages are limited to £500,000 for a newly built home or £250,000 for a converted home. Cover is indexed linked up to a limit of 12% per annum.

- 'Buildsure' scheme exclusive to National Federation of Builders' members, provides a one year defects liability period and a three year structural warranty;

Building Guarantee Scheme (UK) Ltd provides a six month defects liability period followed by a two year period of cover for major structural defects.

13.4   Insurance

Insurance of the contents of a house is at the householder's discretion. However, anyone with a mortgage must insure its structure. Frequently, he will simply ask his building society or bank to do so on his behalf.

For insurance purposes, the value which must be placed upon a property will be the cost of rebuilding it, not its market value. A building society or bank usually works this out by:

- finding out the area of the house;

- multiplying the area by the appropriate building cost per square metre; this figure is found from standard tables, and will vary according to where in the country the building is situated;

- adding on approximately 15% to the total, to allow for professional fees and other add-on costs; and

- allowing for inflation; most house insurance is index-linked to the rate of inflation.

What is Covered by Building Insurance?

Although the cover provided by individual companies may differ somewhat in detail, building insurance should normally provide cover against loss or damage caused by fire, storms, flood, theft and subsidence. A typical list of the **perils** covered by such a policy is:

- fire, explosion, lightning, thunderbolt;

- riot, civil commotion, strikes, labour disturbances;

- aircraft;

- storm, tempest, flood;

- theft;

- bursting or overflowing of water tanks, apparatus, or pipes;

- earthquakes;

- impact by any road vehicle or rail vehicle, or animals;

- breakage or collapse of television and radio receiving aerials, aerial fittings or masts;

- leakage of oil from any fixed oil-fired heating installations;

- subsidence and/or heave of the site;

- malicious damage by any person other than a person lawfully in the private dwelling house;

- falling trees.

The **extent** of the cover, in other words the physical items covered by the insurance policy, may also vary from one policy to another. However, it is usual for building insurance to cover:

- roof, foundations, walls, floors, ceilings, doors and windows;

- outbuildings and garages as well as other garden structures, such as sheds and greenhouses;

- central heating, plus all plumbing and ancillary domestic fittings, such as w.c. pans, bidets and wash-basins;

- external items, such as retaining walls, fences, gates, paths and steps.

Building insurance will not cover normal wear and tear or the maintenance of woodwork, gutters, roofs and so forth. It remains the responsibility of the owner to keep the house in good repair; insurance only provides against specific damage. In this respect it is very similar to car insurance, which provides cover only in the case of accident or damage.

Who Provides Building Insurance?

Most insurance companies offer building insurance, although it might actually be arranged by a building society or bank. In the past, it used to be the responsibility of someone taking out a mortgage to obtain appropriate building insurance through an insurance company. The owner-occupier would pay his monthly mortgage repayments to the building society or bank and his building insurance premiums to the insurance company, usually as a single annual lump sum. Nowadays, it is more common for a building society or bank to arrange building insurance for an owner-occupier, often at preferential rates. The owner-occupier makes monthly payments to the building society or bank which include the mortgage repayments and the building insurance premiums. Apart from anything else, this has the advantage of spreading out the insurance premium over 12 months, instead of paying it out as a single and quite large annual amount.

Types of Building Insurance Policy

There are two main types of building insurance policy:

- Under an **indemnity policy**, an insurance company will undertake to pay enough to restore the building to its former condition before the damage occurred.

- A **new-for-old policy** will in theory provide for the full cost of repairing or rebuilding, provided that the dwelling has been maintained in a good state of repair. A new-for-old policy is therefore a form of index-linked policy, because it guards the owner against the effects of inflation.

The essential difference between these two types of policy is that a new-for-old policy will give you the chance to replace an item at its current cost, whereas an indemnity policy will only pay the original cost. Suppose you had some stereo equipment, which you bought two years ago for £400, and which today might cost £750 to replace. In the event of it being stolen an indemnity policy would only pay £400, whereas a new-for-old policy would pay £750. Not surprisingly, premiums on new-for-old policies are higher than on indemnity policies.

All buildings must be insured at their full value, for a sum sufficient to meet the full cost of rebuilding, sometimes called the **cost of reinstatement**. The cost of reinstatement is the full rebuilding cost of the property, including any VAT payable, plus amounts for:

- the costs of demolition and the removal of debris;
- architect's, surveyor's and legal fees;
- extra costs of rebuilding to comply with current local authority requirements.

The cost of reinstatement of a house may be higher than its market value.

- Some costs, such as those mentioned above, would not be included in its market value.

- Where the demand for houses is poor, the market value may be less than the cost of rebuilding them.

- If the house was built some time ago, the cost of even partial reinstatement in the original style may be substantially greater than the market value.

- The rebuilding of one house is likely to be more expensive than if several houses of a similar type are being built at the same time.

The Insurance Ombudsman

Inevitably, disputes between policyholders and insurance companies arise. Such cases may be referred to the Insurance Ombudsman for an impartial investigation.

The Insurance Ombudsman is an individual supported by a small group of staff. He is independent of building societies, banks and insurance companies. His work is funded by the Insurance Association.

The procedure involving the Insurance Ombudsman is as follows:

- The policyholder lodges his complaint with the Ombudsman. He must do so within six months of failure to agree with the relevant insurance company.

- If the Ombudsman, after investigation, considers that the complaint is justified, he can require the insurance company to settle the claim.

- If the policyholder is unhappy with the decision arrived at by the Insurance Ombudsman, he can institute legal action against the company concerned.

13.5 Value Added Tax (VAT)

Value added tax was introduced in 1973. The current standard rate of VAT is 17.5%. All traders registered for the tax must charge VAT on sales, referred to as outputs or supply. They account for the tax collected by making quarterly payments to the Customs and Excise VAT office, after first deducting any tax they themselves have paid on their purchases or inputs during the period. Businesses trading in goods or services whose taxable outputs exceed £57,000 p.a. must register for VAT with the Customs and Excise office. Any registered trader must show his VAT registration number on the face of any invoice in which VAT is included.

For those who build and supply new domestic dwellings in the private sector, the effect of the legislation is that no VAT is normally payable. This activity is not exempt from VAT, but is charged at a zero rate: when the builder sells a new house, he makes a zero-rated supply. Providing that he is registered for VAT, he will be able to recover any VAT suffered on his inputs. Other arrangements apply for the public sector, but here too VAT suffered can generally be reclaimed.

The government has considered reports about VAT on housing including Lord Rogers' Report *Towards an Urban Renaissance* (detailed in Unit 10) and has recently given builders and property developers incentives to encourage them to upgrade derelict and unoccupied properties to provide residential accommodation.

- As from 1 August 2001, sales of renovated dwellings that have been empty for ten years prior to the sale qualify for zero-rating. (This allows the developer to reclaim the VAT incurred on the renovation works.)

- As from 12 May 2001, VAT is payable on the renovation works at the reduced rate of 5%, provided the dwelling has been empty for at least three years.

- As from 12 May 2001, VAT is payable at the reduced rate of 5% for work carried out on various residential conversions:

  - converting a residential property into a different number of dwellings (eg converting a house into flats);

  - converting a non-residential property into a dwelling or number of dwellings;

  - converting a dwelling into a care home or into a house in multiple occupation, such as bed-sits.

13.6   Building Control

The main legislative control over building in the UK is exercised through the Building Regulations, the latest version of which came into effect on 1 April 1990. A detailed knowledge of these regulations is not required for examination purposes, so we shall look only at their background, purpose, and general content.

These new regulations have two main concepts:

- to encourage energy saving; and

- to avoid pollution of the atmosphere.

Background

Up until the late 1800s, there was virtually no control over any aspect of housing. Legislation on housing began only after a great deal of pressure from social pioneers on public health issues, as we saw earlier in this book. In time, the legislation affected building standards and practices, as well as more general problems in public health and sanitation.

Because it was health issues that prompted the growth in housing legislation, building was controlled mainly through bye-laws made by local authorities under the Public Health Acts. The bye-laws introduced by various authorities were all supposed to be based on models issued by the relevant Minister, but inevitably they differed in detail from authority to authority. As time passed, the differences became more and more marked, until eventually it became obvious that some uniformity would have to be imposed.

In 1962, a Building Regulations Advisory Committee was set up. The old bye-laws were replaced by the Building Regulations, which are set by the Secretary of State and supervised by him. However, they are administered by local authorities.

The Building Regulations were revised in 1965, 1966, 1976 and 1985. The current versions were issued in 1990, although they have been amended to cover encouragement of energy saving and the avoidance of pollution of the atmosphere.

In 1984, a consolidation Act was passed called the Building Act which brought together all the previous fragmented legislation relating to building under one cover. These Acts include the Public Health Acts 1936 and 1961, the Health and Safety at Work etc Act 1974 and the Housing and Building Control Act 1984. This Act gave the Secretary of State the power to make regulations, known as the Building Regulations. These regulations were cast in a radically different format from previous building regulations and consisted of a set of short functional requirements backed up by a series of approved documents as a method of achieving these functional requirements.

Building Regulations are divided into following headings:

Part A: Structure

Part B: Fire Safety

Part C: Site Preparation and Resistance to Moisture

Part D: Toxic Substances

Part E: Resistance to the Passage of Sound

Part F: Ventilation

Part G: Hygiene

Part H: Drainage and Waste Disposal

Part J: Heat-producing appliances

Part K: Stairs, Ramps and Guards

Part L: Conservation of Fuel and Power

Part M: Access and Facilities for Disabled Persons

Part N: Glazing - Materials and Protection

Regulation 7 - Materials and Workmanship

Below are details of some of the purposes of Building Regulations:

Structural Stability	So that buildings do not collapse.
Fire Resistance and Means of Escape	So that buildings do not burn down quickly, fire spread between buildings is limited and people can escape in the event of a fire.
Prevention of Dampness	So that roofs, walls and floors of buildings are weather-resistant and prevent rising dampness.
Toxic Substances	So that the injection of cavity walls with ureaformaldehyde foam is permitted only in certain types of construction.

Sound Insulation	So that separation is provided between new dwellings .
Ventilation	So that rooms are properly ventilated and roof spaces are ventilated to avoid condensation.
Hygiene	So that property bathrooms, hot water storage and sanitary conveniences are provided.
Drainage	So that adequate foul and rainwater drainage are provided.
Heating Appliances	So that heating appliances have sufficient air supply, proper flues and are not a fire risk to the building.
Stairways, Ramps, etc	So that stairways and ramps are of suitable dimensions and are safe.
Thermal Insulation Energy Conservation	So that new buildings can be heated to comfortable levels without using a lot of energy.
Access for Disabled People	So that new buildings have property access for disabled people and existing buildings are not altered to remove such access.

The purposes for which the Secretary of State is empowered to make regulations, with respect to the design and construction of buildings and the provision of services, fittings and equipment in connection with buildings, are set out in Section 1 of the Building Act 1984 as:

● securing the health and safety, welfare and convenience of persons in or about buildings and of others who may be affected by buildings or matters connected with buildings;

● furthering the conservation of fuel and power; and

● preventing waste, undue consumption, misuse or contamination of water.

The shortened regulations provided applicants with the option of either employing an 'approved inspector', or using the local authority to ensure that the works comply with Building Regulations.

Building Regulation M has been amended recently to cater for the changing needs of households from the use of buggies for children to wheelchairs for the disabled. All new dwellings are now regarded as 'lifetime homes' and will include accessible entrances, downstairs wcs accessible to wheelchairs.

Areas of Private Certification

An **approved inspector** is not required to submit his plans, but merely to deposit a site plan showing the layout, sewers, roads etc, together with an 'Initial Notice' or a combined 'Initial Notice and Plans Certificate'. The local authority does not provide forms etc for their perusal, and no fee is required. The local authority has ten working days to reject the initial notice, but approval need not be given. An **approved person** can certify certain specialist areas of works like structural stability, thermal insulation, etc, on plans deposited with the local authority. No checking or consultation with structural engineers is required by the local authority's building control inspectors.

Public bodies such as British Rail, British Airways, etc, can act in a similar way to the approved inspectors.

In all categories, certain items have to be checked and a file kept of all insurance certificates, independence declarations, consultations with the fire authority and the actual approval to act in a private capacity.

Local Authority Deposits

These are considered below.

Full plans

These are very similar to the applications that local authorities receive at present, apart from the fact that certain works may be certified by 'approved persons'.

Building notice

This is a totally new method of submission, and has been used successfully for many years in Inner London. Applicants complete a Building Notice form, and must give 48 hours notice prior to starting work. The Building Surveyor can require plans or details to be submitted when he makes his first inspection. He can also specify the time in which the plans must be provided. No approval or rejection notice will ever be issued – the local authority will only be monitoring work for compliance with regulations, as it proceeds on the site.

No fees are required for any of the privately certificated works. Full plan applications are still the subject of a separate plan and inspection fee. Building Notice applications are subject to only one fee, paid after the first inspection, which is the same amount as a full plans fee.

Contraventions of Building Regulations

The powers of local authorities to enforce the Building Regulations are contained in the Building Act 1984. Section 91(1) imposes on local authorities the general duty of carrying the Act into execution, and Section 91(2) states that it is their function to enforce the Building Regulations in their area.

Under Section 35, any person contravening a provision contained in the Building Regulations is liable on summary conviction to a fine not exceeding £2,000. He is also liable to a further fine, not exceeding £50, for each day on which default continues after his conviction. Proceedings may be taken for contraventions in individual parts of a building, even before completion of the whole. Any proceedings must be taken within six months of the authority becoming aware of the completion of the works, not from the date of a subsequent inspection.

As well as taking proceedings for a fine, the local authority may, by notice under Section 36 (served within 12 months of the completion of the work, or part of it), require an owner to pull down or alter work carried out in contravention of the Regulations. Should the owner fail to comply with the notice within 28 days (or such longer period as may be allowed on application to the magistrates' court), the authority may carry out the work and charge the cost to the owner.

Exemptions from Building Regulations

Some works are exempt from Building Regulations approval. The following works do not require approval, although planning permission may be needed.

A small **detached** building which contains no sleeping accommodation not exceeding 30 m² (300 sq ft) and is either wholly non-combustible; or if combustible (timber roof, etc) is more than 1 metre from any boundary.

A single-storey building which is a greenhouse, not exceeding 30 m² conservatory with translucent roof, porch, covered yard or covered way, or a carport open on at least two sides (doors do not count as open sides).

Repairs: Minor repairs. Major repairs or use of different materials may need approval.

Boundary and other walls that do not form part of a building.

You should assume all other work requires Building Regulations approval including:

Use of a conservatory as a kitchen or living room.

Removal of internal load-bearing walls.

New bathrooms or kitchens.

Conversion to flats.

Widening of window openings.

Alterations within roof space.

Alterations to drains.

Any alterations to an existing building that affects stability, means of escape, fire precautions or access for people with disabilities.

Case Law

In *Murphy v Brentwood District Council* (1990), it was held that a local authority was in breach of its duty of care under Section 64 (passing or rejecting of plans and power to retain plans) of the Public Health Act 1936 when it relied on the opinion of its consultants as the basis for approving plans for a new house constructed in 1970.

The semi-detached house concerned had been built on filled and levelled ground and careful consideration had been given to the foundations. Foundation plans and calculations had been submitted by civil engineers on behalf of the contractors. These had been checked by the local authority's consultant engineers and the plans subsequently approved.

It was common ground that the council's consultants were competent and fit to be trusted in the matter but differential movement of the concrete raft foundations had taken place after construction causing it to distort and cracks had appeared.

By virtue of the wording of the legislation (now repealed by the Building Act 1984), the council was found to be at fault in the matter and £38,777 was awarded to the plaintiff.

Summary

This unit has covered smaller topics of housing; although these topics are smaller, they are equally as important as earlier topics dealt with in this book.

We have looked at the professional personnel involved in housing, and what their responsibilities are. We have considered building contracts and insurance in some detail. Finally, we have outlined current building control.

INDEX

Index